Modern Japanese Fiction and Its Traditions

Modern Japanese Fiction and Its Traditions

AN INTRODUCTION

J. THOMAS RIMER

PRINCETON UNIVERSITY PRESS

PRINCETON, NEW JERSEY

Copyright © 1978 by Princeton University Press
Published by Princeton University Press, Princeton, New Jersey
In the United Kingdom: Princeton University Press, Guildford, Surrey

Taketori monogatari, copyright © by Donald Keene

All Rights Reserved

Library of Congress Cataloging in Publication Data will
be found on the last printed page of this book

Publication of this book has been aided by the
Paul W. Mellon Fund of Princeton University Press

This book has been composed in VIP Bembo

Printed in the United States of America
by Princeton University Press, Princeton, New Jersey

Preface

WHAT follows here has a double purpose. I hope first of all to indicate certain structural principles important in the tradition of Japanese narrative fiction. Secondly, I have enjoyed writing in some detail about works that I genuinely admire, works I would like to call to the attention of readers who may not have read them. For both reasons I have included copious quotations from the translations of the original texts, perhaps more than some readers may require or desire. Still, I would insist that a close reading of texts of this quality is the first requisite step toward any proper analysis of their larger purposes, and I hope that my readers will share my enthusiasm for the particular examples I have chosen.

There are, of course, some omissions. Ihara Saikaku, the Tokugawa novelist, has been written about so often, and so well, that there seemed little point in repeating the same information. Among modern writers I have set aside Akutagawa Ryūnosuke for much the same reason. Shimazaki Tōson, on the other hand, cannot be dealt with in such a study as this because as yet, regrettably, no major work of his is available in translation other than *Hakai* (The Broken Commandment), an admirable but somewhat atypical youthful work. I have also omitted Mishima Yukio, first, because he has been so much discussed elsewhere (although his texts have not been given careful scrutiny on any systematic basis), secondly, because I do not happen to share the enthusiasm of many others for his work.

My greatest regret of all is that I have not had the profit and pleasure of consulting Professor Edward Seidensticker's new and complete translation of Lady Murasaki's *The Tale of Genji*, which, at the time of writing, was not yet available. My analysis has been based rather on Arthur Waley's earlier translation; but that translation too has become a classic in its own right and, as such, surely deserves detailed treatment.

My thanks for help in preparing this study go to many. In

particular I would like to thank Professor Masao Miyoshi for a number of trenchant comments that were most useful to me in revising the manuscript. Professors Earl Miner and Makoto Ueda also made helpful suggestions, and both Miss R. Miriam Brokaw and Mrs. Arthur M. Sherwood of Princeton University Press have provided me with the utmost support with the production of the book. Professor Eugene Soviak's questions stimulated me to take up many of the matters dealt with in this study, and I have to thank Mr. Robert Tuggle of New York for one key sentence and the very important concept that lies behind it. My wife Laurence, through her own studies in French literature, did a great deal to help me in refining my own conceptions, as she read through and commented in detail on the manuscript chapter by chapter. I wish also to acknowledge the generous financial support provided me by Washington University for the preparation of the manuscript, in several stages. Professor Donald Holzman, of the École des Hautes Études en Sciences Sociales, Paris, was also most helpful to me at several crucial junctures in the preparation of the manuscript.

Finally, I want especially to thank Professor Donald Keene for his kind permission to print here his revised version of his translation of *Taketori monogatari* © Donald Keene, 1977. Its inclusion greatly enhances the usefulness of my study.

Grateful acknowledgment is also made to the following for permission to reprint extracts from previously published material:

Alfred A. Knopf, Inc.: excerpts from Tanizaki Junichirō, *Seven Japanese Tales*, translated by Howard Hibbett, copyright © 1963 Alfred A. Knopf, Inc.; excerpts from Yawabata Yasunari, *Snow Country*, translated by Edward G. Seidensticker, copyright © 1956 Alfred A. Knopf, Inc.; excerpts from Kaiko Takeshi, *Darkness in Summer*, translated by C. S. Seigle, copyright © 1973 Alfred A. Knopf, Inc.; excerpts from Abe Kōbō, *The Box Man*, translated by Dale Saunders, copyright © 1974 Alfred A. Knopf, Inc.

University of Tokyo Press: excerpts from *The Tale of the Heike*, translated by Hiroshi Kitagawa and Bruce T. Tsuchida, copyright © 1975 University of Tokyo Press.

Saint Louis
March 1976

T.R.

Contents

Modern Japanese Fiction and Its Traditions

I

Introduction

I

SINCE the Second World War, an increasing number of translations have made available to the Western world an ever broader range of Japanese fiction, ranging from the early poem tales to the newest existentialist fashions of Abe Kōbō. These translations find readers, and some have achieved lasting reputations. Still, the comments often made in the press or in reviews suggest a certain dissatisfaction felt by readers. The forms in which these narratives are cast—short story, novella, novel, reminiscence—seem familiar yet somehow malformed with respect to our expectations. We are attracted, yet disconcerted by what we find.

Or so the argument goes. Actually, such a statement of the problem suggests a proper answer. A certain amount of critical attention has been focused on the question of what Japanese fiction is *not*. More effort is needed to determine what the general principles of the traditions of that fiction might be. There are several obvious ways to pursue such a topic. One might, for example, examine the larger role of fiction in Japanese culture and society. Japanese fiction had an aristocratic beginning in the Heian court. In particular, the tonality given to narrative prose by Lady Murasaki and her *The Tale of Genji* created an aesthetic that can readily be traced all the way down to the postwar novels of Dazai, Kawabata, and Tanizaki. Another method might be to examine the readers of Japanese literature. Court attitudes and aristocratic self-images certainly conditioned the artistic milieu from which *The Tale of Genji* came; in the early twentieth century, writers of the stature of Natsume Sōseki wrote their most sustained efforts for serial publication in newspapers. All such questions might be regarded as a way to study Japanese literature through its sociology. The information available through such analysis is immensely revealing and helps to give a sense of the limits of creativity in each successive social setting.

Such critical procedures make it possible to use these works of literature as documents in cultural, intellectual, and philosophical history. Much modern Japanese literary criticism is of this variety, and some excellent Western scholarship has been written from a similar point of view. Among recent studies in English, one might mention *The World of the Shining Prince* (New York, 1964) by Ivan Morris, which attempts to recreate the social and spiritual milieu of Lady Murasaki and her generation. Another first-rate treatment of problems in Japanese literary history is Masao Miyoshi's *Accomplices of Silence* (Berkeley, 1974), a study of modern fiction in terms of its social and linguistic contexts.

The forms of Japanese fiction possess a literary history of their own, one that has given rise to a series of changing styles. Further, as contemporary Western criticism has been at pains to point out, style itself not only determines the content but is often synonymous with it. An analysis of style and content, and of the nature of the relationship between them, would seem to constitute the basis for an understanding of the purposes of Japanese fiction, or of any other. The task of providing any such analysis is a formidable one, and what follows is merely a modest attempt to suggest certain necessary directions of inquiry. My conviction, in sum, is that the great works of Japanese literature succeed brilliantly on their own terms. It is up to us to find out what those terms are.

II

In determining the necessary means to discuss the framework that sustains this literary structure, we may put forth two larger problems. Both have a bearing on every work examined here. The first is the problem of originality. Certainly originality remains the often unspoken yet ultimate criterion for the success of much contemporary Western art, music, and literature. A work is judged by the extent it can break away from what has come before. Some of the satisfactions found among Western readers of Japanese fiction in translation are due to the very fact that different traditions make a given work seem original in terms of Western sensibilities. Read in their proper context, however, the Japanese works are bound to make a different impression. Japan, like other cultures that bear the burdens of a long and complex history, seems to favor a more classically oriented literary tradition. Originality is highly valuable, but within certain limitations imposed by a developed and inherited taste. Certainly originality has never been the ultimate criterion in Japanese tradition. Western perceptions as to the nature of Japanese originality are sometimes muddled because of the reputation that Japan has earned during the earlier years of the century as a country of imitators. By such a definition, works of literature are sometimes dismissed as mere imitations of available models—*The Tale of Genji* is copied from Chinese works, Tanizaki from Edgar Allan Poe, and Dazai perhaps from Dostoevsky.

In terms of literary craftsmanship, however, such influences (and their extent is always less than might be supposed) are rather a sign of Japan's longstanding cosmopolitan attitude toward other civilizations. China, Japan's most powerful neighbor and culturally her greatest source of influence until the late nineteenth century, took little interest in literary and artistic traditions other than her own, but the Japanese, who never saw themselves as the center of world culture, always maintained a lively interest in the variety of experiences available to them. This fundamental attitude was as visible in the early Japanese chronicles as it was in the latter half of the sixteenth century, when the Portuguese missionaries came to Japan, and as it has been since the 1850s, when Japan began to open her doors to the West.

Moreover, such a lively interest in other cultures—or more specifically for the present purposes, in other literary styles and systems of aesthetic and philosophic ideas—must certainly come as no surprise to those who know anything of the history of the European intellectual traditions. No one finds unnatural the enormous impact of Goethe and Shakespeare on all of European culture; Sartre seems no less an important figure for having been stimulated by Kierkegaard and Heidegger. In the European tradition, cosmopolitanism is assumed to be a positive virtue. Japanese literary culture be-

haves no differently, but the distances are greater and the traditions further apart. The borrowings therefore often seem
more apparent and the eclecticism more striking, even when
the results are altogether successful. Exchanges bring riches:
what we admire in our own literary tradition we can scarcely
condemn in another.

In addition, we must realize the added difficulties imposed
on our understanding by such a literary tradition. Quite simply, one must know more. In particular, Japanese modern
writers who draw on three pasts at once (European, Japanese,
and Chinese) make any simple judgments on their work difficult to render; indeed, the untutored Western reader may
not even be aware of the challenges set, the rules of the game.
In particular, structural elements that often seem completely
missing often turn out to be operating most effectively, but in
terms defined by canons of taste and tradition wholly un-
familiar to us. Until some understanding of that tradition can
be achieved, individual works of Japanese literature, for the
Western reader, must be made to stand, frail and perilously
alone, in a fashion never anticipated by their original authors
or readers.

The second preliminary problem that might be raised concerns the ever-changing relationship between the past and the
present for each individual author. For the Japanese, the past
performs an endlessly complicated function. In the first place,
the past never served them as a monolithic tradition, a cultural carpet rolling down through the ages, to provide a kind
of homogeneous blanket covering the warts and idiosyncratic
bumps of each succeeding age. The changes that have come to
Japan in modern times are well known and enormous, but the
changes Buddhism brought to early Japanese culture, or those
brought about as a result of the social restructuring of the
country during the medieval period, were in some ways just
as profound. The question, in literary terms, of what to do
with the past was just as important then as it is now. Further,
the literary past was usually perceived not as a burden but as a
precious thread of continuity and sophistication in a world
that all too often seemed full of upheaval and continuous,
ominous change. The Japanese literary tradition, and the psy-

chological and stylistic attitudes it fostered, retained a kind of dialectical energy that has provided vitality for almost a thousand years.

Of course every civilization retains its literary past in some fashion, even if only as a stereotype ripe for destruction and ridicule. Writers who feel empty and bereft are usually those who have no sufficient tradition behind them, as Hawthorne once insisted. In Japan, the literary past always plays some active function, even if an unconscious one, in the composition of fiction. An attempt to define the functioning of that past provides one major theme of this study.

With these remarks as a preface, a Western reader, faced with the range of Japanese fiction now available to him in English, might well go on to pose a number of additional questions. The first area of concern involves the relationship of fiction to reality. Long accustomed to holding up as a criterion the "willing suspension of disbelief" in making judgments on the efficacy of a work of fiction, the Western reader here faces a new set of conventions that define that relationship. Not only is the relationship between fiction and reality of a somewhat different nature in the Japanese tradition; the ultimate sense of reality itself, as perceived by the various writers discussed in the present study, can in no way be defined in the same terms as our own. The Japanese sense of the continuity of personality in time, the relationship of the individual to others, and of the individual to nature, stands at a considerable distance from our Western experience. Many Japanese writers have been found disappointing by Western critics who find the narratives shapeless, without climax. The Japanese response might well be (although I must confess I have never seen it so succinctly formulated) that reality is indeed shapeless and that Japanese literary conventions are thus closer to ultimate truth than are our own. In any case, the Japanese literary mechanisms for apprehending reality permit the creation of works that, read carefully, possess the ability to shake us loose from our usual preconceptions.

A related question concerns the relation of language to narrative. Perhaps the fact that the Western novel is bound up in conveying our own perceptions of "reality" has imposed the standards of prose on the linguistic structures of our fiction; and, indeed, writers who move toward a use of heightened prose or poetry (Hesse, Rilke, on occasion Gide) in an attempt to produce "poetic" novels have done so, to some extent, at their peril, for such hybrid genres have not always received the modern reader's full sanction. The Japanese novel, on the other hand, draws on poetry as much as on prose for its literary mechanisms and for its language, and our expectations must be altered accordingly.

Still another issue involves the nature of causality in the Japanese tradition. Our notion of cause and effect goes back, no doubt, to Aristotle; by the nineteenth century, causality, in its artistic aspects, was such a central conception in fiction that Henry James could declare "What is character but the determination of incident? What is incident but the determination of character?" Gide may have struck a glancing blow at this central concept with his *acte gratuite*, but the close reciprocal relationship between character and action is still of crucial importance in Western fiction. One's first response on reading Japanese fiction is that this relationship, whatever its ultimate nature, is certainly more loosely perceived in the literary mechanisms involved. Determining the qualities and limitations of the nature of this causality will help considerably in explaining the ranges of artistic sensibility found appropriate to narrative in the Japanese tradition.

Another area of exploration might be that of coherence, or total effect. Tightly structured Western fiction often makes its impact, and sets in motion its deepest reverberations, through the architectural structure of its various parts. Again, our contemporary sense of reality makes us more appreciative of the Japanese looser structure; we tend to prize the Poussin sketch over the formal painting, and, as Charles Rosen has pointed out, Flaubert's real art may now seem to lie in his letters rather than in his novels.[1] Nevertheless, the literary structures in Japanese fiction are assembled in strikingly different ways, and the coherence they are marshalled to suggest is of a different order than that to which Western readers are accustomed.

[1] See Rosen's article "Romantic Documents," in *The New York Review of Books*, May 15, 1975, p. 15.

All of these concerns might be summed up as cautionary in nature—a desire to remove false expectations for Western readers. Yet one can hope for more than that: only by approaching these works of Japanese fiction with the proper expectations can their humor, lyricism, and philosophical profundity be perceived. An analysis of their literary structures may be a most helpful way to create the proper expectations.

III

If the role of creating proper expectations is one normally assigned to literary criticism, then one might next discuss the accomplishments of Japanese traditions of criticism. As in Europe, criticism has played a part in the Japanese literary tradition since its beginnings, and a study that could provide even a modest outline of the history of Japanese literary criticism would make a book far longer than this one. No such attempt is provided here, but a few remarks on the concerns of Japanese criticism might be useful at this point.

If we look briefly at what might be termed traditional literary criticism in Japan—that is, from the earliest periods through the incursions of the West in the 1850s and after—we find that one prominent fact stands out. The highest genre of literature was poetry, and most critical attention was focused on this form. What Japanese criticism on fiction existed (and there was a certain amount at all times, especially concerning *The Tale of Genji*) tended to define and make use of critical terms borrowed from the poetic vocabulary. One genre was defined in terms of another.

A closer look at the tradition suggest that two basic types of criticism maintained an ascendancy. One was didactic and moral, often with a heavy religious cast, Confucian, Buddhist, or Shintō. Like much of what the good Christian bishops have told us down through the centuries about Western literature, most of these homilies can now be put aside. A second type of criticism dealt more closely with the problems of art and might be termed a kind of technical criticism. A modern reader will find this older criticism quite practical in nature and often surprisingly contemporary in feeling. In the Heian period (794-1185), which saw the creation of *Genji, Tales of Ise*, and several great anthologies of 31-syllable *waka* poetry, the critics were the poets. The whole aristocratic class wrote poetry. Literary criticism was written by practicing poets for practicing poets. Questions as to the worth of literature, or debates over the relative worth of literature in relation to history or philosophy, were seldom pursued, since the aristocratic class shared the same assumptions about the fundamental importance of poetry. Criticism stressed such questions as the choice of proper means to suggest allusive effect, or the creation of techniques permitting the inclusion of a poetic reference without giving a newer poem too great a literary burden.

The patterns and expectations of literary criticism were laid down in such a fashion for an aristocratic audience. Later, even when that society began to change, the earlier canons of taste and the limitations set on the functions of literary criticism continued to prevail. Adaptations, however, were made for each successive audience. Indeed, the simplest way to grasp the general nature of the changes and developments in Japanese literary criticism is to observe for whom the criticism was being composed. In the Heian period, the poet-critics mostly wrote for each other, but in the long period from 1185, after the disastrous civil wars that virtually destroyed the political power of the court, down to 1600, when the country was reunified under the Tokugawa Shogunate, several new factors became important. A new warrior class arose. Fighting men who had spent their lives far from Kyoto, the capital, they took the political power from the court and felt they needed to adopt the high culture of their predecessors as well. Now the court poets had others to whom to teach literature besides themselves, and the new military rulers proved to be, on the whole, avid students and generous patrons. Social status, of course, remained all important. Even such a fine poet as Kamo no Chōmei (1153-1216) could complain that his work was not properly appreciated because of his inferior social status.

Criticism, because of a new audience, also developed certain new concerns that were of vital importance in the growth of the Japanese aesthetic sensibility. During most of the Heian period, contemporary values were the most important—put baldly, what was newest was best. After destruction and civil war, however, the past seemed, as it receded, to have been far better than a troubled and uncertain present. The virtues of the literary past began to replace those of the present in the hierarchy of values. Indeed the actual social values of the past often seemed in danger of slipping away altogether, and thus evoking the earlier Japanese aristocratic culture became, according to medieval Japanese criticism, one of the important duties of the literary tradition. Criticism urged writers to understand the past and use it as a means to choose appropriate precedents for new literary departures. The Western image of the medieval Christian monk preserving what he could of European culture while brutal wars raged outside his monastery is one that is not markedly different from the Japanese example. Nevertheless, although literary criticism was written by a somewhat larger group than in the Heian period (indeed the "socially inferior" Kamo no Chōmei wrote the most satisfactory medieval thesis on poetics) and for a somewhat larger audience, the nature of the criticism remained predominantly practical. The critical dialogue remained basically one between teacher and student, although the nature of both was now slightly altered. Still, the underlying assumptions concerning the purposes of that relationship were not questioned.

In the Tokugawa period (1600-1868), when the country was united and at peace, the range of literary consumers was extended still more. Domestic tranquillity brought increased commerce, and the rising class of town merchants possessed the money, the leisure, and the desire for status that led them to follow literary pursuits. This new group of students required proper instruction, like the warriors who preceded them, and courtly literary values were again adapted and transformed accordingly.

The continuing preoccupation with an ever-receding past also caused an intellectual movement of considerable importance that in turn was to provide a link with the later development of the modern Japanese sensibility. The influence of Chinese ideas on Japan (like European ideas on America) was

always profound, although far less than on the civilizations of
Vietnam or Korea. The study of Chinese literature and philosophy was particularly popular in the Tokugawa period,
since these writings, because of their more synthetic nature,
seemed to supply a cohesive view of philosophy and literature
that Japanese commentaries could not provide. Japanese
writers and historians admired these Chinese examples and
tried to emulate them by turning back to examine their own
earliest traditions, just as the Chinese had done. In the process, however, the Japanese found that many widely accepted
Chinese philosophical and historical canons of thought and
interpretations actually did considerable injustice to the early
Japanese sensibility. This school of research, often called "National Studies," produced important results in political and
social philosophy. In the field of literary studies, the scholars
began to identify the early Japanese sensibility as a virtue to be
defined neither in the didactic forms suggested by other
Japanese critics in earlier periods nor by any significant reference to Chinese literary premises. The greatest of these
critics, Motoori Norinaga (1730-1801), was perhaps the first
to lift Japanese literary criticism from the level of the brilliant
particular observation to the level of general aesthetic (but not
didactic) consideration. He was a major figure, and much of
his work can still be consulted with profit. In many ways,
Motoori was the prototype of the modern literary intellectual
now so familiar in contemporary Japan and elsewhere.

Motoori's observations were made within the context of
traditional Japanese culture; with the coming of Western ideas
about literature toward the end of the nineteenth century, an
enormous upheaval brought to the fore questions concerning
the role of literature and of the critic as well. Some of these
issues seem unresolved in Japan even today. The dislocations
of the times produced a new role for the Japanese writer. In
the Meiji period (1868-1912), novelists, aware of the vast
changes in their society, were forced to look intellectually at
the problems they faced: economically, socially, and spiritu-
ally. The literary traditions of the past seemed to offer little in
the way of help. The modern critic Nakamura Mitsuo has described the position of these writers very clearly.

For them, the novel was not merely an artistic representation of human life. Rather, it was a means of searching for a new, true way of living. At the same time, it was a record of this search. This was the hazardous quest for the sake of which the writers of the Meiji and Taisho periods risked tragedy in their real lives. They had high, probably exaggerated expectations of the novel, and they dared to believe in them and to *live* them.

For them, art was a path of mental and spiritual training, and the search for truth meant living without pretense. This ethical passion made these people, eking out their meager lives in obscure corners of society, the conscience of their society. By speaking out their own minds honestly, they succeeded in grasping the very nature of the civilization in which they lived in ways which were possible to none other of their contemporaries.[2]

Some novelists wrote for others who, like them, felt the ambiguities and difficulties of a dislocated existence. For these readers the writers often seemed heroes in a struggle to search out some kind of truth about the meaning of life. Novelists now became cultural heroes, and literary criticism began to include the collection of materials appropriate to such hero worship. A general educated public, an intelligentsia, for whom such criticism could be written, began to develop in the Meiji period, and this public still seeks to identify its heroes today. The arrival of a general reader on the Japanese literary scene has produced a critical vocabulary and a set of concerns considerably different from those found appropriate in earlier periods.

Having said this much about the audience for literary criticism and the effect of that audience on the changing nature of criticism, we might sketch briefly the kind of critical postures that have been assumed. In the case of traditional criticism, composed on the whole by professionals for professionals, argument often centered around critical terms, "virtues" perhaps, that literary works ought to possess. A given work (poem, diary, novel, etc.) was judged within the framework

[2] Nakamura Mitsuo, *Modern Japanese Fiction* (Tokyo, 1968), pp. 7-8.

of these critical values. Definitions of these terms in English are inevitably slippery. In the first place, many of the words used were used as early as the Heian period. The meanings of many words began to change during the subsequent expansion of the traditional critical vocabulary. Secondly, definitions of the terms usually revolved on matters of taste: they must be grasped, felt, responded to, not merely elucidated. Most of these critical terms strike a Western reader as basically aristocratic in nature; they suggest virtues to be appreciated through leisure, cultivation, and self-reflection.

Some examples may make the general tonality of the traditional critical vocabulary more explicit. Most of these terms remain (perhaps by other names) as a part of Japanese literary taste even today.

Aware (or, in its fuller form, *mono no aware*) is perhaps the most important term of all, and the most difficult to define in any concise fashion. A literal translation suggests "ahness," a clumsy word in English. *Aware* was an exclamation, "ah!" perhaps; *mono no aware* might thus become the "ahness of things." Such terminology suggests the ability of the discerning writer to find great and fundamental significance in the ordinary things of life and the further ability to pass such feelings along to discerning readers. *Mono no aware* might be said to represent a deep sensitivity to things, an ability to grasp the movements, the possibilities, the limitations of life in the context of a single incident, sometimes of a trifling nature. This intuitive yet cultured response to life represented the highest aesthetic virtue, and the artistic operation of the principle is as visible in the work of Tanizaki and Kawabata as in so many earlier works, notably in *The Tale of Genji*.

A second literary virtue was that of *makoto*, or sincerity. The idea of categorizing a work of literature, perforce an artificial construction, as "sincere" may seem curious at first, but the term actually reflects a sense of the peculiar virtues of the Japanese spirit in literature. Against the subtleties and profound learning of the Chinese were posited the spontaneity and the natural response to situations and surroundings unique to the Japanese. For many writers and critics, such a spirit was best embodied in the earliest collection of Japanese poetry, the *Manyōshū*, compiled in the eighth century, at a time when many poems could be included that showed little, if any, influence from Chinese poetics. Generation after generation of critics (Motoori Norinaga among them) praised this "Manyō spirit" as representing the best and truest strain in Japanese culture. Sincerity was often seen as a court of last appeals in a literary debate. Even in the modern period, motive can count for as much, or more, than accomplishment.

Another critical term, often associated with early medieval poetry and later important to the *nō* theater, is that of *yūgen*, sometimes defined as "mystery and depth." The concept is an elusive one, yet of central importance in the history of Japanese aesthetics. Shōtetsu, a medieval poet and critic, defined *yūgen* as "feelings that cannot be put into words, for example the effect of the moon veiled by a wisp of cloud or of scarlet mountain foliage enshrouded in autumnal haze." Such a definition might suggest the beauty of overtones, but the meaning of *yūgen* goes deeper still. Kamo no Chōmei explains it as follows:

> . . . it should be evident that this is a matter impossible for people of little poetic sensibility and shallow feelings to understand. . . . How can such things be easily learned or expressed precisely in words? The individual can only comprehend them for himself. Again, when one gazes upon the autumn hills half-concealed by a curtain of mist, what one sees is veiled yet profoundly beautiful; such a shadowy scene, which permits free exercise of the imagination in picturing how lovely the whole panoply of scarlet leaves must be, is far better than to see them spread with dazzling clarity before our eyes. What is difficult about expressing one's personal feelings in so many words—in saying that the moon is bright or in praising the cherry blossoms simply by declaring that they are beautiful? What superiority do such poems have over mere ordinary prose? It is only when many meanings are compressed into a single word, when the depths of feeling are exhausted yet not expressed, when an unseen world hovers in the atmosphere of the poem, when the mean and common are used

to express the elegant, when a poetic conception of rare beauty is developed to the fullest extent in a style of surface simplicity—only then, when the conception is exalted to the highest degree and "the words are too few, will the poem . . . have the [necessary] power. . . ."[3]

Such an explanation practically serves as a poem in itself; but whatever the ultimate meaning of *yūgen* may be (a meaning which in any case is heavily dependent on the taste and cultivation of the reader), the term suggests a transcendental beauty, a beauty behind the surface that exists on another plane of reality to which the work of art may help to lead the reader. Such ideas are not entirely foreign to our own culture. One need think only of Wordsworth's "Intimations of Immortality":

To me the meanest flower that blows can give
Thoughts that do often lie too deep for tears.

The difference, however, is that for Wordsworth the transcendental experience produces thoughts; for Chōmei an emotional and intuitive response is required, no matter how transformed by necessary cultivation and self-reflection. One poem often cited as possessing *yūgen* is the following *waka* by Fujiwara Teika (1162-1241):

miwataseba	In this wide landscape
hana mo momiji mo	I see no cherry blossoms
nakaikeri	And no crimson leaves—
ura no tomaya no	Evening in autumn over
aki no yūgure	A straw-thatched hut by the bay.
	(tr. Donald Keene)

Teika here excludes all the usual symbols of the beauties of nature and the seasons, pushing his poetic vision above and behind the open grey scene that provides the surface images. The criteria for the proper evocation of *yūgen* are subtle. The effects of *yūgen* can be profound, even in the kind of seemingly simple poem cited above.

[3] Quoted in Brower and Miner, *Japanese Court Poetry* (Stanford, 1961), p. 269.

A fourth term often employed in traditional literary criticism is *sabi*. The word is related to the Japanese word for "rust," which immediately says a good deal about the literary virtues it suggests. One modern rendering of the term that captures something of the feeling meant to be conveyed is "tranquility in the context of loneliness." Like *yūgen*, the word was first associated with poetry and later was given a wider application. The term was particularly important with reference to the *haiku* of Matsuo Bashō (1644-1694) and his followers. The art of *haiku* writing, which reached its first great heights with Bashō, was a more popular art than the poetry practiced by the earlier courtiers; and for some critics, *sabi* is a more homely version of the aristocratic *yūgen*. Bashō himself identified the virtues of *sabi* in a poem by his disciple Kyorai:

hanamori ya	Under the cherry blossoms
shiroki kashira o	The guardians of the trees
tsukiawase	Lay their white heads together.
	(Nippon gakujutsu shinkōkai trans.)

Bashō liked Kyorai's juxtaposition of the pale fresh blossoms with the white hair of the old gentlemen who, sent out to keep the tree safe from those who might pluck its branches, sit gossiping underneath its boughs. Bashō himself defined *sabi* as the feelings one might experience in seeing an old warrior, weary and battle-scarred, dressed for an elaborate occasion in fresh bright robes. *Sabi*, like the other terms mentioned above, demands a proper artistic response to the thrust of the writer's own cultivated intuition.

All of the examples (and there are many more, some equally significant, that might be provided) obviously serve best as touchstones of taste. Ultimately, in Japanese terms, they provide the basis for a critical stance, but the gap between such a recognition of this realized feeling and our familiar concepts of literary prose structure—and we can certainly sense principles of structure in the works of Japanese fiction we read—poses certain difficulties for the Western reader. Passages of prose, for example, can be said to express *mono no*

aware or *yūgen*; yet even after such an acknowledgment is
made, the question remains as to how such an effect was accomplished. The Western reader seeks, in effect, a poetics of
prose.

With the coming of Western influences at the time of the
Meiji period and after, one might assume that the critical
stance of Japanese literary critics would come closer to that
employed in the West. In broad outline, certain *rapprochements*
were created, but many of the similarities, in fact, seem to
exist only on the surface. The first systematic Western critical
methodology was introduced in a celebrated book *Shōsetsu
shinzui* (The Essence of the Novel), written in 1885 when its
author, Tsubouchi Shōyō, was a mere twenty-six years old.
Shōyō went on to become the most distinguished translator
of Shakespeare into Japanese. His attack on Tokugawa didactic fiction and his insistence on the central importance of the
psychological realism he found in his reading of Western, particularly British, fiction, had a profound effect on young
Japanese readers and writers. His book literally launched the
modern literary movement. The break with the literary past
was enormous. The poet and actor Shimamura Hōgetsu
wrote with the firmest of convictions in 1908 that in the past
Japanese literature had chosen beauty as the highest ideal;
now, with the advent of naturalism, the ideal was truth.[4]

Despite the change in the literary climate, however, much
modern Japanese literary criticism remains closer in spirit,
whatever its current fashionable verbal trappings, to the older
criticism than to the systematic criticism of the West. Modern
Japanese literary criticism can be roughly divided into three
categories. None performs precisely the functions a Western
reader might expect. The first of these might be described as
academic criticism. Time has wrought enormous changes in
the Japanese language, and works written even as late as the
early years of this century require considerable quantities of
notes and explanations. For the older texts, variants must be
compared, definitions of archaic terms clarified, manuscripts
sought out. A whole academic industry has sprung up to pre-

[4] See Hisamatsu Sen'ichi, *The Vocabulary of Japanese Literary Aesthetics*,
(Tokyo, 1963), p. 69.

serve and protect the national literary heritage. The expenditure of energy on the details of these varieties of critical problems has not produced as powerful a parallel concern with the larger significance of the works so carefully being explicated. This particular critical world is a miniature one. Small questions are answered brilliantly. Large ones are seldom posed.

Some of this larger function has been taken over by a second category of critics, those who have adopted a Marxist stance. Many of them, but by no means all, are associated with universities. For those educated in the period from roughly 1920 to the 1960s, Marxism seems to provide the same psychic satisfactions Confucianism did for their ancestors: a love of orthodoxy, a rigid abstract framework within which any particular reality may be fitted, and a sense of possessing the truth. On the whole, Marxism brought to the consciousness of literary critics a sense of the social forces that lie behind individual acts and helped them understand the changing possibilities for interpreting literature in a rapidly industrializing society. But there have been no Marxist critics of Japanese literature, in academic circles at least, with the sort of temperament that might have led them to look beyond the structures of the intellectual system they adopted. As yet, Japan has produced no Lukács, no Adorno.

A third type of contemporary criticism is that produced by the best of those men who might be called, for want of a better term, literary journalists. Many such writers make criticism their vocation and have achieved the kind of status among discerning readers that a man like Edmund Wilson gained in this country during his lifetime. The criticism written by these men is intensely personal and powerfully stimulating. Etō Jun, himself a highly accomplished critic, describes the paradigm as follows:

> I think that a literary theory, if it is to be called a theory at all, can be discovered only *a posteriori* through the critic's ethical as well as aesthetical experiences as he reads a particular work. Once discovered, however, this "theory" does not necessarily work again in the same effective manner in its application to another work. This is, I think, the fate of any literary theory, for a theory cannot be alive un-

less it is rooted in the critic's own experience of an actual work. By its own nature, this kind of experience can hardly be repetitive.[5]

The emphasis again remains on a personal, highly intuitive response to literature by one who has cultivated himself by study and reflection. The greatest of the modern Japanese literary critics, Kobayashi Hideo (born 1902), has composed a number of essays that are as poised and as moving as any texts in modern Japanese literature; yet as these works reveal the meeting of his sensibility with the work under examination, the result seems as much a map of Kobayashi's own spiritual landscape as of the work under discussion.

In sum, in modern Japanese literary criticism there exists a natural and tacit understanding that much can be assumed. For those of us who do not share that tradition, our task is to grasp as precisely as possible what those assumptions are.

IV

In attempting to provide an explication of certain important literary structures and themes in the Japanese tradition, I have (as the subsequent text will make clear) employed concepts taken from a variety of traditional and modern Japanese writers and critics, in order to make the discussions that follow as meaningful as possible. In particular, I have adopted the method used by such critics as Kobayashi: that of choosing for analysis individual texts that I much admire. The works I have chosen date from all periods in Japanese literary history. Using each work as a point of departure, I have attempted to show, by citing various other texts, both literary and critical, how the Japanese tradition, as it developed, produced a close interplay of thematic and narrative structures, an interplay that in turn came to represent the central element in a highly coherent literary aesthetic, with its carefully wrought sanctions of thought and expression. Further, I would suggest as well, such modes seem in some ways closer

---

[5] Etō Jun, "Modern Japanese Literary Criticism," *Japan Quarterly*, XII, April, June 1965, p. 177.

to our own contemporary view of literature than to certain conventional ideas in our own tradition.

I would add a final note of caution. Works as rich as those discussed in the pages that follow cannot be dealt with in any reductionist fashion. In emphasizing the tradition from which they come, I do not wish to suggest in any way that their principal significance lies merely in their relationship to that tradition. Each is unique: each can be read and interpreted in a variety of ways, as can any great work of literature. Knowledge of the Japanese tradition, however, helps center each work more precisely, so that its special beauties and accomplishments can be more justly appreciated. Roman Jakobson has justly observed that "the reader of a poem or the viewer of a painting has a vivid witness of two orders: the traditional canon and the artistic novelty as a deviation from that canon. It is precisely against the background of that tradition that innovation is conceived. . . . This simultaneous preservation of tradition and breaking away from tradition form the essence of every new work of art."[6] In terms of the Japanese tradition, Jakobson's example of painting is particularly apt. Our familiarity with the traditions of craftsmanship so important in the history of Western painting (a necessary study of the great masters, for example, or a self-imposed apprenticeship with an older painter) can serve as a means to permit us to better grasp similar attitudes held by a great majority of Japanese writers toward their own art, from the earliest times down to the generation of Kawabata and his "disciple," Mishima Yukio.

The present study is chiefly concerned, then, with an articulation of the Japanese tradition. Such a study has value because, precisely as Jakobson suggests, a comprehension of that tradition will help make clear in turn the innovatory nature of the works of literature discussed here. Each possesses such qualities, and not only with respect to the Japanese tradition. A careful reading of these texts can provide us, as Western readers, with a means to expand our own comprehension of reality as well.

[6] Roman Jakobson, "The Dominant," in Matejka and Pomorska, ed., *Readings in Russian Poetics* (Cambridge, 1971), p. 87.

II

Tanizaki Junichirō: The Past as Homage
A Portrait of Shunkin and *The Bridge of Dreams*

FOR many readers, the work of Tanizaki Junichirō (1886-1965) remains the most absorbing in modern Japanese literature, and in many ways, for its period, the most contemporary in spirit. Tanizaki examined the foibles and obsessions of his time with an elegant and ironic spirit that continues to give his work a surprising freshness. Yet an analysis of his writing indicates a powerful interest on his part in the themes and techniques of older Japanese literature. His perception of these older traditions, and his use of them, help provide the richness of texture that gives his narratives their grace and their weight. His works may thus lead in several directions at once. An examination of two of them, the novella *A Portrait of Shunkin*, and the short story, "The Bridge of Dreams," both of which contain elements of the past and the present, may therefore serve as an appropriate means to begin an examination of the larger tradition.

Tanizaki's life spanned the entire modern period. He began writing early in the century, often, it is said, under the "Satanic" influences of Edgar Allan Poe and Oscar Wilde. Fascinated by Western culture, he enjoyed visiting the foreign shops, stores, and hotels in Tokyo and nearby Yokohama, and he witnessed the destruction of that "modern" civilization he so appreciated when Tokyo burned after the great earthquake of 1923. Tanizaki left to live in a quiet area in the vicinity of Osaka, the large industrial city near Kyoto, the old capital. He wrote a considerable number of works during the increasingly difficult period of the 1930s; during the Second World War he finished composing what is perhaps his masterpiece, the long and evocative novel *Sasame yuki* (Thin Snow) as a tribute to the world he saw crumbling around him. In the vastly different postwar era he continued to produce novels as provocative as *Kagi* (The Key) in 1956, and, in 1962, the novel that provides a last ironic look at himself and his generation, *Fūten rōjin kikki* (The Diary of a Mad Old Man).

For Japanese readers of his generation, Tanizaki's works often seemed scandalously "modern." He himself commented that his extensive reading of Western literature (by which he may have meant such writers with a Naturalist bent as Ibsen, Zola, and Strindberg) gave him the ability to portray the liberation of sexual desire. Tanizaki seems to have meant that he had been liberated to portray a new set of relationships between men and women. Women in his work often became fierce and demanding creatures; if not quite jealous goddesses, they certainly remain larger than life. His male characters often find themselves most comfortable when groveling at their feet. In this respect, Tanizaki's celebrated short story *Shisei* (The Tattooer), written in 1910, can serve as a paradigm for much of his later work. When the beautiful heroine is about to have a spider tattooed on her body, the tattooer warns her of the pain involved. "I can bear anything for the sake of beauty," she replies simply. The thrust of much of Tanizaki's work is suggested by the overtones of that one sentence. His ability to push his reader into a peculiar psychological state, as well as his highly developed dramatic sense (he was a promising playwright early in his career) remained enormous assets for him throughout his creative life.

For all his interest in overtures toward sex and psychology, Tanizaki was always careful to stress the ultimate importance of careful literary construction. In 1927, he provided an explicit statement of the value of such methods in his own literary work, in the midst of a literary debate with Akutagawa Ryūnosuke, the author of *Rashōmon* and other celebrated stories. Tanizaki speaks as though he were a musician, explaining the importance of a fugue:

> According to Akutagawa, I am excessively given to novel, fanciful plots. I wish to write only of the perverse, the fantastic, what excites the masses. This is not good. This is not what a novel should be. There is no artistic value in plot interest. Such, I think, is Akutagawa's general view. Unfortunately I disagree. Plot interest is, described differently, the way in which a work is assembled, interest

in structure, architectural beauty. It cannot be said that this is without artistic value. . . . It is of course not the sole value, but I myself believe that among the literary forms the novel is that which can possess the greatest sense of structural beauty. To do away with plot interest is to throw away the special prerogatives of the form known as the novel.[1]

Those readers who seized on the more outrageous aspects of Tanizaki's thematic concerns (some would term them obsessions) failed to take note of the means by which their interest was inevitably caught and sustained in those narratives. The means Tanizaki often chose owe much to traditional Japanese literature.

A PORTRAIT OF SHUNKIN

In *Shunkinshō* (A Portrait of Shunkin), Tanizaki explores to the full the psychological relationships between master and slave. The composition of such a work of fiction, with its eerie artistic and erotic insights, would doubtless have been impossible in Japan before the twentieth century; but its creation in 1933 would also have been impossible without a desire to render a certain literary homage to the past.

The narrative is presented in the first person by a learned man of this century with a taste for the traditional arts. He attempts to assemble various documents in order to recreate, and to understand, the life of Shunkin, the blind daughter of a rich Osaka merchant in the early nineteenth century, who became an expert player on the samisen. The narrative focuses on the relationship between Shunkin and the young boy Sasuke, who, having joined the family to learn a merchant's trade, is eventually assigned as a servant and pupil to the difficult daughter. The story chronicles the relationship between this extraordinary pair, from childhood and adolescence through adulthood, when Shunkin herself becomes a teacher. The two live together as mistress and servant until

[1] Quoted in Edward Seidensticker, "Tanizaki Jun-ichirō, 1886-1965," *Monumenta Nipponica*, xxi, 3-4 (1966), p. 261.

the beautiful Shunkin, scalded on the face by an unknown assailant, is able, through her own first experience with humility, to begin to accept Sasuke as her equal. Sasuke's own sacrifice is to blind himself, so as never to see the scarred face of his beloved. They finish out their lives together in the embrace of mutual darkness.

Shunkin is an extraordinarily rich narrative that can intrigue and move the reader in a variety of ways. The subject matter itself stands as a particularly powerful example of Tanizaki's predilection for creating forceful and autocratic women for his central characters. Sasuke, who is reduced to a kind of psychological slave, fondles her feet, takes her to the lavatory, and performs every conceivable function (including the sexual) to insure her comfort and well-being. Shunkin is not grateful. Tanizaki uses his psychological study of the relationship between the two, his literary manifestation of the special closed world in which they live, to suggest that the relationship between "Teacher" and "Taught" operates in any human situation. Although in *Shunkin* all such elements seem pushed to extremes, the characters remain believable: the reader, perhaps to his discomfort, is forced to recognize that he finds himself in familiar territory, no matter how purposefully exotic the trappings.

Tanizaki's own taste and learning create in *Shunkin* a document that reveals much about the quality of life in the late Tokugawa period. The various distinctions between social classes and the general compartmentalization of life are carefully delineated. All of society seems a series of airless rooms. Art (in this case the musicality of Shunkin) in such a social context, suggests Tanizaki, may have provided the most delicious of dangers, since it cut across all social distinctions and barriers—as it does in a number of important moments in the novella. The deepest level of thematic structure in *Shunkin* reveals Tanizaki's convictions concerning the necessary rigors of all art: only unrelenting efforts, and often the most painful ones, can produce any genuine results. Once attained, however, the continuing sacrifice seems justified. For Tanizaki, beauty is never far from pain.

When Sasuke begins to learn the samisen, he studies at

night, in a dark closet, so as not to disturb the other sleeping apprentices. His difficulties are enormous.

> . . . Sasuke would wait until he was sure they were sound asleep then get up and practice in the closet where the bedding was kept. The attic room itself must have been hot and stuffy, and the heat inside the closet on a summer night almost unbearable. But by shutting himself up in it he could muffle the twang of the strings and at the same time avoid the distraction of outside noises, such as the snoring of his roommates. Of course he had to sing the vocal parts softly and pluck the strings with his fingers, instead of with a plectrum: sitting there in the pitch-dark closet, he played by his sense of touch alone.[2]

Later, Shunkin's very abuse spurs Sasuke on to greater skills:

> "You're such a weakling!" she told Sasuke scornfully. "You're a boy, and yet you can't stand the least thing. It's all because of your crying that they blame me and think I'm being cruel to you. If you really want to become an artist you've got to grit your teeth and bear it, no matter how much it hurts. If you can't, I won't be your teacher."
>
> After that, however badly she abused him, Sasuke never cried.[3]

Only after Sasuke has blinded himself can he feel that he has attained a proper level of understanding:

> Always before, even while they were making love, they had been separated by the gulf between teacher and pupil. But now Sasuke felt that they were truly united, locked in a tight embrace. Youthful memories of the dark world of the closet where he used to practice came flooding into his mind, but the darkness in which he now found himself seemed completely different. Most blind people can sense the direction from which light is coming: they live in a

---

[2] Tanizaki Junichirō, *Seven Japanese Tales*, tr. by Howard Hibbett, (New York, 1963), p. 22.

[3] *Ibid.*, p. 34.

faintly luminous world, not one of unrelieved blackness. Now Sasuke knew that he had found an inner vision in place of the vision he had lost. Ah, he thought, this is the world my teacher lives in—at last I have reached it![4]

Shunkin as well only achieves the highest pinnacle of her art through suffering. The narrator comments on this fact:

> How ever blessed with talent, she could scarcely have attained the ultimate mastery of her art without tasting the bitterness of life. Shunkin had always been coddled. Though severe in her demands on others, she herself had never known hardship or humiliation. There had been no one to humble her. But then Heaven had subjected her to a cruel ordeal, endangering her life and smashing her stubborn pride.[5]

Indeed, Tanizaki ultimately suggests, the beauty of the lives of these two people seems to lie in their suffering, however perversely inspired.

In constructing *Shunkin*, Tanizaki solves with consummate skill the chief artistic problem such an account proposes: he has made the fantastic world of the heroine credible. In this regard, the unnamed narrator plays a key role, although his presence contributes little of real importance to the theme of the story. He serves rather as a bridge between the commonplace world of the reader and the bizarre world of Tanizaki's heroine. The narrator begins by explaining that he has become quite interested in the musician Shunkin and that he has managed to visit the grave-site of the woman and her pupil Sasuke, also a fine musician. He goes on to tell the reader that he has located an old biography of Shunkin and a dim photograph of her as well. He has also spoken with an old woman who knew the pair when she was very young. The narrative that follows is constructed of juxtapositions of portions of that biography, along with statements made by the old woman, plus an extensive commentary provided by the narrator himself. Some statements contradict each other. Often the narrator speculates on the psychological meaning of

[4] *Ibid*., p. 74.   [5] *Ibid*., p. 81.

the actions outlined in the biography. Raising questions about aspects of the meaning of the events makes the reader more willing to assume that the events actually took place; such questions act as a device to cast over the somewhat fabulous and hallucinatory narrative a thin semblance of ordinary reality.

For example, after an extraordinary account of the birth of Shunkin's illegitimate child, during which Shunkin's wanton cruelty toward Sasuke is first revealed, Tanizaki halts the flow of narrative so that his narrator can make the following comment.

> Why did Shunkin treat Sasuke in this fashion? To be sure, Osaka people have always been more concerned about questions of family background, property, and status, when it comes to marriage, than those to Tokyo: Osaka is famous for its proud old merchant families—and how much prouder they must have been in the feudal days before Meiji! A girl like Shunkin would doubtless have regarded Sasuke, whose family had served hers for generations, as someone immeasurably beneath her. Then too, with the typically embittered attitude of a blind person, she must have been determined not to show any weakness, or let anyone make a fool of her.
>
> I suppose she felt that she would be insulting herself irreparably by taking Sasuke as her husband. Probably she was ashamed of sleeping with an inferior, and reacted by behaving coldly toward him. Then did she consider him nothing more than a physiological necessity? As far as she was aware of her own feelings, I dare say she did.[6]

The narrator's speculations here seem to provide the reader only a partial explanation for Shunkin's cruel behavior. In previous sections of the narrative, Tanizaki has already let the reader see further into the real nature of Shunkin than the narrator himself seems prepared to do. There seems something more, something terrible to state, that the narrator cannot quite bring himself to envision. Yet the reader quickly realizes

[6] *Ibid.*, p. 41.

that he can sense certain depravities in the couple's relationship. Forced to take cognizance of his own ability to recognize the presence of such abnormalities, the reader is shocked at himself and his own reactions. Tanizaki, of course, has sought all these results.

Sophisticated as the use of such a narrative technique may be in developing a contemporary psychological portrait of Shunkin and Sasuke, such methods owe some debt to earlier traditions. The first person narrator is perhaps the oldest organizing device used in what might be termed traditional Japanese fiction. The functions of such a narrator will be taken up in later chapters. In *Shunkin*, Tanizaki avoids the use of an omniscient narrator. The reader is shown his attitudes, foibles, tastes, curiosities. His personality is sketched to the extent that he can help propel the narrative along; yet his personal characteristics are not sufficiently obtrusive that they risk distracting the reader's attention from the couple. This reflective solo voice, so much a part of the traditional Japanese modes of narrative, is here fitted with great skill into a framework in which the device functions to produce precisely the complex effect desired.

A narrative constructed from so many diverse elements requires some kind of overall unity to which the various parts of the story can be related. Tanizaki adopts a number of strategies to bring this unity about. One involves the use of images and objects that recur again and again in his narrative. Such symbolism is a familiar enough device for Western readers. Blindness, for example, serves as one unifying image helping to link various levels of meaning.

Sasuke is first drawn to darkness when he learns to play at night:

. . . Sasuke never felt inconvenienced by the darkness. Blind people live in the dark like this all the time, he thought, and Shunkin has to play the samisen the same way. He was delighted to have found a place for himself in that dark world of hers. Even afterward, when he could practice freely, he was in the habit of closing his eyes whenever he took up the instrument, explaining that he felt he had to do exactly as Shunkin did. In short, he wanted to suffer the same handicap as Shunkin, to share all he could of the life of the blind. At times he obviously envied them.[7]

A Portrait of Shunkin thus becomes, in one sense an account of how Sasuke's wish was eventually granted. The language of the narrative is filled with diverse images of blindness as the story progresses.

Tanizaki's most poetically effective symbols, however, are those of birds. Shunkin keeps caged nightingales and larks. When she listens to them sing, her spirits brighten. She often takes her caged larks to the roof of her house and, in accordance with custom, lets them out of their cages to soar into the sky and sing. The birds normally soon return, but, at the end of the story, her favorite lark does not come back. Shunkin falls into a despondency that eventually brings about her death. The birds have one meaning for her, but another for the reader, who comes to see Shunkin as a caged bird who finds the only release possible in her music. The lyrical images of the birds singing in flight may seem to provide too obvious a parallel to the blind samisen player. But they function well within the context of the atmosphere of the story.

An allied technique Tanizaki employs shows a great reliance on traditional Japanese aesthetics. No Western critical term serves to define such a device. He chooses one moment, one revelation, when the thrust of the whole narrative, its largest significance, seems suggested in a critical central moment. Such a moment creates, in modern prose, precisely that sense of *aware*, that deep sensitiveness to things, so highly prized by traditional Japanese writers. The whole is rendered visible by the revelation of one small element. The narrative microcosm that fulfills this function in *Shunkin* takes place at a party to which Shunkin (accompanied by Sasuke) has been invited by a wealthy young student. The gathering is boisterous. All the guests are fascinated by the beauty and *hauteur* of the blind woman. Suddenly, an untoward incident occurs:

> That afternoon while they were all out strolling in the garden Sasuke led Shunkin among the plum blossoms,

---

[7] *Ibid.*, p. 22.

guiding her slowly from tree to tree and stopping before each of them. "Here is another!" he would say, as he held her hand out to stroke the trunk. Like all blind people, Shunkin depended on her sense of touch to make sure that something was really there; it was also her way of enjoying the beauty of flowers and trees. But when one of the jesters saw her eagerly caressing the rough bark of an old plum tree with her delicate hands, he cried out in a queer, shrill voice: "Oooh, I envy that tree!" Then another jester ran up in front of Shunkin, threw himself into a grotesque pose, arms and legs aslant, and announced: "I'm a plum tree too!" Everyone burst out laughing.[8]

Up until now the pressures of vulgar humanity have been carefully excluded from the story. Until this moment, the reader has unwittingly come to inhabit the closed world of Shunkin and her companion. Now the reader is shocked into the realization that, whatever the nature of Shunkin's cruelty and obsessive demands for excellence, she is a great artist. And now she is being made fun of. The reader's sympathies for her are crystallized, fully engaged. They remain so for the rest of the narrative. This means of creating *aware* in prose, of producing a shock of realization which can suggest the significance of a narrative and so push it forward, finds many antecedents in Japanese fiction, stretching back to *The Tale of Genji*, that classical text which most occupied Tanizaki during the course of his own artistic career. He read and studied that work continuously, and first translated it into modern Japanese before the war.

"THE BRIDGE OF DREAMS"

Shunkin is an altogether modern piece of writing and indeed seems a thorough vindication of James's dictum quoted earlier, "What is character but the determination of incident? What is incident but the illustration of character?" Yet it owes much to the Japanese past, not only for the choice of subject matter but because of the author's occasional use of traditional

[8] *Ibid.*, pp. 62-63.

literary methods. *Yume no ukihashi* (The Bridge of Dreams),
however, a later story written in 1959, after Tanizaki's profound involvement with *Genji*, seems an even more effective
literary experiment, for here Tanizaki attempts a recreation of
some of the themes from Lady Murasaki's novel, paying
homage (albeit in his own way) to the classic, while maintaining with great flair his own literary identity.

More than any other work of Tanizaki, "The Bridge of
Dreams" seems difficult to summarize. The peculiar power of
the story lies in the creation and in the sustaining power of a
special atmosphere. At a climactic moment, the young man
Tadasu, who narrates the entire account in the first person,
cries out, "I was back in the dream world that I had longed
for, back in the power of the old memories that had haunted
for so many years."[9] As a small child, Tadasu lived in an elegant and secluded house in Kyoto with his father and his
mother Chinu. His mother died when he was five, and his
father remarried another woman so like his own first mother
that the child's memories become completely confused and
blurred. He reestablishes the same relationships with his new
mother, some of them abnormal and erotic. When Tadasu is
eighteen, his father dies and asks his son to take his place,
marrying another girl his own age for the sake of appear-
ances. This bizarre relationship continues until the demise of
his second mother, who is bitten by a centipede and dies.
Tanizaki's tangle of erotic relationships may seem perverse
and arbitrary when subjected to such summary treatment.
They are, however, part and parcel of the atmosphere of the
story. And the atmosphere is the subject of, and the justification for, the entire narrative.

Tanizaki has created a world as close to that of the court
depicted in *The Tale of Genji* as might be possible in a
twentieth-century setting. The reference to *Genji* is clear from
the title of the story, "The Bridge of Dreams," itself the name
of the very last book of Lady Murasaki's novel. Indeed
Tanizaki's story opens with a quotation, a poem written by
one of the mothers on the subject of *Genji*. The house in

---

[9] *Ibid.*, p. 134.

which Tadasu is brought up seems to exist in a timeless world. The descriptions of the rooms and gardens have nothing contemporary about them. The sense of the past is always powerful; indeed it is the present that seems ambiguous and arbitrary. Tanizaki creates his links with the present through his characters, who cool their beer in the garden pond and, reluctantly, visit a physician when care is needed. But the world of the house, with its silences, the occasional *koto* music, and the sound of the old-style bamboo clapper in the pond, seems as complete as that of those secluded chambers in which so many of the characters of *Genji* live and, occasionally, die.

Tanizaki's treatment of his characters and of their interrelationships provides an equally effective reworking of certain themes in *Genji*, Tanizaki's musical variations on an earlier theme. That theme, so skillfully developed by Murasaki, concerns the love shown by several important male characters for their mothers, or, perhaps one should say stepmothers. Murasaki relates the discovery by these male characters of this love to their own ability to understand themselves. More often than not, Lady Murasaki uses the theme to show the eternal appeal of certain types of beauty and to suggest the interdependence of all human affection. The emotional and moral world of *Genji*, created when it was, contains much that suggests an ultimate openness and innocent good will in many kinds of human relationships. For Tanizaki, living in the twentieth century, the recreation of a modern version of this earlier world brings with it a strong odor of decadence and decay. This too, for Tanizaki, is beautiful, and such are the elements that make up his own contribution to the world of *Genji*.

Along with the theme of loving one's mother, muted and etherealized in Murasaki, eroticized in Tanizaki, is a second theme common to both narratives, that of children concealed and discovered. Again, in Lady Murasaki's novel, this motif is often used (along with its value as a plot device) as a means by which a character can achieve self-definition and self-enlightenment. For Tanizaki, the lost child serves rather as a means to permit the others (especially Tadasu) to turn ever more inwards upon themselves. Some Japanese writers and critics have pointed out that Tanizaki is, in fact, a moralizer; to the extent that a foreign reader may agree that this might be the case about so atmospheric a story as "The Bridge of Dreams," such a penchant for moralizing might be seen in Tanizaki's discreet suggestion (certainly nowhere stated) that he is depicting a culture that has lived too long.

Tanizaki's care in selecting every proper detail in order to create the atmosphere he desires shows his literary skill and learning at its best. The story is filled with references to *Genji* and the whole history of Kyoto, just as *The Tale of Genji* itself is filled with earlier literary and cultural references. A discussion on calligraphy, one of the arts most prized in Lady Murasaki's novel, opens Tanizaki's story. Poems by Kamo no Chōmei are mentioned; and indeed Chōmei himself, who, in his *Hōjōki* (An Account of My Hut) created a celebrated (and fictionalized) account of his own retirement, seems a perfect prototype for Tadasu, who is keeping a record of his own spiritual existence. Rai Sanyō (1780-1832) and Ishikawa Jōzan (1583-1672), two other learned writers and poets from the Tokugawa period, are also cited, expanding the world of taste and learning in which the characters of the story live. Even when Tadasu leaves the house in search of the mysterious younger brother he has never seen, his trip takes him to villages in the countryside famous in classical literature through references in *The Tale of the Heike* and the medieval *nō* plays. Indeed, the only thoroughly modern element in the story is the occasional intrusion of the doctor, who heralds births and deaths. His appearance always seems startling and usually (despite his personal kindness) disagreeable.

Tanizaki's most elusive homage to *Genji* may lie in his tacit adoption of certain of Lady Murasaki's attitudes. In the earlier novel, the world created by the author is one inhabited by the women of the court, retired from the world, who have the leisure to dream and to reflect. Largely cut off from the world of politics and court activity, they learn of events outside their purview slowly and imperfectly. Tanizaki has made his main character a man, but, despite the change in sex, Tadasu remains far more a part of the world of his strange home than

he does of any world at large. Both he and Shunkin exist in
terms of the atmospheres surrounding them. Toward the end
of "The Bridge of Dreams," the reader is casually informed
that Tadasu graduated from high school and studied law at the
university, but elements from the outer world have nothing
to do with what he perceives to be his real existence. Tanizaki
has remained quite faithful to Lady Murasaki in this respect.

What is more, Tanizaki has absorbed and made use of one
of Lady Murasaki's major literary devices, and one so appropriate to the atmosphere in which she lived and wrote: that of
indirection. In *The Tale of Genji*, the truth about the various
characters and their mutual relationships are revealed in
pieces; the reader comes to know the truth, or a variety of
truths, quite slowly. Overarching relationships—physical,
psychological, or spiritual—are slowly suggested as the narrative moves forward. The reader of Lady Murasaki's novel
thus comes to be enlightened in somewhat the same fashion
that he might hope to be in real life.

In "The Bridge of Dreams," indirection and reticence make
it possible for Tadasu to tell his story. Before the final revelation of his relations with his second mother and of his marriage of convenience to the daughter of the family gardener,
Tadasu makes the following statement.

> I have tentatively given this narrative the title of "The
> Bridge of Dreams," and have written it, however amateur-
> ishly, in the form of a novel. But everything that I have set
> forth actually happened—there is not one falsehood in it.
> Still, if I were asked why I took it into my head to write it
> all, I should be unable to reply. I am not writing out of any
> desire to have others read this. At least, I don't intend to let
> anyone see it as long as I am alive. If someone happens
> across it after my death, there will be no harm in that; but
> even if it is lost in oblivion, if no one ever reads it, I shall
> have no regret. I write for the sake of writing, simply be-
> cause I enjoy looking back at the events of the past and try-
> ing to remember them one by one. Of course, all that I
> record here is true: I do not allow myself the slightest false-
> hood or distortion. But there are limits even to telling the

truth; there is a line one ought not to cross. And so, although I certainly never write anything untrue, neither do I write the whole of the truth. Perhaps I leave part of it unwritten out of consideration for my father, for my mother, and for myself. . . . If anyone says that not to tell the whole truth is in fact to lie, that is his own interpretation. I shall not venture to deny it.[10]

Tadasu's words are, at least in part, an ironic reworking of the well-known passage in *The Tale of Genji* in which Genji defines the art of fiction:

I have a theory of my own about what this art of the novel is, and how it came into being. To begin with, it does not simply consist in the author's telling a story about the adventures of some other person. On the contrary, it happens because the storyteller's own experience of men and things, whether for good or ill—not only what he has passed through himself, but even events which he has only witnessed or been told of—has moved him to an emotion so passionate that he can no longer keep it shut up in his heart. Again and again something in his own life or in that around him will seem to the writer so important that he cannot bear to let it pass into oblivion. There must never come a time, he feels, when men do not know about it.[11]

Tanizaki's passage reflects something of Murasaki; but, more than that, Tadasu's words reveal certain artistic principles involved in the composition of much Japanese poetry and prose. ". . . I certainly never write anything untrue, neither do I write the whole of the truth." Such a principle of adhering closely to the "truth" of one's natural materials but shaping them to the ends of art is one alive in the earliest poetic diaries and is still visible in contemporary fiction. Instinctive selectivity from all the possible materials that the observation of life might offer: in the art of Tanizaki, at least, reticence and

[10] *Ibid.*, pp. 140-141.
[11] Murasaki Shikibu, *The Tale of Genji*, tr. by Arthur Waley, (London, 1937), p. 501.

taste join together at this point to produce, not verbal photographs, or confessions, but literary evocation.

A *Portrait of Shunkin* and "The Bridge of Dreams" will surely strike a Western reader as contemporary in their explicitness and profound in their artistic concerns. And the stories explain themselves. No footnotes on Japanese culture are required to penetrate these peculiar worlds that Tanizaki has created. The author's mastery of the intimate connections between character, incident, and atmosphere permit each element of these stories to reinforce the others; each word of the text seems inevitable, exquisitely appropriate. Nevertheless, Tanizaki's work satisfies profoundly because behind his own personal accomplishment lies a long literary heritage to which his art pays the ultimate compliment of constant reference.

III

Natsume Sōseki: The Past as Style
Kusamakura

THE homage Tanizaki paid to the past was an important aspect of his art; but in Natsume Sōseki's remarkable 1906 novel *Kusamakura* (translated by Alan Turney as *The Three-Cornered World*), traditional literary techniques are recast in the light of Sōseki's own modern sensibility to produce not only a satisfying novel in its own terms but a virtual handbook of traditional aesthetic attitudes and methods. Sōseki (1867-1916) is one of the two great literary figures of his period (Mori Ōgai is the other). Both loved Western literature, went abroad, and did much to introduce the best of nineteenth-century European prose and poetry to their contemporaries. Sōseki began his career as a teacher of English, but after his three-year sojourn in England, where he suffered numerous psychological difficulties, he returned to Japan and became a novelist. Most of his work is somber, filled with a high moral and social purpose that gives his late works, in particular, a powerful philosophical thrust. These aspects of Sōseki's art have come to be relatively well understood in the West, through an excellent series of translations and commentaries.

Sōseki's earlier, more openly aesthetic, work, exemplified by *Kusamakura*, some short stories, and his *haiku* poetry, have been relatively less well represented. Like Mori Ōgai, he grew up when it was still possible to receive an education that involved the study of traditional Chinese and Japanese literary texts and a study of traditional literary and philosophical values. He learned to write accomplished poetry in classical Chinese, the mark of a good Tokugawa education. Perhaps his travels to Europe gave him the perspective on those traditions to permit him to examine them with the kind of enthusiastic clarity seen in *Kusamakura*. In any case, Sōseki came in this novel as close as any modern writer has done to creating pure aesthetic responses in his readers.

The word *kusamakura* Sōseki chose for the title might be translated as "the traveller's pillow," and, in traditional Japanese poetic vocabulary, the term suggests a journey, possibly a search. Sōseki provides both. The Western reader who stumbles on the novel unaided may feel at first that he is wandering around in a maze, somewhere between art criticism and a mystery story. Fortunately, *Kusamakura* explains itself as it goes along, and what it is "about" becomes clear as the narrative progresses. Sōseki himself considered his novel an experiment; he called it a *haiku*-novel and commented that his experiment involved having the protagonist stand still as events moved around him, rather than following a more normal pattern of moving a protagonist through those external events. Such a structure, worked out so carefully in the course of the novel, brings with it new demands on the reader, whose own sense of relationships between thought and action must alter themselves accordingly.

Sōseki chose to write *Kusamakura* in the first person. Whatever psychological or philosophical congruences there may be between Sōseki and the "I" of the novel, however, the two must never be confused. The artistic technique of what might be called the "false I" in Japanese fiction goes back to the beginnings of their literature and continues in importance today. Certain artistic problems concerning the use of the "false I" and its relationship to the author are dealt with elsewhere; in the case of *Kusamakura*, Sōseki uses a traditional narrative technique with a considerable lineage in order to suggest to his readers the atmosphere of certain classic works. This atmosphere helps thrust the reader into the interior—but not too far into the interior—of the narrator's mind. Sōseki's aim here is to project an artistic and creative consciousness, mixing observation, action, and reflection. In such a construction, style is of the utmost importance. *Kusamakura* is widely regarded as a model of elegant modern Japanese prose. Alan Turney's translation inevitably falls short of giving full satisfaction on this level, but it is more than serviceable.

Sōseki's "I" is an artist who paints in oils, in the Western style increasingly practiced in Japan by the turn of the century. This very fact sets the artist at some objective distance

Among the flowers
Of white poppy.[1]

The prose section fulfills functions as close to poetry as to narrative, creating a reflective environment that permits the poem literally to spring forth; the surrounding prose justifies and explains that poetic impulse.

Kusamakura takes this kind of prose as its model. The protagonist does, psychologically at least, stand still as he responds to the various events around him. The first chapter of the novel is a *tour de force*, presenting the thoughts of the artist on a mountain walk, ranging over Eastern and Western art and philosophy. The treatment given is elegant, psychologically astute, and lightly ironic, in Sōseki's finest fashion.

Art, muses the artist, involves transcendence.

There is no escape from this world. If, therefore, you find life hard, there is nothing to be done but settle yourself as comfortably as you can during the unpleasant times, although you may only succeed in this for short periods, and thus make life's brief span bearable. It is here that the vocation of the artist comes into being, and here that the painter receives his divine commission. Thank heaven for all those who in devious ways by their art, bring tranquillity to the world, and enrich men's hearts.[2]

Tranquillity, above the mundane and vulgar world, is the goal sought. The artist goes on, however, to remind himself that to know life must inevitably require a knowledge of sorrow; and that knowledge as well is at the beginning of all art:

After twenty years of life I realized that this is a world worth living in. At twenty-five I saw that, just as light and darkness are but opposite sides of the same thing, so wherever the sunlight falls it must of necessity cast a shadow. Today, at thirty, my thoughts are these: In the depths of joy dwells sorrow, and the greater the happiness the greater

[1] Matsuo Bashō, *The Narrow Road to the Deep North and Other Travel Sketches* (Baltimore, 1960), pp. 87-88.
[2] Natsume Sōseki, *The Three-Cornered World* (London, 1965), pp. 12-13.

the pain. Try to tear joy and sorrow apart, and you lose your hold on life.[3]

The inexorable blending of joy and sorrow eventually gives the artist his sense of reality. Both must be accepted. This fundamental attitude is, of course, the principal concomitant of the term *aware*, discussed earlier, that literary virtue which, lightly touched on here, finds its most powerful expression in the concluding sections of *The Tale of Genji*.

The quality of the relationship of man to nature is also crucial. Man exists as a part of nature in the traditional Japanese view, and his best means of living is to accommodate himself to it. The celebrated incident of the abandoned child in Bashō's 1684 travel diary *Nozarashi kikō* (The Records of a Weather-Exposed Skeleton) provides one classic statement of the "divine indifference" of nature to the preoccupations of man:

> As I was plodding along the River Fuji, I saw a small child, hardly three years of age, crying pitifully on the bank, obviously abandoned by his parents. They must have thought this child was unable to ride through the stormy waters of life which run as wild as the rapid river itself, and that he was destined to have a life even shorter than that of the morning dew. The child looked to me as fragile as the flowers of bush-clover that scatter at the slightest stir of the autumn wind, and it was so pitiful that I gave him what little food I had with me.
>
> > The ancient poet
> > Who pitied monkeys for their cries,
> > What would he say, if he saw
> > This Child crying in the autumn wind?
>
> How is it indeed that this child has been reduced to this state of utter misery? Is it because of his mother who ignored him, or because of his father who abandoned him? Alas, it seems to me that this child's undeserved suffering has been caused by something far greater and more

[3] *Ibid.*, pp. 13-14.

massive—by what one might call the irresistible will of heaven. If it is so, child, you must raise your voice to heaven, and I must pass on, leaving you behind.[4]

The protagonist's path in *Kusamakura* is also difficult, although in a more literal fashion:

This is a terrible road. If it were only plain earth it would not take all that long, but imbedded in the ground are large stones. You can smooth the soil out flat, but the stones will stick up. You can break the stones to pieces, but not the rocks. There is nothing you can do about getting rid of the rocks. They sit atop the mound of broken earth unconquered, and with an almost contemptuous air of self-assurance. There is nowhere here where Nature will yield us a road without a struggle. Thus since our opponent is so unaccommodating, and will not step aside, we must either climb over, or go round.[5]

In accommodating oneself to the larger and inscrutable purposes of nature, one can transcend one's own concerns and join the larger, higher world. When his thoughts reach this point, the protagonist quotes a few lines from Shelley's "To a Skylark":

We look before and after
And pine for what is not:
Our sincerest laughter
With some pain is fraught,
Our sweetest songs are those that tell of saddest thought.[6]

It is precisely nature's indifference to those human concerns that permits man to lose himself in it and to draw strength from his own smallness. The protagonist continues to muse:

Looking at the landscape, it is as though you were looking at a picture unrolled before you, or reading a poem on a scroll. The whole area is yours, but since it is just like a painting or a poem, it never occurs to you to try to develop

[4] Bashō, *Narrow Road*, p. 52.   [5] Sōseki, *World*, p. 15.
[6] *Ibid.*, p. 17.

it, or make your fortune by running a railway line there from the city. You are free from any care or worry because you accept the fact that this scenery will help neither to fill your belly, nor add a penny to your salary, and are content to enjoy it just as scenery. This is the great charm of Nature, that it can in an instant discipline men's hearts and minds, and removing all that is base, lead them into the pure unsullied world of poetry.[7]

Distance from mundane concern permits worldly values to be set aside. For the protagonist, it is the lack of such distance that sets off Western art from Eastern art,

> I want a poem which abandons the commonplace and lifts me, at least for a short time, above the dust and grime of the workaday world; not one which rouses my passions to an even greater pitch than usual. There are no plays, however great, which are divorced from emotion, and few novels in which considerations of right and wrong play no part. The trade-mark of the majority of playwrights and novelists is their inability to take even one step out of this world. Western poets in particular take human nature as their corner stone, and so are oblivious to the existence of the realm of pure poetry. Consequently, when they reach its borders, they come to a halt, because they are unaware that anything lies beyond.[8]

In response, the artist quotes to himself lines from two famous poems of meditation by two great classic Chinese poets, Tao Yuan-ming (365-427) and Wang Wei (699-761).

> Happily, oriental poets have on occasion gained sufficient insight to enable them to enter the realm of pure poetry.

Beneath the Eastern hedge I choose a chrysanthemum,
And my gaze wanders slowly to the Southern hills.

> Only two lines, but reading them, one is sharply aware of how completely the poet has succeeded in breaking free

---

[7] *Ibid*., p. 18.   [8] *Ibid*., p. 19.

from this stifling world. There is no girl next door peeping
over the fence; nor is there a dear friend living far away
across the hills. He is above such things. Having allowed all
consideration of advantage and disadvantage, profit and
loss, to drain from him, he has attained a pure state of
mind.

Seated alone, cloistered amidst bamboo
I pluck the strings;
And from my harp
The lingering notes follow leisurely away.
Into the dim and unfrequented depths
Comes bright moonlight filtering through the leaves.[9]

The artist goes on to remark that, "within the space of
these few short lines, a whole new world has been created.
Entering this world is not at all like entering that of . . . popular novels . . . it is like falling into a sound sleep, and escaping
from the wearying round of steamers, trains, rights, duties,
morals and etiquette."[10]

[9] *Ibid.*, p. 20. The reader may enjoy seeing the full texts of the poems
quoted by the artist.
Tao Yuan-ming's famous poem has been translated as follows by James
Hightower in *The Poetry of T'ao Ch'ien* (Oxford, 1970), p. 130:

I built my hut beside a traveled road
Yet hear no noise of passing carts and horses.
You would like to know how it is done?
With the mind detached, one's place becomes remote.
Picking chrysanthemums by the eastern hedge
I catch sight of the distant southern hills:
The mountain air is lovely as the sun sets
And flocks of flying birds return together.
In these things is a fundamental truth
I would like to tell, but lack the words.

Wang Wei's poem has been rendered as follows by G. W. Robinson in his
volume *Poems of Wang Wei* (Baltimore, 1973), p. 31:

Bamboo Grove House
I sit alone in the dark bamboos
Play my lute and sing and sing
Deep in the woods where no one knows I am
But the bright moon comes and shines on me there.

[10] *Ibid.*, p. 20.

This essential desire for transcendence and tranquillity, then, becomes the object of the artist's tour. "I wish," he concludes, "if only for a brief period, to wander at will through a land which is completely detached from feelings and emotions."[11]

Such are the aesthetic boundaries sketched out by Sōseki in his opening chapter, and he uses the rest of his novel to let the protagonist, and the reader, decide what the real limitations of such a trip might be.

Throughout the course of the narrative Sōseki provides short and vivid glimpses into the traditional aesthetic processes behind the creation of art and literature. To discuss the hundreds of examples he provides would require a book as long as the novel itself, but a few examples may suffice to show the gratifying range of his sympathies.

The relation of man to nature, or, in the case of painting, of man to landscape, is a concept instantly familiar to those who have looked at a Chinese or a Japanese scroll painting and sought out the tiny figures that find their modest place in the vast symmetries about them. The philosophical (and indeed scientific) relationships suggested in these proportions were profoundly upset because of the influences brought to the Far East by the intrusions of the West in the latter part of the nineteenth century. The fact that the problems engendered have not yet been resolved in the artistic sphere can easily be seen in contemporary drawings and paintings from the People's Republic of China, where tiny trucks often replace the wandering philosophers in vast panoramas of nature. They look ridiculously out of place.

Sōseki wanted to convey these reciprocal relationships and he managed to do so with an affecting simplicity. In the second chapter, for example, the artist meets an old woman who runs a dingy shop by the side of the road. She points out to him a local landmark, a large rock shaped like a Japanese goblin. He defines the woman in terms of art and the scenery:

> There, rising majestically into the air, was a tall tapering rock like a pillar from which large chips have been cut. This

[11] *Ibid.*, p. 21.

apparently was the Tengu rock. I gazed first at the mountain, then at the old woman. Finally, I looked half at one
and half at the other, comparing them.

As an artist, I have only two impressions of old women's
faces in my mind. The first is that of the old woman in
Takasago, and the second that of the mountain witch drawn
by Rosetsu. Having seen Rosetsu's picture, my conception
of an old woman was as a rather weird creature; a person to
be seen against a background of autumn-tinted leaves, or in
a settling of cold moonlight. Thus when I saw the Noh
play at the Hosho theatre, I was astonished that an old
woman could have such gentle features . . . depicted in such
a way, even an old woman looks handsome, and has an air
of gentle kindliness. Such a person would not be out of
place on a gold-leafed screen, and is not at all inconsistent
with the idea of soft spring breezes and cherry-blossom. At
all events, as I looked at the old woman standing beside me,
her arms bare, her back straight, one hand shading her eyes
and the other pointing away off into the distance, I thought
how much more in keeping she was with the scenery of a
mountain track in springtime, than with the Tengu rock. I
picked up my book and began to sketch her.[12]

The old woman is seen (at least at this juncture of the narrative) in terms of such relationships, not in terms of her own
personality; indeed what the protagonist is seeking is a larger
propriety outside the realm of the individual.

Such assimilation of the individual into art and nature is an
important principle in traditional Japanese aesthetics. In a famous passage Bashō told his students that only such a process
could create real *haiku* poetry:

Go to the pine if you want to learn about the pine, or to
the bamboo if you want to learn about the bamboo. And in
doing so you must leave your subjective preoccupation
with yourself. Otherwise you impose yourself on the object and do not learn. Your poetry issues of its own accord
when you and the object have become one—when you

[12] *Ibid.*, pp. 30-31.

have plunged deep enough into the object to see something like a hidden glimmering there. However well phrased your poetry may be, if your feeling is not natural—if the object and yourself are separate—then your poetry is not true poetry but merely your subjective counterfeit.[13]

The artist in *Kusamakura* echoes the same sentiments and sees such an attitude as a means to escape the materialism of modern life. Assimilation into nature purifies because nature, with that divine indifference, sets aside human perspectives, human understandings. At a point late in the novel, the protagonist, seated by a quiet pond, comes to just such a realization:

> That is the beauty of Nature. It is true that if forced Nature can act ruthlessly and without remorse, but on the other hand, she is free of all perfidy, since her attitude is the same towards everyone who harasses her. There are any amount of people with the ability to judge without fear or favor between Iwasaki and Mitsui [two of the largest industrial firms in Japan], but only Nature could, with icy indifference, set at nought the might of all the princes since time began. Her virtue is far beyond the corrupting reach of this world, and she looks down with an absolute impartiality from the seat of judgment which she has established in infinity.[14]

Sōseki uses the concept of the great assimilating powers of nature as a means to provide a lyric rhythm in his narrative. Nature frames each incident presented and places each in a larger perspective. For example, a long and chatty conversation between the artist and a foolish barber who once lived in Tokyo concludes as follows:

> The scenery and the barber had nothing at all in common, and had he been a more forceful personality, strong enough to impress me as powerfully as my natural surroundings, then I would surely have been struck by the incongruity of their co-existence. Fortunately, however, he

[13] Quoted in Bashō, *Narrow Road*, p. 33.   [14] Sōseki, *World*, p. 133.

was not a very striking character, and for all his brash city ways, and his caustic wit, he was certainly no match for the perfect harmony and serenity of Nature. He had persistently tried to shatter this aura with his interminable chatter, but so formidable was his opponent that he had been reduced to the level of a barely perceptible speck of dust hovering in a ray of spring sunshine. . . .[15]

The artist, able to put the barber in his proper place, is now freed of him:

My barber at the moment was playing out some ridiculous farce, with the whole limitless scenery of springtime as his backdrop. He, who was doing his uttermost to destroy the tranquillity of spring, had only succeeded in adding to it. I felt that I had fallen into the company of a meddling fool. This braggart with all his cheap talk was no more than a component colour in the landscape, blending perfectly with his surroundings on that peaceful spring day.[16]

The fact that the protagonist senses these proportions shows that he is an artist. For, as Sōseki indicates in a later passage in the novel, the artist is not afraid to abandon his own preoccupations to join with nature. Such an attitude of mind is fundamental to the aesthetics of the traditional poetic arts, especially for the writing of *haiku*. Throughout the text, Sōseki's protagonist composes *haiku* and discusses their means of composition. In these passages, Sōseki comes as close as any writer has done to show in prose the mental processes involved in the composition of this deceptively simple form. As sensation becomes art, the identification of the poet fuses with the matter before him; ego and self are forgotten:

Presently, as I sat there beside the mountain path, beneath a sky already dimmed by the early evening of spring, the gentle and soothing sound of a packhorse driver's song broke through into my reverie. It was a song full of tenderness and compassion, yet somewhere locked in the depths there pulsed an irrepressible lightheartedness. I could not

[15] *Ibid.*, p. 81.   [16] *Ibid.*

get it out of my head that the voice was coming from a
figure in a painting. I scrawled the following lines slantwise
across the page.

Swifter than the deer, a song comes on ahead through
    the spring rain.
Leaving the packhorse to follow with tinkling bells.

When I read this poem through, however, I had the feeling that it had not been written by me at all.[17]

Later in the novel, the artist composes a whole sequence of
haiku poems, thereby showing the relation of one succeeding
sensation to another. In each case, a glimpse of beauty produces an instantaneous vision that results in a poem. At one
point Sōseki has his protagonist catch a glimpse of Onami,
the lovely girl who lives at the inn. He sees her through an
open door; what comes then to his mind is not the inspiration
for a *haiku*, but a few lines from a poem by George Meredith.
The artist then adds a few lines of his own, just as a traditional
haiku writer would "cap" a verse by another poet by adding
an additional poem to a sequence. Sōseki repeats the sequence
when Onami "caps" the verses written the night before by
the artist, who has left his tablet out while he slept.

The relationships that link one *haiku* to another vary
widely: season, hour, some small detail of nature, color, or
any other point that provides for an emotional movement,
even if not a strictly logical one. What a Western mind terms
the "association of ideas" is so expanded in the world of *haiku*
composition that, for most Western readers at least, the reasons for the linkages often seem difficult to determine at first
glance. What such progressions reflect, however, is the means
by which the mind instinctively associates one thing with
another. Sōseki often uses this seemingly random means to
connect paragraphs in his narrative. Lying in his bath, the artist hears the sound of a samisen, which quickly suggests to his
half-dreaming consciousness a neighbor girl who played the
samisen when he was a child. She lived in a nearby wineshop,

[17] *Ibid.*, p. 33.

and the artist's memories move to the smell of the rice wine, the swallows in the trees, and the vast pine trees themselves. These random recollections are in each case linked together by sights, sounds, or smells that move the narrator's consciousness from one sensation, one memory, to another. As does Proust, Sōseki uses the seemingly arbitrary workings of the mind to conjure up a whole childhood. His technique in doing so (although not unlike Proust's) is traditionally Japanese.

The central role of poetry in the literary conception behind *Kusamakura* is paramount. The artist never finishes a painting during his "non-human" tour. Yet, as Sōseki is at great pains to suggest, all forms of art are interrelated, and a visual or aural stimulation may produce a poem as easily, and as appropriately, as a picture. The protagonist writes many poems in traditional styles, both in Japanese and in classical Chinese, a form of poetry much favored in most periods of Japanese literary history for certain modes of philosophically directed expression. The protagonist has memorized not only snatches of Meredith, but large chunks of Chinese poetry and prose; at one point he recites a long passage concerning a journey written by Ch'ao Pu-chih (1053-1110). The artist remarks that he learned the passage as a boy, and he can still quote it from memory. He often recites classical Chinese poetry to match precedent with his own experience, and, on several occasions, he composes Chinese poetry himself.

The beauty and efficacy of many other Japanese artistic forms are discussed throughout the book, ranging from calligraphy to *nō* and the tea ceremony. The tonalities of traditional Japanese art pervade the atmosphere of the novel; that aristocratic sensibility alive to the nuances of environment that provides the special world in Tanizaki's "The Bridge of Dreams" is equally visible here. Sōseki's account of emotions engendered by the passing of time finds antecedents as far back as *The Tale of Genji*:

> The voice had at first sounded near the verandah, but had now faded away into the distance. It is true that when something comes to an end suddenly it gives a feeling of

suddenness, but you do not, however, feel the loss too keenly. When a voice ceases cleanly and decisively, it arouses a corresponding feeling in the listener. However, when faced with a phenomenon like this song, which can go on and on becoming fainter and fainter until eventually it disappears without your realizing it, you find yourself breaking the minutes up into seconds and dividing the seconds into fractions, trying to pinpoint the exact time at which it will end; and all the time the pain caused by the anticipation of the loss grows more and more acute. It is like being with a sick man who appears ever on the verge of death but never dies, or watching a flame which gutters continually but never quite goes out. It throws your feelings into complete confusion, and drives every thought save the one: Is this the end? Is this the end? There was something in this song which embodied all the regrets of mankind at the transience of spring in this ephemeral world.[18]

Sōseki often contrasts Eastern and Western aesthetics. The contrasts are often ironic, a word that perhaps describes better than any other the author's stance throughout the novel. *Kusamakura* is by no means merely a plea for traditional Japanese attitudes. The artist, like Sōseki, is trained in and committed to Western methods of art, and the trip remains an experiment on the traveller's part. Throughout the novel Sōseki shows he is well-versed in Western art and Western attitudes, and his Western examples are often most appropriately chosen. Nor is he always in deadly earnest in making such comparisons. There is, for example, a long series of amusing remarks scattered throughout the book comparing the mysterious Onami to Ophelia; in his mind, the artist replaces her Japanese hairstyle with the one used by J. E. Millais in his then-famous painting of Ophelia floating down the stream.

The attitudes of the artist must not be confused with those of the author. The protagonist may complain that Western artists merely show ". . . their inability to take even one step

[18] *Ibid.*, p. 45.

out of this world," yet at the time Sōseki wrote *Kusamakura* he expressed elsewhere his great admiration for Ibsen. Indeed, most of the rest of Sōseki's novels might be said to have been indirectly inspired by his growing concerns over problems in his own society first examined in Europe by Ibsen. *Kusamakura* is a remarkable attempt to define traditional Japanese aesthetics at least in part by contrasting them with those inherent in the kinds of lives led by Sōseki and his contemporaries. Such contrasts are never presented in any pejorative fashion, yet are sharply rendered nevertheless. The non-human is set against the human, ironic detachment against human involvement, leisure against speed, the aristocratic against the democratic. In particular, the sense of contrast shown between the painter's attempt to "stand still" and the throbbing vitality of Onami in her search for self-realization gives the book, through Sōseki's careful structuring, its narrative energy and turns what might have been a treatise into a novel.

THE WORLD OF HUMAN RELATIONS

The protagonist of *Kusamakura* does make discoveries as the novel progresses. Despite his desire to remain uninvolved (almost a passion in itself), he manages to come closer and closer to understanding the character of Onami, the mysterious young woman concerning whom he first hears a few rumors from the old woman he meets in the second chapter. He penetrates through layer after layer, sifting information, most of it conflicting, as he comes closer and closer to understanding what kind of a person she might be. The truth almost always moves faster than his intuition. His mental "sketch" of her, which he feels must precede any actual sketch, remains unfinished until the last page of the novel. Sōseki creates an atmosphere of suspense that provides a certain ironic perspective on the mental world of the protagonist: his doubt about the nature of Onami serves to render arbitrary many of his other suppositions as well. He is slowly drawn into human involvements despite himself, and the movement of the narrative shows that such a course is inevitable.

The old woman tells the artist something about Onami's unsuccessful marriage, into which she had been forced, adding that her banker husband later lost all his money. "After that she went back to live with her father, and since that time people have been saying what a callous, unfeeling woman she is. She used to be such a retiring, gentle girl, but lately she's become quite spirited and wild."[19] Despite these earthy details, however, the artist continues to regard Onami as a subject for a picture; he hears Gembei the packhorse driver reminiscing with the old woman over Onami's wedding day, when he carried the bride over the mountain in her wedding finery. "Although I had a clear impression," thinks the artist to himself, "of the clothes, the hair-style, the horse and the cherry tree, the one thing I just could not picture was the bride's face."[20] The image of Ophelia comes to his mind and he continues to associate that image with her until the end of the novel.

The artist learns other views concerning Onami at various points in the narrative. For Gembei, the packhorse driver, she is a madwoman, from a long line of madwomen; for the barber, she is a harlot; for the Abbot of a nearby Zen temple, she is a wise and enlightened woman. Such widely divergent images are constantly juxtaposed against the artist's own discoveries about Onami, discoveries that also serve as a means to self-discovery for him.

In his first real encounter with Onami, the artist realizes that she is too complex a person to be quickly understood. He has gone to stay as a guest in a large house, now being used as an inn, where Onami and her old father now live. She appears at the door of the bath in the morning. In trying to describe the effect she has on him, the artist recognizes tension and the lack of any resolution in the forces at war within her personality:

> Thus it was that behind the look of contempt I could see a desire to cling to someone, and beneath her sneering attitude I caught a glimpse of prudence and good sense. She tried to appear as though if she gave free rein to her wit and

[19] *Ibid.*, p. 38.   [20] *Ibid.*, p. 35.

high spirits she could handle a hundred men with ease, but in spite of herself she could not contain the gentle compassion which seeped through the hard exterior. There was absolutely no consistency in her expression. She was a person in whom understanding and bewilderment were living together under the same roof and quarreling. This lack of consistency in her expression was evidence of the conflicting nature of her feelings, which in turn reflected the instability of the life she had lived. Hers was the face of one who is oppressed by misfortune, but is struggling to overcome it. She was undoubtedly a very unhappy woman.[21]

At their next encounter, Onami comes to suggest that the artist might enjoy looking at her father's collections of antiques. Now the artist begins to realize that she is a woman of education and of discernment as well:

". . . by the way, from your language, I would say you were not a country girl."

"Meaning that from my character you would say I was?"

"As far as character is concerned it's better to be a country girl."

"Then I have something to be proud of."

"You've lived in Tokyo though, haven't you?"

"Oh yes, in Kyoto too. I'm rather a vagabond. I've been all over the place."

"Which do you like best, here or Tokyo?"

"There's no difference."

"But surely life must be more comfortable in a quiet place like this?"

"Whether you are comfortable or not depends entirely upon your frame of mind. Life is whatever you think it is. What is the use of running away to the land of mosquitoes, because you are uncomfortable in the land of fleas?"[22]

Onami's final words in fact express in different words the meaning of the poem by Tao Yuan-ming on which the artist mused in the opening chapter. Yet Onami is certainly searching for something and with an ardent desire that the artist, in

[21] *Ibid.*, p. 56.   [22] *Ibid.*, p. 69.

his current frame of mind, continues to find unsettling. He shows her the unfinished sketch of the bride on the horse by the cherry tree; she thrusts it back with the words, "what a cramped and uncomfortable world. It is all width and no depth. Do you like a place like this where the only way to move is sideways? You must be a regular crab."[23] She has divined precisely what is lacking in the artist's own vision and in doing so shows considerable wisdom.

Later in the novel, the protagonist sorts out his thoughts on Onami and tries to compare them with the wildly different accounts he has heard. He realizes that he has not yet grasped her personality and cannot yet understand what is lacking in her expression, something missing that prevents him from painting her beautiful face:

> Having thought over various other possibilities, the answer suddenly dawned on me. I had forgotten that there exists among the many emotions one called compassion. It is unknown to the gods, and yet it is the very emotion that can elevate man to near-deity. There was not a trace of compassion in O-Nami's expression; that was what was missing. The instant I saw a flicker of this emotion pass across her features roused by some momentary impulse, I would be able to complete my picture; but when or even if that time would come I had no way of knowing. Her usual expression was only a faint mocking smile accompanied by a frown which showed a burning determination to win at all costs. This by itself was useless to me.[24]

The protagonist cannot see what Sōseki shows the reader: the deficiency of perception may be on the artist's part. Sōseki's ironies now become more obvious. In the following chapter, the Abbot of the Zen temple tells the artist something more about Onami: "She had so much weighing on her mind when she came back to her father's place after her divorce, that she could not bear it; and because she could not bear it she eventually came to me and asked for religious instruction. Recently she has improved tremendously. Look at her, she's now a highly rational woman."[25]

[23] *Ibid.*, p. 70.   [24] *Ibid.*, p. 138.   [25] *Ibid.*, p. 155.

By now the reader begins to understand that Sōseki has set up the artist and Onami as parallel cases. Her study of Zen is an attempt to withdraw and to transcend, just as the artist is making a similar attempt on his "non-human" tour. The rhythm of their encounters, reinforced by Sōseki's ironic treatment of the pair, suggests that, to him, withdrawal from human concerns is not finally possible.

Despite the congruity of purposes with Onami, the artist is still unable to see her objectively. If each chapter of the book might be likened to a *haiku* that gives the reader a sharp impression, the most brilliantly focused of all is Chapter 12, when the artist goes sketching on a path overlooking the sea. That morning he had seen Onami with a knife in her hand and he made the now almost automatic artistic transferral: "I left the hotel feeling that I had been watching a very early morning performance of *kabuki*." Now, from a vantage point on the hill, he sees Onami talking with a stranger, a shabbily dressed man. Suddenly she reaches into her clothing. The artist expects the knife; instead she presents the man with a bag of money. The artist's "objectivity" has again blinded him from realizing the human truth of the situation. The man is Onami's former husband. He is on his way to Manchuria, and she has given him money to help with his trip. The knife turns out to be a farewell gift from Onami's father for her nephew Kyuichi, who has been drafted to serve in the Russo-Japanese War. The artist might, had he felt a sense of involvement and compassion himself, have quickly understood both things, but his self-inflicted "objectivity" has betrayed him.

The last image of the novel ties all the strands together. The artist's trip is over, and he accompanies Onami, her father, and the unfortunate Kyuichi down to the city, where the young man will take a train to join the army. As the train departs, there is a last surprise:

> . . . the train started to move. One by one the carriage windows passed by, and Kyuichi's face gradually grew smaller. As the last third-class carriage went past, another face emerged. There was the shaggy beard and well-worn brown Homburg of the "soldier of fortune" who, filled

with the sadness of parting, was taking one last look out of the window. Just then, he and Onami happened to catch sight of one another, but the engine continued to chug on, and very soon his face disappeared from view.

Onami gazed after the train abstractedly, but strangely enough the look of abstraction was suffused with that 'compassion' which had hitherto been lacking.[26]

Onami has shown compassion and the painter has seen it. Emotion has entered the non-human world. Significantly, the Japanese word employed by Sōseki for "compassion" is *aware*, that term defined earlier as perhaps the highest virtue that can be mirrored in literature:

> "That's it! That's it! Now that you can express that feeling, you are worth painting," I whispered, patting her on the shoulder. It was at that very moment that the picture in my mind received its final touch.[27]

So the book ends.

THE END OF THE PAST

In bulk if nothing else, *Kusamakura* may seem more a sketch than a serious work. There is nothing remotely portentous about the text, and in its more lively sections it creates the kind of atmosphere familiar to those who appreciate the work of the Tokugawa *nanga* painters, or that of Sōseki's contemporary, the artist Tomioka Tessai (1836-1924), who created humorous, colorful landscapes and wore their often considerable learning lightly. Yet Sōseki's humor and delicacy do not make his novel merely slight; indeed, Sōseki's artist begins his journey in the same way that Dante's hero does his. And the return journey from the mountain to the railroad, with the hint of the coming slaughter in the Russo-Japanese War, seems planned, artistically, to serve the same purposes in *Kusamakura*, as does the final descent from the mountain in Thomas Mann's *The Magic Mountain*. Both show war and the end of a civilization. For Sōseki, the modern

[26] *Ibid.*, p. 184.   [27] *Ibid.*

world exists and we must simply live in it, with whatever wisdom and compassion we can muster.

The young man, Kyuichi, on whose forehead Death had already made his putrid bloody mark, was dragging us all relentlessly along with him. The rope of Destiny was pulling him towards a distant, dark and grim land to the north, and so we too, who were inextricably bound to him by the circumstances of a certain day, month or year, would be drawn on until such time as the sequence of events set in motion by these circumstances should arrive at its inevitable conclusion.[28]

In a later and far more somber novel, *Mon* (The Gate), written four years later in 1910, Sōseki again takes up the theme of the impossibility of drawing away from life in our century. Sosuke, the protagonist, takes his troubles to a Zen monastery, hoping to cure himself through meditation. He fails. The Abbot releases him:

Through the years he had relied solely upon his own powers of discretion. It was cruelly ironic that it should be this very self-reliant discretion that had proved to be a curse to him now. In his present mood he envied the unsubtle simplicity of the fool, who follows a course of action without having to weigh the possibilities or puzzle over the means; and he looked with near reverence upon the dedication of the simple good men and women who were firmly anchored in their beliefs and undisturbed by intellectual doubts. It seemed to him that he had been fated from birth to stand forever outside the gate, unable to pass through. There was nothing he could do about it. But if the gate were really impassable, then it had been a contradiction to come here in the first place. He looked behind him and he lacked the courage to retrace his steps along the road he had come. He looked ahead at the firmly bolted door that would never open to reveal the view beyond. He was not a man, then, to pass through, nor yet was he yet one who could be content to remain on the outside. In short, he was

[28] *Ibid.*, p. 177.

a poor unfortunate doomed to squat before the gate waiting for night to fall.[29]

Mon is a powerful novel and its themes are explicitly stated. *Kusamakura*, however, maintains a peculiar charm because Sōseki's serious concerns are so concealed in the structures of the book. Both the artist and the reader are educated to understand that any escape into the past is at best a tour, a spree; the present must command our attention, and our compassion. Sōseki's artist comes to this awareness only at the end of the novel, but the reader is shown from the beginning the disparity between what the artist thinks and what he feels. This gap becomes a source of humor for Sōseki, who often makes fun of that disparity. For example, in the long monologue that forms the first chapter of the novel, the artist's thoughts on the nature of joy and sorrow rise to a point of foolish exaggeration ("gorge yourself and later you will feel uncomfortable . . .") when he trips:

> It was just as my meandering thoughts reached this point, that my right foot came down suddenly on the edge of a loose angular rock, and I slipped. To compensate for my left foot, which I had hastily shot out in an effort to keep my balance, the rest of me—dropped! Fortunately I came down on to a boulder about three feet across, and all that happened was that my colour-box, which I had been carrying slung from my shoulder, jerked forward from under my arm. Luckily no damage was done.[30]

The real terrain forced a loss of "detachment." At the end of the same chapter, a rain shower destroys his objectivity altogether:

> When I think of it as happening to someone else, it seems that the idea of me soaked to the skin, surrounded by countless driving streaks of silver, and moving through a vast grey expanse, would make an admirable poem. Only when I completely forget my material existence, and view

[29] Natsume Sōseki, *Mon*, tr. by Francis Mathy (London, 1972), pp. 204–205.
[30] Sōseki, *World*, p. 14.

myself from a purely objective standpoint can I, as a figure in a painting, blend into the beautiful harmony of my natural surroundings. The moment, however, I feel annoyed because of the rain, or miserable because my legs are weary with walking, then I have already ceased to be a character in a poem, or a figure in a painting, and I revert to the uncomprehending, insensitive man in the street I was before. I am then even blind to the elegance of the fleeting clouds; unable even to feel any bond of sympathy with a falling petal or the cry of a bird, much less appreciate the great beauty in the image of myself, completely alone, walking through the mountains in spring.

At first I had pulled my hat down over one eye and walked briskly. Later I gazed down fixedly at my feet. Finally, very subdued, I hunched my shoulders and took one dejected step after another. On all sides the wind shook the tree-tops, hurrying a solitary figure on his way. I felt that I had been carried rather too far in the direction of detachment from humanity![31]

Ironic contrast serves Sōseki here, as it does throughout the novel, as a means to comment on the unreality of withdrawal. Irony is a coloration found throughout much of his best work and in *Kusamakura*, too, irony is the usual means to suggest larger perspectives. The reader feels an ache, of course, as the party leaves the delights of the mountain village for what seems the inevitable pain to follow. Sōseki wanted that ache to be felt. The novel serves as a farewell to the author's younger enthusiasms and to his own love for his traditional culture. How fitting that Sōseki should render so clearly a multitude of traditional literary attitudes, using so many traditional techniques, in this slight, profound, and very modern novel.

[31] *Ibid.*, pp. 25-26.

IV

Antecedents: The Tale, the Diary, the *monogatari*, the Essay

THE use of the word "novel" in Japanese (*shōsetsu*, literally something approximating "short account") can be extended backwards only for a hundred years or less. What a Western reader might roughly consider as fiction in the earlier periods spreads itself among a number of traditional genres of Japanese literature, most of which seem to have definitions that show considerable variance during their own long histories. In general, the tale, the diary, the *monogatari*, and the essay all seem to possess in varying amounts certain characteristics of Western fiction; on the other hand, these forms contain elements that often seem to prevent them as well from qualifying for such a definition. A work that seems to begin as created narrative often begins to mix with sober fact, slide perhaps into didactic abstractions, and finally finish without any climax at all. Nevertheless these four forms have contributed greatly to the tradition of Japanese letters. Their structures and the quality of their general contents have been instrumental in forming what might be termed the psychology of Japanese literature. They are well worth examining, not only because of their own considerable merits, but because of their importance in shaping the perimeters of the possibilities for literature down to the present day.

The early history of these literary forms is baffling, obscure, and complex, as any reader will discover when consulting any of a number of excellent specialized works on the subject.[1] What follows here is merely a series of reflections on

---

[1] See in particular the excellent prefatory essay in Helen Craig McCullough's *Tales of Ise* (Stanford, 1968), Edwin Cranston's long introduction to *The Izumi Shikibu Diary* (Cambridge, 1969), and the introduction to D. E. Mills's *A Collection of Tales from Uji* (Cambridge, England, 1970). There is also a great deal of good information to be found in various sections of *Translations from Early Japanese Literature* (Cambridge, 1951), by Edwin O. Reischauer and Joseph K. Yamagiwa.

a possible psychological spectrum relating these forms together in terms of their contribution to a tradition close to
what we might term as fiction. A thorough study of any one
of these genres in and of itself will, and should, produce
somewhat different results.

There are a number of various factors to consider in examining these earlier documents. For example, one must observe
the language in which the story or the account was written.
Some were written in Chinese, some in Japanese, and some in
a mixture of both. In turn, the type of language used helps
define the limitations and possibilities of the genre in question. In the Heian court, when Japanese literature reached its
first great heights of perfection, men were educated in
Chinese and wrote basically in that language. Religious documents, state papers, philosophical poetry, Confucian essays,
and other similar compositions were written in Chinese. A
phonetic alphabet for the Japanese language (*kana*) had, of
course, been developed but was usually considered fit only
for women, who were not usually given the privilege of
learning the complicated Chinese characters. Lady Murasaki's
own comments on the subject are revealing:

> There is a lady, Saémon no Naishi, who unreasonably
> cherished hatred of me. I was not at first aware of it, but
> later heard of much criticism of me in my absence. Once
> the Emperor was listening to a reading of my *Genji
> monogatari* and said, "She is gifted, she must have read the
> Chronicle of Japan." This lady heard of it and unreflect-
> ingly spread abroad among the courtiers the idea that I am
> very proud of my learning, giving me the name of "The
> Japanese Chronicle Lady"—it is laughable, indeed! I am re-
> served even before the maids of my own house; how then
> should I show my learning in court? When my elder
> brother Shikibu no Jō was a boy he was taught to read the
> Chinese classics. I listened, sitting beside him, and learned
> wonderfully fast, though he was sometimes slow and for-
> got. Father, who was devoted to study, regretted that I had
> not been a son, but I heard people saying that it is not beau-
> tiful even for a man to be proud of his learning, and after

that I did not write so much as the figure one in Chinese. I grew clumsy with my writing brush. For a long time I did not care for the books I had already read. Thus I was ashamed to think how others would hate me on hearing what Lady Saémon said, and I assumed an air of not being able to read the characters written on the royal screen. But the Empress made me read to her the poetical works of Li Po, and as she wished to learn them I have been teaching her since the summer of two years ago the second and third volumes of that collection very secretly, when none were present. Her Majesty and I tried to conceal it, but His Majesty and the Lord Prime Minister finding it out, the latter presented to the Empress many poetical books which he had had copied. I think that bitter Saémon does not know it yet. If she did, how she would criticise me![2]

One explanation for this split use of language concerns the division between "public" and "private." Chinese was considered most suitable for use when questions of logic and clarity were concerned; but in order to express the nuances of personal emotion, the native vernacular, supposedly however poor in literary possibility and in tradition, was felt to be superior. The fact that the court contained for many generations cultivated and thoughtful women with both the time and the inclination for introspection and for writing, helped to develop the Japanese language as a means not only for communication but for literary art. One Chinese legacy, however, was carried over into literature in Japanese: a belief in the supremacy of poetry. The 31-syllable *waka* (literally "Japanese poem," to set the form off from those of Chinese verse) became the most prestigious form of literature written: collections of the best poems were made at Imperial sanction, and to have one's poems included in these classic collections was the highest honor to which a writer (that is to say, a courtier) might aspire. Prose works were thus often judged in terms of their relationship to the canons of poetic style. To a Western reader, judging one form by another may seem to

---

[2] See Donald Keene, ed., *Anthology of Japanese Literature* (New York, 1955), p. 155 (slightly adapted).

suggest misplaced assumptions. But, in fact, poetry domi-
nated the other forms, shaping them in a fashion that put the
lyrical moment at the center of the Japanese literary tradition.
Various implications of such an emphasis will be discussed
later; here, let it suffice to say that the language in which a
work was written determined its style, its contents, and, to a
considerable degree, its audience. The four genres below
were for the most part written in the Japanese language, and
they made the greatest contributions to the tradition of narrative fiction.

THE TALE

What is commonly called in English a *tale* (some examples
of which are called *setsuwa* in Japanese) covers a wide spectrum of fictional material, ranging in content from pious accounts of the lives of Buddhist saints to miraculous stories of
ghosts, monsters, and great heroes. In this regard, at least,
early Japanese tales bear some resemblance to the Chinese
ch'uan ch'i, usually translated as "tales of the marvellous."
Stories of this variety, written in classical Chinese during the
T'ang Dynasty (618-907), were known to have circulated
among the educated readers in Heian Japan, and Japanese language versions of certain of these tales were included in early
collections of stories compiled at the time. The T'ang stories
were often written by candidates for examinations leading to
Imperial office who used the writing of short fiction as a
means to practice composition, develop skill in narrative
technique, exposition, and versification. The best of the
Chinese stories were exceedingly well composed, psychologically acute, and quite sophisticated in tone and content.

Japanese scholars of the early literature of tales have suggested that four kinds of these "tales of the marvellous" had
an important effect in stimulating the creation of independent
Japanese stories: love and dream tales, adventure stories, tales
of knights and chivalry, and accounts of ghosts and the
supernatural. The categories seem rather vague, but they do
suggest at once the fact that the contents of these stories is
closer to what is usually termed in the West "the romance"

than to realistic fiction. Northrop Frye's well-known definition of romance and of the romantic hero provides a set of
concepts useful in analyzing both the Chinese and early
Japanese tales:

> If superior in *degree* to other men and to his environment,
> the hero is the typical hero of *romance*, whose actions are
> marvelous but who is himself identified as a human being.
> The hero of romance moves in a world in which the ordi-
> nary laws of nature are slightly suspended: prodigies of
> courage and endurance, unnatural to us, are natural to him,
> and enchanted weapons, talking animals, terrifying ogres
> and witches, and talismans of miraculous power violate no
> rule of probability, once the postulates of romance have
> been established. Here we have moved from myth,
> properly speaking, into legend, folk tale, *märchen*, and
> their literary affiliates and derivatives.[3]

The most famous of the early Japanese tales, the *Taketori
monogatari* ("The Tale of the Bamboo Cutter"), the authorship of which is uncertain, dates from the late ninth or early
tenth century. The story is usually regarded as the oldest sur-
viving work of fiction in the Japanese language. Whatever its
historical importance, however, the tale is a delightful and
amusing work that has justly retained its popularity until today. "The Tale of the Bamboo Cutter"[4] bears many of the
hallmarks pointed out by Frye. The story is as follows: a
kindly old bamboo cutter finds a tiny, mysterious child at the
base of a stalk of bamboo; he brings her up and is rewarded by
growing very rich. When the lovely magical princess (named
Nayotake) grows up, she is courted by five celebrated lovers,
who demand her hand in marriage. She gives each an impossible task to fulfill, and each one fails, although each tries to
trick her into believing that he has succeeded. Eventually the
Emperor hears of her beauty and manages to arrange a royal
hunt so that he can pass by the bamboo cutter's home, where
Nayotake still lives. Struck by this extraordinary girl, "so

[3] Northrop Frye, *Anatomy of Criticism* (Princeton, 1957), p. 33.
[4] For a full text of the story, see Appendix I.

beautiful that she filled the room with light," the Emperor tries to steal her away. She vanishes and he realizes that she is no ordinary mortal. Afterwards she permits a correspondence, but they do not meet again. Nayotake begins to weep at the sight of the moon. She tells the bamboo cutter that her real home is in the moon, and that she is only visiting the earth. She realizes now that she must return. The Emperor sends troops to keep her on earth, but, on the appointed day, she tearfully bids farewell to her earthly companions and rises into the sky, leaving the distraught bamboo cutter and the Emperor behind.

Many of the features of the story sound familiar to those who have studied Western fairy tales, but neither the humor nor the general sophistication of the original text is obvious from such a brief summary. In particular, the tricks played by, and on, the five suitors are amusing in themselves and apposite to the characters of the men portrayed. The account of the seasick Grand Councillor, off searching for a jewel in the head of a dragon, is particularly amusing.

The theory has been advanced that the story may have been written first in the Chinese language by a well-educated Japanese courtier, then "translated" into the Heian vernacular for wider distribution. Such an explanation helps to account for the general air of sophistication, perhaps, but there are many folk elements in the story as well, such as the etymology provided for the name of Mt. Fuji that closes the story. Nayotake's voyage back to the moon is the kind of magical trip common to many folk legends, including those of Southeast Asia. Whatever the diverse origins of the story may be, however, "The Tale of the Bamboo Cutter" is satisfying from a literary point of view. The mysterious atmosphere surrounding the girl is suggestively conveyed, and the plot is carried forward with certitude and a genuine rhythm. The tonality of the story provides a judicious mixture of romance and irony, both nicely controlled in terms of the characters presented. For all her witty coquettishness with the suitors, Nayotake never loses her dignity. The suitors, on the other hand, are described by one who had a highly developed sense of the foibles of human vanity.

"The Tale of the Bamboo Cutter" is arguably the best of
the early tales, but many of its important attributes, especially
the combination of an emphasis on a worked-out plot with a
predilection for the miraculous, became important ingre-
dients in the work of many writers in various periods, from
Bakin and Ueda Akinari down to Mori Ōgai and Akutagawa
Ryūnosuke in the modern period. Ultimately this combination of qualities sets off the tale from the other genres discussed below.

THE DIARY

The diary (*nikki* in Japanese) is a second important genre of
early Japanese literature. But is a diary, properly speaking, literature at all? The answer in this case would be affirmative,
and again the reasons are related to the split in language in
early Japan. During the Heian period, two types of diaries became common. The first category might be termed "public,"
to continue that earlier terminology. Kept in the Chinese language, such diaries served as court records, indicating cere-
monies, visits, and other official information of the sort.
Courtiers may also have kept personal diaries or accounts in
Chinese—whom they met, what functions they attended, and
so forth. Such accounts by prominent men (most of whom
were not writers in the artistic sense at all) provide historians
with considerable valuable information about the habits of the
society in which they lived, but they were never conceived of
in literary terms at all.

There also developed, however, what might be called literary diaries. Such diaries, written in Japanese, often bore some
resemblance to prosaic truth but often slid smoothly from fact
to fiction; indeed, a good deal of modern Japanese literary
scholarship on the subject has involved complicated attempts
to separate out the two. These literary diaries, usually written
in the first person, provide remarkably vivid views of the interior emotional world of their authors, and in that sense are
much truer to life than a more prosaic account of a day's
events.

The earliest of these literary diaries is the *Tosa nikki*, or

"Tosa Diary," written around 936. The "Tosa Diary" is a
fine work of art in its own right and can serve as well as a
paradigm for the form. Its structure suggests a number of
problems that confront a Western reader in placing the form
in a context comfortable to him. The opening entry begins as
follows: "Diaries are things written by men, I am told.
Nevertheless I am writing one, to see what a woman can
do."[5] Despite this statement, other literary evidence makes it
clear that the diary was written by Ki no Tsurayuki (869-945),
a courtier and leading poet of his day. One explanation for the
creation of such a "false I" as narrator is that Tsurayuki did
not wish, as a government official, to write a literary work in
women's language. Whatever the reason, the emotional flow
of the first-person narrative is consistently sustained.

The "Tosa Diary" concerns the return to Kyoto, the capital, of the Governor of Tosa province, on the then-remote island of Shikoku. Tsurayuki served as Governor himself, and
the cogent details given concerning the trials of the journey
are obviously recorded from experience. The diary chronicles
the farewell, the departure of the party, and the regret felt by
the narrator over the fact that "her" young daughter, who has
died, will never again see the capital. The passengers wait out
their time on board ship, compose poetry about the beauties
of the scenery, suffer storms, try to avoid encounters with pi-
rates, and make offerings to the gods for a safe journey. The
traveller finally returns home to the capital, only to find "her"
home in ruin. The narrator, musing on the sadness of death
and neglect, writes, "One who shares our inmost thoughts"
composed this poem:

> When one, whose home is here, has not returned,
> How sad to see these new young pines![6]

The "one who shares our inmost thoughts" is presumably
the actual author, Ki no Tsurayuki, who comes forth here to
take his rightful place as a poet, even though he relinquishes

---

[5] Keene, *Anthology*, p. 82. There is another excellent translation, with various useful notes, in Earl Miner's *Japanese Poetic Diaries* (Berkeley, 1969).

[6] *Ibid.*, p. 91.

his role as narrator throughout to a feminine "false I." The "Tosa Diary" therefore lies somewhere between truth and fiction. Most of the later literary diaries follow variants of this same pattern. Bashō, for example, whose celebrated poetic journey provide a unique record of his sensibilities in a similar mixture of poetry and prose, did not hesitate to alter the truth when it suited his larger artistic purposes. Lavish mansions become miserable hovels, distances are changed, even famous objects not seen are described. Such falseness seems somehow shocking; by Western standards, the alteration of fact for literary purposes may be possible in drama or fiction but not in such firsthand "actual accounts" as these.

The common denominator of these diaries may well lie in the fact that they all include poetry, both expressly written for the diary and sometimes quoted from other sources. Earl Miner has written that any satisfactory definition of the form must be based on the fact that poetry is included.[7] The centrality of poetry and the use of the "false I" may be at the bottom of the discomfort felt by Western readers when considering the diary as a form of creative literature. In Western poetry, the assumption is normally made that the narrator, or *persona* in a poem is the poet. When Wordsworth writes, "My heart leaps up when I behold/ A rainbow in the sky," the average reader assumes (rightly or wrongly) that the "I" somehow equals the poet. In drama of course, the author cannot be associated directly with all his characters; Shakespeare is speaking of Hamlet, not necessarily himself at all, when he writes, "O, what a rogue and peasant slave am I." In the Japanese diary, however, the poems too can often have a "narrator" who may actually be somewhat different from the author; the poet, it might be said, assumes a *persona*, or at least a particular set of emotional attitudes, for the purpose of his poem. Perhaps a random example will make the point more clearly. Here is an entry from a well-known literary diary of the thirteenth century, the *Izayoi nikki* ("Diary of the Waning Moon") by the nun Abutsu (1209-1283).

At a place where we stopped around noon, there was a small poor pillow of boxwood. Since I felt miserable, I lay

[7] See *Japanese Poetic Diaries*, p. 16.

down and, seeing an ink-stone, wrote on the sliding doors beside the pillow as I lay:

naozari ni	It was but a trifling meeting,
mirume bakari o	Oh temporary pillow.
kari makura	Tell not to others
musubi okitsu to	That we made promises.[8]
hito ni kataru na	

Abutsu has turned a prosaic situation into a dramatic one; she has imagined the "author" of the poem (not necessarily herself) as a woman who has just undergone some sort of romantic encounter. The poem is certainly not an account of Abutsu's own mood, clearly described previously, where indeed she seems to suggest that she wrote the poem as much as for a diversion as for anything else. The poem then becomes a test of her imagination and her poetic technique, not of her truthfulness.

The "false I" becomes an important element in much of Japanese fiction (indeed the use of such a narrator has been noted in the works of Sōseki and Tanizaki already discussed). Obviously the narrators in such works resemble their authors in some fashion, but maintain their differences as well. This combination of dramatization and self-dramatization surely has its *locus classicus* in the literary diaries; and indeed the interplay of fact and fancy makes both the diaries and their modern descendants more psychologically real than the tales, which are overtly fantastic and romantic. The ascent of Nayotake to the moon is charming, but the lament of the narrator in the "Tosa Diary" for "her" dead child is truly moving because interior emotional states have been elucidated in the most intimate way.

The subject matter of the literary diaries varies widely. In the Heian period, many of the diaries written by women take the form of memoirs, ranging from a document such as Lady Murasaki's diary, which seems an accurate description of her own view of herself, to the diary of Izumi Shikibu (966?-1030), a famous poetess of the period, which contains a great deal of poetry and shows little concern to explicate any purely

---

[8] Reischauer and Yamagiwa, *Early Japanese Literature*, p. 79.

factual treatment of its subject matter. By the Kamakura period, travel accounts by pilgrims became more prominent. In the Tokugawa period, Matsuo Bashō traced the antecedents for his own literary journey and spoke of the inspiration he gained from a study of these earlier accounts:

> From time immemorial the art of keeping diaries while on the road was popular among the people, and such great writers as Lord Ki [no Tsurayuki], [Kamo no] Chōmei, and the nun Abutsu brought it to perfection. Later works are by and large little more than imitations of these great masters, and my pen, being weak in wisdom and unfavored by divine gift, strives to equal them, but in vain. It is easy enough to say, for example, that such and such a day was rainy in the morning but fine in the afternoon, that there was a pine tree at such and such a place, or that the name of the river at a certain place was such and such, for these things are what everybody says in their diaries, although in fact they are not even worth mentioning unless there are fresh and arresting elements in them.[9]

Bashō's diaries perhaps represent the high point in the development of this form, not only because of the beauty and profundity of many of the *haiku* included there, but because of the evocative *haibun* prose style he developed to accompany them.

MONOGATARI

This combination of prose and poetry suggests in turn a third prototype of the modern novel, the *monogatari*, of which the *Genji monogatari* is the most celebrated example.[10] The word *monogatari* means literally *mono-o kataru*, "tell about something." Scholars have divided the *monagatari* into a

---

[9] From *Oi no kobumi* (The Records of a Travel-worn Satchel). See Matsuo Bashō, *The Narrow Road to the Deep North and Other Travel Sketches*, tr. by Nobuyuki Yuasa (Baltimore, 1966), pp. 73-74.

[10] Note that "The Tale of the Bamboo Cutter" is also often classed as a *monogatari*. Nevertheless, the story best serves as a prototype for the literary tale.

number of categories. The one closest to the diary, and the one which undoubtedly also served Bashō as a model, is the *uta monogatari*, or, literally, "telling about poetry."

The origins of the *uta monogatari* are obscure. Many Japanese scholars feel that the form developed from headnotes used to accompany poems in early Japanese collections. The *Manyōshū* (compiled in the latter half of the eighth century) contains explanatory prefaces before certain poems. For example, the following poem:

> In the great ship, full-oared,
> I speed this child of mine to the Land of Kara;
> Bless him, O gods!

is given this headnote:

> A poem which the Empress Dowager of Fujiwara composed at the supplication ceremony at the Kasuga Shrine, and gave to [her nephew] Fujiwara Kiyokawa, ambassador to China.[11]

Without it, the meaning of the poem would not be fully clear. The need for headnotes grew even stronger as the shorter poetic forms became more popular. The Imperial collection compiled in 905, the *Kokinshū*, consisted largely of 31-syllable *waka*. In order to give some overall organization to the collection, poems were arranged by subject matter (the seasons, travel, love, etc.) and longer headnotes were often provided. Without such proper prose contexts, many of these short poems seem practically unintelligible. For example, the following poem is included under the category of "Laments":

mina hito wa	Everyone else, it seems,
hana no koromo ni	Is now gaily dressed.
narinu nari	Will you not at least
koke no tamoto yo	Remain dry,
kawaki dani seyo	O monkish sleeve?

The meaning of the poem is fairly cryptic until one consults the headnote, which provides atmosphere and context:

[11] Nippon Gakujutsu Shinkōkai, tr., *The Manyōshū* (New York, 1969), p. 84.

74   ANTECEDENTS

During the reign of the Fukakusa Emperor, the poet was in constant attendance on the throne as Director of the Archivists' Bureau. When the emperor died, he abandoned court life, went to Mt. Hiei, and became a monk. He wrote this poem the following year, when everyone had stopped wearing mourning and he had begun to hear of rejoicings about promotions and the like.[12]

The headnote is, in fact, a good deal longer than the poem. And it could scarcely be omitted. Bashō combines prose and poetry in much the same way, with the same principle of mutuality involved, although the results are infinitely more sophisticated.

The prototype of the *uta monogatari* and one of the most loved and quoted books in Japanese traditional literature is the *Ise monogatari* or *Tales of Ise*, assembled around 950 by its author or authors. Basically speaking, *Tales of Ise* is a weaving together of various poems to tell a story. In this case, the story, such as it is, concerns the various adventures of the courtier and poet Ariwara no Narihira (825-880). Here the same format is employed: a poem is preceded, and sometimes followed, by a prose setting. Here is a particularly well-known section:

> In former times there lived a lady in East Gojō, in the Western pavilion of the Empress Dowager's palace. Narihira visited her there, at first with no specific intentions but later in great infatuation. About the tenth day of the first month, however, she concealed herself elsewhere. Although he heard where her refuge was, it was impossible for him to go to her, and he became increasingly depressed. In the first month of the following year, when the plum blossoms were in their full glory, he went again to the Western Pavilion, remembering with longing the happenings of the previous year. He stood and looked, sat and looked, but nothing seemed the same. Bitterly weeping, he lay on the deserted bare wooden floor until the moon sank in the sky. Recalling the happiness of the year before, he composed the poem:

---

[12] See McCullough, *Tales of Ise*, p. 166.

tsuki ya aranu	Is not that the moon?
haru ya mukashi no	And is not the spring the same
haru naranu	Spring of the old days?
wa ga mi hitotsu wa	My body is the same body—
moto no mi ni shite	Yet everything seems different.[13]

The poem, a complex and musical one, obviously requires some kind of headnote or other kind of explanation. The poem was originally included in the *Kokinshū*, compiled some fifty years earlier than *Tales of Ise*. In the earlier collection, the poem is provided with a much briefer headnote, merely indicating that the writer, without the means to contact a woman he loved, went to the empty rooms in the spring a year after she disappeared. The bare facts are presented in both versions, but in *Tales of Ise*, the author is intent on dramatizing, and personalizing, the lyric experience by, quite literally, telling a story about it. Many of the best poems in *Tales of Ise* were already well known from previous collections; what is consistently new is the provision of prose renderings and expansions.

A close look at the text shows a considerable amount of fictionalizing has been done. In other incidents, for example, poems (especially anonymous ones) are often attributed to Narihira. In some cases, the original atmosphere of a particular poem is wrenched around to suit a new situation. Section 58 begins:

A man who was a great gallant once built himself a house at Nagaoka and took up residence there. Several very attractive ladies were in service at a neighboring imperial establishment, and one day some of them caught sight of the man as he was superintending the rice harvest in his fields—it was after all a rural spot. The ladies came trooping in, calling, "Isn't this a rather odd occupation for a famous lover?" The man retreated in confusion to the privacy of an inside room, whereupon one of his tormenters recited this poem:

| arenikeri | Poor neglected house! |
| aware ikuyo no | No doubt it has seen |

[13] Keene, *Anthology*, p. 71.

yado nare ya   Many generations pass
sumiken hito no   And thus its former resident
otozure mo senu.   No longer cares to come here.[14]

The poem is "spoken" ironically here. Originally it was included in the *Kokinshū* under the heading "Miscellaneous Poems" and was intended, as Professor McCullough points out, to express sadness and nostalgia. In the *Kokinshū* the poem is listed as anonymous; later collections attribute the poem to Lady Ise (fl. ca. 935), a noted poetess and lady-in-waiting to the court of the Emperor Uda. In *Tales of Ise*, however, the poem has been picked up and reassigned to serve a new narrative purpose for which it was certainly not originally designed. *Tales of Ise* is far more than a collection of headnotes; the fictional imperative is already at work, however imperfectly, and the familiar pattern of narrative building to lyric impulse is one that, as has been pointed out earlier, becomes a basic movement in Japanese fiction in many periods. Other *uta monogatari*, such as the *Yamato monogatari*, or *Tales of Yamato*, written around 950, also combine prose and poetry (in that particular case, a mixture of history, legend, and poetry) with similar results.

Along with the *uta monogatari*, several other categories of *monogatari* have been of crucial importance in the history of Japanese literature. Military and historical tales come to play an important role, in particular the *Heike monogatari* (The Tale of the Heike), a work that will be discussed later in a different context. Some didactic fiction, Buddhist fable, and similar material is also sometimes classed as a kind of *monogatari*. The chief model and precedent for later fiction, however, came from those *monogatari* that centered on human relationships. *Genji* is the most famous example, but by no means the only one. At first glance, *Genji* seems to have sprung full-blown and glorious into the world of Heian Japan to enrich and glorify the time forever. The truth, of course, is both more complex and more intriguing than that oversimplification.

The chief fact that must be appreciated about *The Tale of Genji*, and about those other *monogatari* written in the same

[14] McCullough, *Tales of Ise*, p. 107.

style, is the primal importance of poetry in the Heian conception of narrative. This fact has been somewhat obscured in
Waley's translation, where many of the poems are flattened
into prose, but *Genji* in its original form is closer in the spectrum to the *uta monogatari* than it is to a modern prose novel.
Straightforward Japanese prose narration can be traced back
through works like "The Tale of the Bamboo Cutter" to
early accounts of Japanese myth and early history coming
down from the oral tradition and first written down in an
early work like the *Kojiki* (Record of Ancient Matters) (710),
although to the extent that Lady Murasaki and her contemporaries may have known the stories at all, it was doubtless
from the more formal accounts put into classical Chinese,
such as in the *Nihongi* (Chronicles of Japan) (720). If prose antecedents provided the mystical and fanciful, the poetic tradition, through the *Manyōshū*, the *Kokinshū*, and the *uta
monogatari*, produced the interior, lyrically personal vein. One
of Murasaki's great triumphs was surely to combine both in
an evocative narrative style that brought about the con-
vergence of the best from all these disparate elements. The
other *monogatari* of the period for which texts have come
down to us combine them also, but by no means with as sure
a touch. *Genji* remains the dominant influence, not only in its
form, based on such an effective balance between introspection and forward motion, but also for its mood, its philosophy of life, and its awareness of the nature of the self. *Genji* is
the only one of the precedents discussed here that might be
mistaken for a novel in our conventional sense of the word;
and, if it were, what a modern, post-Proustian novel it might
seem! Nothing of the quality of *Genji*, however, ever resembles another work of art. *Genji* is unique unto itself and will
be discussed elsewhere in those terms.

THE ESSAY

The fourth prototype of fiction in early Japanese literature
is the artistic essay, or, in Japanese, the *zuihitsu* (literally, "following the brush"). In many ways the traditional forms of
essay resemble the diary: essays are usually first-person ac-

counts of events witnessed, often combined with philosophical or emotional introspection. Two differences, however, are striking. First of all, the "I" of the essay is not a
"false I." The "I" is not ambiguous. The author purports to
be none other than precisely himself, and the artistic boundaries of the essay are close to those of the Western personal
essay. Secondly, because the essays tend to be extremely personal, they usually show no organization at all. Nothing is
rearranged, as it were, for overall effect. Many collections of
such essays resemble the *Pensées* of Pascal in form: random
jottings, each section more or less complete in itself, linked
together merely by the predispositions and personality of
their author. Nor is any time sequence usually suggested.

The origins of the essay, like those of the other early literary forms in Japan, remain quite obscure. Some Japanese
scholars indicate that personal literary essays, long popular in
China, may have provided the original impetus for the creation of Japanese counterparts. One of the first works in Japan
that might be considered a collection of essays is the brilliant
Makura no sōshi (Pillow Book) of Sei Shōnagon, a contemporary of Lady Murasaki, whose witty observations remain remarkably cogent and evocative even today. Some scholars
speculate that the form of her collection was suggested by a
Chinese custom whereby informal notebooks were kept at
the bedside for the purpose of making informal jottings. Yet
Shōnagon's own observations are far beyond anything remotely suggested by the modest Chinese models available to
her.

The effect of the *Pillow Book*, like other later collections of
essays and comments, seems close to that of a personal diary,
with the items of observation and reflection prepared for
others to read in terms of content rather than of chronology.
The form seems an especially suitable one for the Japanese
literary sensibility. Some of the finest works in the whole
literary tradition, such as the *Hōjōki* (An Account of My Hut)
written by Kamo no Chōmei, or the *Tsurezuregusa* (Essays in
Idleness) by Yoshida Kenkō (1283-1350) are two of the more
obvious examples of works that are still held up as models of
style, language, and expression. The essay form in many

ways resembles the diary, and, in particular, certain sections of Bashō's reflective *haibun* prose seem closest to the ideal of the essay writer. Bashō, however, shapes his entire diary for an overall artistic purpose; and although the "I" of his travel diaries is closer to the true "I" of the essays than to the "false I" of the literary diaries, Bashō does not, as was indicated earlier, hesitate to change and to adapt the literal truth for his own artistic purposes. Bashō mentions his debt to Kamo no Chōmei, but he also cites Ki no Tsurayuki and Abutsu, both of whom wrote literary diaries but not the more "truthful" essays.

GENERAL CONSIDERATIONS

Any scheme that attempts to analyze literature in terms of its forms is bound to be arbitrary and imperfect. However loose the definitions that have been here employed, however, the tale, the diary, the *monogatari*, and the essay each exhibit in their own particular way certain characteristics that manage to set them off from each other. These prose genres began in the early periods in the long literary history of Japan, and they continued to remain important forms, with certain inevitable modifications, down into the latter part of the nineteenth century. Each of these forms contains elements that relate to Western conceptions of fiction. When the form of the Western novel began to be imported into Japan in the 1880s in reasonable translations, even through the unlikely medium of Jules Verne and Bulwer-Lytton, the Japanese sensibility found much that could be immediately recognized and appreciated. The modern Japanese novel, in turn, grew out of a contact with the West. Thus from the perspective of the modern Japanese novel, and from that of the nature of Western narrative itself, the structural features of the four prototypes discussed here suggest certain principles at work, principles that have obviously maintained an important role in the Japanese literary sensibility. Three might be mentioned here:

(1) "collecting." All the forms discussed seem to attempt to achieve artistically satisfying methods of relating various individual items together. Each form seems to choose a differ-

ent means to accomplish those ends. The essay merely juxtaposes each individual item; the *uta monogatari* attempts to create a continuity through prose added to poetry; the diary attempts to maintain chronology. The close interrelationship between the narrative and the lyrical impulse remains an important artistic problem even in modern fiction, solved (or not) by different authors in different ways.

(2) the "literary I" or the "false I." The use of the first person goes back to the earliest traditions. Elements of self-dramatization visible in the poetic *waka* tradition, discussed above, found their way into the structure of the diary and eventually into the form of the ubiquitous "I novel" so popular in modern Japan. That floating "I" that, wandering as it does back and forth between fiction and reality, thereby confusing many Western readers, can be understood only if the psychological and literary antecedents are kept in mind.

(3) "circular structures." The lyric impulse, plus its prose surroundings, in the diary or in the *monogatari* provides a basic pattern that gives to the Japanese narrative tradition a circular form. Rather than building to a climax, a text tends to follow the pattern of preparation → heightened emotional insight → commentary and transition. The influence of the basic pattern of the *uta monogatari* not only on a work like *Genji* but indirectly on later writers as diverse as Saikaku, Nagai Kafū, and Kawabata Yasunari, remains profound.

Further, examining the spectrum of these forms also makes possible some additional speculation on the unique nature of Japanese narrative. One may range the forms as follows:

tale → *monogatari* → diary → essay

Two overall principles of organization then suggest themselves: first of all, the range from "tale" to "essay" goes from romance (Nayotake's adventures) to an acute psychological accuracy (Yoshida Kenkō's observations). The *monogatari* is certainly more fanciful than the diary, which, although containing much that represents an artistic transposition of reality, nevertheless seeks to give rise to a sense of reality. The romantic characters in *Genji*—Genji himself, the haughty Lady Rokujō, the mysterious Yugao, and the others—are slightly larger than life, and the narration is created so that they will seem so; on the other hand, Bashō, in his travel diaries, is able, for all the profundity of the lyric insights expressed in his *haiku*, to dramatize himself as a real man, with all the foibles of a real man.

Such an observation may seem a commonplace; the second, combined with it, makes for a more surprising pattern. Again beginning with the tale, the principles of narrative organization (plot development, irony, *dénouement* and so forth) are tightly arranged. Indeed, in this respect, the tale seems closest to Western models of fiction. As one moves away from the more romantic forms to the more psychologically realistic ones—the diary and the essay—the materials are less and less tightly organized. The closer one comes to the real workings of the mind and of the emotions, the less narrative organization is found to be of value. The psychology behind such literary structures views nature, and the self, as in flux. In such a view, total coherence and unity become not the norm but an artificial construct. Such a conception of the world is more familiar to us, with our contemporary ideas of existential psychology, than it would have been even fifty years ago. In literary terms this complex of attitudes helped shape the various forms of traditional literature along the diverging lines sketched above. Modern Japanese writers, inheriting such attitudes, continue to pay homage to the same patterns. Some differences with the Western literary tradition now become apparent. The bulk of Western fiction usually combines organization with psychological realism to achieve its ends. Japanese fiction tends to separate them. Thus the differences between these two codes of literary etiquette are at times profound.

V

Source Books I: *Tales of Ise*, *The Tale of Genji*

THE *monogatari*, in its prose and poetic forms, bears the closest resemblance of any traditional genre to modern Japanese fiction, and indeed this form provided a certain actual prototype in terms of the formation of psychological and aesthetic sensibilities in writers and readers alike. From the end of the Heian period until the end of the nineteenth century, to be cultivated meant to have read and studied these works and to have absorbed the kind of expectations and pleasures they provided. Both *Tales of Ise* and *The Tale of Genji* served as sourcebooks for later periods in Japanese literature (and indeed, for all the fine arts), and their influence seems not yet exhausted. Both served in a sense as books of aesthetic etiquette, providing a series of emotional situations and artistic predispositions toward those situations that quickly came to form the basis for measuring the artistic accomplishment in other works of literature. Both *Ise* and *Genji* often served as a last court of appeals in the canons of Japanese traditional taste.

TALES OF ISE

Tales of Ise is an earlier work than *Genji* and, both by the nature of its construction and its mixed form of poetry and prose, it is far less skillful. Many of the 120-odd sections retained in the standard version seem lightly sketched, and the prose settings that accompany the poems seem somewhat arbitrary in conception. Nevertheless, *Ise* provides a number of striking short scenes that became the models for later works, either in subject matter or in structure.

Perhaps the most famous incident in *Tales of Ise* has to do with the transcience of time, quoted in full in the previous chapter. Narihira's celebrated poem that closes it is, again, as follows:

tsuki ya aranu	Is not that the moon?
haru ya mukashi no	And is not the spring the same
haru naranu	Spring of the old days?
wa ga mi hitotsu wa	My body is the same body—
Moto no mi ni shite	Yet everything seems different.[1]

Nothing remains the same; the movement of time inevitably produces not only a sense of personal loss but an awareness of the terrible arbitrariness of all human attachment, even to one's own desires. The greatest loss, of course, is death. Narihira's response to death is captured in one of the great poems from this period of Japanese literature.

tsui ni yuku	This road,
michi to wa kanete	I have long been told,
kikishikado	Man travels in the end—
Kinō kyō to wa	Yet I had not thought to go
omowazarishi o.	Yesterday or today.[2]

Transcience, itself an important ingredient making up the conception of *aware*, is here only lightly sketched; but transcience becomes one of the major themes of *Genji*, where it provides the emotional impetus behind much of that elaborate literary conception. Any reflection on time forces a heightened sense of self: the self views its own image at two different points, emotionally speaking, and the difference between them gives rise to a strong sense of the movements of the inner life. This sense of flux in turn brings with it a feeling of melancholy over the arbitrary quality of any permanent attachment, any attempt to arrest the ceaseless motion of time. To try to stop the flow and to achieve permanence is in itself a human movement that, although it may even involve the exercise of virtue (in *Genji* one thinks of the character Murasaki's devotion to her husband), cannot conquer the erosions of time. This cluster of attitudes is as much a part of a novel like Kawabata's *Snow Country* as of *Tales of Ise*. Kawabata's novel is in prose and concerns characters who live

[1] Keene, *Anthology of Japanese Literature*, p. 71.
[2] McCullough, *Tales of Ise*, p. 149.

in this century, but the lyrical impulses at the basis of his sensibility can be traced back to these early Heian sources.

If transcience and self-awareness are linked, then the passage from childhood to adult status represents a particularly important area for literary observation, since it is precisely at such a time that feelings of this sort first arise. The personality of the adolescent, caught at the moment of expansion into adulthood but not yet hardened into fixed emotional attitudes or burdened down by spiritual or material cares, is a perfect subject for such artistic concerns.

The opening portions of section #23, another of the most famous sections from *Tales of Ise*, present these concerns with a touching and poetic delicacy:

> A boy and a girl, the children of two men who travelled over the countryside, once used to play together beside a well. As they grew up they both felt rather self-conscious about continuing the old relationship, but the boy had set his heart on marrying the girl, and she too was determined that she would be his wife, and refused to agree when her father tried to betroth her to someone else. The boy sent the girl this poem:

tsutsui tsu no	My height that we measured
izutsu ni kakeshi	At the well curb
maro ga take	Has, it seems,
suginikerashi na	Passed the old mark
imo mizaru ma ni.	Since last I saw you.

She replied,

kurabekoshi	The hair parted in the middle
furiwakegami mo	That I measured against yours
kata suginu	Now hangs below my shoulders.
kimi narazu shite	For whom shall it be put up,
tare ka agubeki.	If not for you?[3]

The children realize that time will turn them into adults and that the changes coming to them are subtle and complex; their exchange amounts to a renewed avowal of affection. (Unfor-

[3] *Ibid.*, p. 88.

tunately the incident continues less happily after their marriage; but the remaining passages in the section are not relevant to the mood created here.) Indeed, the passage seems to
suggest, the consciousness of time's passing seems itself to be
a sign that adulthood has been reached. Adolescence and a
sense of one's relationship to the past form an important
thematic emphasis in Tanizaki's story "The Bridge of
Dreams" and is part of the basic conception of Nagai Kafū's
"The River Sumida." The incident of the two children at the
well became the basis for the nō play *Izutsu* (The Well-Curb)
by Zeami and, much later, provided the Meiji-period author
Higuchi Ichiyō (1872-1896) with the materials for one of the
finest short works in modern Japanese fiction, her *Takekurabe*
(Comparing Heights). Adolescence is always a popular subject for literature in any culture, but the self-awareness, reticence, and delicacy contained in this early literary model have
helped make the Japanese artistic conception of adolescence a
reflective, almost an elegiac, one.

Relations between young people are one source of literary
inspiration in *Tales of Ise*. Another is the relationship between
children and parents. The Confucian virtues of filial piety
were known and appreciated in Japan during the Heian period
(and were more formally adopted in later times). In *Tales of
Ise*, the coloration given these attitudes are more affectionate,
and more pragmatic than the formal Confucian values themselves suggest:

> Once there was a man of rather low rank whose mother
> was an imperial princess. The mother lived at Nagaoka,
> and since the son was in imperial service at the capital, he
> found it hard to visit her as often as he would have liked.
> He was her only child, and she loved him dearly. In the
> Twelfth Month of a certain year, a letter came from her; it
> was, according to the messenger, a matter of the utmost
> urgency. In great alarm the man opened it and read this
> poem:

> oinureba   More than ever
> saranu wakare no   I yearn to see you,
> ari to ieba   For old age is said to bring

| iyoiyo mimaku | A parting |
| hoshiki kimi kana | None can evade. |

Weeping bitterly, the son wrote,

yo no naka ni	For the sake of sons
saranu wakare no	Who pray that their parents
naku mo gana	May live a thousand years
chiyo mo to inoru	Would that in this world
hito no ko no tame.	There were no final partings.[4]

The son's reply is, of course, formally "correct," but in addition to his maintaining a proper attitude toward his mother, which poetic (and real) decorum would require, his poem, and his emotional state as he wrote it, are meant to suggest a real affection and pain at separation. Parent-child relationships are often positive in Japanese fiction and on occasion serve as a contrast to other less successful relationships. Mutual love and respect between children and parents is the basic relationship that sustains Mori Ōgai's *Sanshō Dayū*, and the same patterns are important in Dazai's *The Setting Sun*. The affection felt between uncle and nephew in Kafū's "The River Sumida" and the love between father and daughter suggested in *Kusamakura* reflect those attitudes as well. In all of these diverse works, the goal of the parent-child relationship seems a kind of calm trust, precisely what is suggested in this incident from *Tales of Ise*.

A third item of importance in *Tales of Ise*, and indeed in much early poetry, concerns the beauty of nature. Nature can set the mood and the tonality of a segment of narrative and thus provide the proper setting for the lyric impulse. Narihira is the first of a long line of Japanese heroes sensitive to the beauties around him. Portions of Section 87 show clearly how sensitivity to nature can create an ambiance suitable to the poems presented. In this particular case, indeed the poems are rather too modest for the setting:

One day, as the gentlemen were cantering on horseback across the beach in front of the host's house, with no par-

---

[4] *Ibid.*, p. 128.

ticular destination in mind, someone proposed an ascent into the mountains for a view of Nunobiki Falls. The falls were spectacular—a rock face 200 feet high and 50 feet across, swathed, it seemed, in white silk. From the top jutted a rock the size of a straw cushion, against which the rushing waters dashed and shattered in cascades of globules as big as tangerines and chestnuts. The host called for waterfall poems, and the Guards Commander recited,

wa ga yo o ba	Which, I wonder, is higher—
kyō ka asu ka to	This waterfall or the fall of my tears
matsu kai no	As I wait in vain,
namida no taki to	Hoping today or tomorrow
izure takaken.	To rise in the world.

Next the host composed this:

nukimidaru	It looks as though someone
hito koso arurashi	Must be unstringing
shiratama no	Those clear cascading gems.
ma naku mo chiru ka	
	Alas! My sleeves are too narrow
sode no sebaki ni.	To hold them all.[5]

Narihira journeys to many places in *Tales of Ise*, and a number of these places thus became famous "literary" spots in later works of Japanese poetry and fiction. In particular, the area stretching from Ashiya west to Suma (that roughly corresponds to the location of the modern city of Kobe) became an important area for an incident in *Genji*. Lady Murasaki, using that etiquette of emotional response already available to her in *Tales of Ise*, expanded the mood of natural beauty and solitude to suit the larger purposes of her novel. The area figures in *The Tale of the Heike*, in the nō play *Matsukaze*, and in Bashō's 1687 travel diary, "The Records of a Travel-worn Satchel." Each work pays homage to its predecessors while adding new layers of emotional and aesthetic response.

The emotional possibilities of a natural setting receive perhaps their most evocative example in the prose setting

[5] *Ibid.*, pp. 130-131.

created for a verse by Narihira, taken from the latter half of
Section 83:

> Such was the manner in which this Commander made
> himself useful to the prince; but one day, while he was still
> in constant attendance at the palace, he was astonished to
> learn that his patron had become a monk. When the First
> Month came around, he resolved to go and pay his respects
> to him at Ono, a place blanketed with snow at the foot of
> Mount Hiei. With much difficulty he made his way to the
> hermitage, and found the prince looking bored and forlorn.
> He lingered on and on, reminiscing about the past; but
> though he would have liked to remain still longer, his offi-
> cial responsibilities obliged him to start back at nightfall.
> As he set out he recited,

wasurete wa	When for an instant I forget,
yume ka to zo omou	How like a dream it seems . . .
omoiki ya	Never could I have imagined
yuki fumiwakete	That I would plod through snowdrifts
kimi o mimu to wa	To see my lord.

> He went back to the capital in tears.[6]

The hero seeks out his former patron, making his way
through a landscape that echoes perfectly the forlorn, and
possibly stern, mood of the prince. Narihira shows his un-
swerving loyalty, and the setting itself is naturally expressed
in the poem through the mention of snowdrifts. This passage
has been justly admired for the overtones of emotion captured
in such a brief space, as well as for the consonance of visual
and emotional themes chosen, each set reinforcing the other.

The poem itself questions the differences between dream
and reality, the confusions of which have been brought about
by time, and this ambiguity too is another legacy of *Tales of
Ise* to later Japanese literature. The encounter of Narihira and
the Virgin of Ise (a court lady sent to live at the imperial

[6] *Ibid.*, pp. 127-128.

shrine there) most probably gave the title to the entire collection and contains an expression of this shifting sense of reality. Here is the opening portion of Section 69:

Once a man went to the province of Ise as an Imperial Huntsman. The Ise Virgin's mother had sent word that he was to be treated better than the ordinary run of imperial representatives, and the Virgin accordingly looked after his needs with great solicitude, seeing him off to hunt in the morning and allowing him to come to her own residence when he returned in the evening.

On the night of the second day of this hospitable treatment, the man suggested that they might become better acquainted. The Virgin was not unwilling, but with so many people about it was impossible to arrange a meeting in private. However, since the man was in charge of the hunting party, he had not been relegated to some distant quarter, but had been lodged rather close to the Virgin's own sleeping chamber, and so the Virgin went to his room around eleven o'clock that night, after the household had quieted down. He was lying on his bed wide awake, staring out into the night. When he saw her by the faint light of the moon, standing with a little girl in front of her, he led her joyfully into the bedchamber; but though she stayed from eleven o'clock until two-thirty, she took her leave without exchanging vows with him.

The man, bitterly disappointed, spent a sleepless night. The next morning, despite his impatience, he could not very well send a message, and was obliged to wait anxiously for word from the Virgin. Soon after dawn she sent this poem without an accompanying letter:

kimi ya koshi	Did you, I wonder, come here,
ware ya uukikemu	Or might I have gone there?
omōezu	I scarcely know . . .
yume ka utsutsu ka	Was it dream or reality—
nete ka samete ka.	Did I sleep or wake?

Shedding tears of distress, he sent her this:

kakikurasu	I too have groped
kokoro no yami ni	In utter darkness.
madoiniki	Can you not determine tonight
yume utsutsu to wa	Which it might have been—
koyoi sadameyo.	Whether dream or reality?[7]

The context is frivolous, but the use of the unreal to define the real, here so lightly touched upon, continues to serve as a literary device and, as often, as a genuine philosophical concern in virtually every work discussed in this volume, from Ueda Akinari to Sōseki's *Kusamakura*, where the protagonist's dream-like glimpses of Onami delude and inform him in equal proportions. The set of paradoxes underlying this dichotomy between reality and dreams is no doubt traceable through the influences of Buddhism back to the example of Chuang Tzu, the ancient Chinese Taoist philosopher whose writings were as influential in Japan as in China. One of his most famous passages runs as follows:

> But when a man is dreaming, he does not know that he is dreaming; nor can he interpret a dream till the dream is done. It is only when he wakes, that he knows it was a dream. Not till the Great Wakening can he know that all this was one Great Dream. . . .
>
> Once Chuang Tzu dreamt that he was a butterfly. He did not know that he had ever been anything but a butterfly and was content to hover from flower to flower. Suddenly he woke and found to his astonishment that he was Chuang Tzu. But it was hard to be sure whether he really was Chuang Tzu and had only dreamt that he was a butterfly, or really was a butterfly and was only dreaming that he was Chuang Tzu.[8]

Every educated writer and reader in Japan knew the fables of Chuang Tzu and many improvised on his original themes. Bashō, for example, wrote a charming *haiku*.

---

[7] *Ibid.*, pp. 115-116.

[8] Arthur Waley, *Three Ways of Thought in Ancient China* (New York, 1956), p. 32.

okiyo okiyo	Arise, arise
waga tomo ni sen	And be my companion,
nuru kochō.	Sleeping butterfly![9]

Chuang Tzu's texts, however, are lean and sharp in their paradoxes. The Japanese sensibility, even at the time of the composition of *Tales of Ise*, tended to mist them over; night and shadow dimmed the powerful wit and added an element of elegy and nostalgia to those concepts of primal emptiness.

These examples of the influence of *Tales of Ise* on Japanese fiction have centered on poetry and seem to emphasize again what may seem to a Western reader to be a confusion of genres. The key to each section of the narrative has been a poem: the lyric impulse has justified the incident, and the central themes expressed and reflected in the text are lyrical and introspective in nature. Within the context of *Tales of Ise*, such preoccupations are natural. What seems remarkable is that such conceptions could have made such a strong imprint on later works conceived more or less purely in terms of prose narrative. The confusion, of course, is merely our own; Western authors often dramatize a novel but seldom, as is the case here, "novelize" a poem. Poetry has here, and to an equal if not to a greater extent in *Genji*, set many of the standards for prose, and the general compendium of emotions expressed in these two works provide the tonality for most serious forms of literary accomplishment—prose, poetry, and drama—down to the present century. Indeed, fiction and drama that consciously pay homage to such ideals are dignified through such an association. Even a comic writer like Ihara Saikaku (1642-1694), who wrote for a broad public and made fun of old attitudes, knew those traditions and attitudes well. In fact, he began as a *haiku* poet himself.

THE TALE OF GENJI

Genji is, of course, not only a sourcebook but a supreme work of fiction in its own right, and it will be discussed at

---

[9] See R. H. Blyth, tr., *Haiku, Vol. 1, Eastern Culture* (Tokyo, 1949), p. 43.

length later in that regard. What should be mentioned in the
present context, however, is the fact that Lady Murasaki took
up many of the themes first broached in *Tales of Ise* and developed their prose possibilities, achieving an extraordinary
level of sophistication. The poetic ideals—and the poems
themselves (some eight hundred in the original, often buried
in the Waley translation)—remain at the literary center of the
author's conception. The opportunity to compose long prose
sections permits a leisurely and sensitive examination of the
attitudes and inner mental workings of the many characters in
the novel, those who write, and read, those poems. And important as the narrative itself is, the lyrical impulses scattered
through the text serve as the flowers in the field that lure the
fascinated traveller on.

For a book as renowned as *Genji*, even in its own time, it is
surprising how little is known about its author and the circumstances of its composition. We know relatively little
about the external career of Lady Murasaki, and some critics
have even debated the fact that she wrote the book. There are
many textual problems and a certain number of variants exist.
Another controversy over the text (explained at some length
by a *Genji* scholar, Tamagami Takuya, in a 1949 article) concerns the possibility that Lady Murasaki may have told her
story orally, and that what is today a written text was originally meant to be listened to by a select and cultivated audience.[10] The question is of some importance in terms of certain matters of internal organization (length of chapters, level
of vocabulary, etc.), and dramatic recitation might certainly
have helped develop the narrative potentialities in the text, as
was certainly the case with *The Tale of the Heike*. Whatever
the original form of *Genji*, it soon assumed fame in its written
version, and manuscript copies were prizes eagerly to be
sought. This lyrical and introspective work almost immediately set a pattern for the high purposes of fiction. A definitive
text was collated about a hundred years later by the famous
arbiter of taste and poet, Fujiwara Teika (1162-1241), and
his version has remained the standard since. Teika himself

[10] See her article "monogatari ondokuron josetsu—Genji monogatari no
honsei," *Kokugo kokubun*, Vol. 19, #3, March 1949, pp. 1-12.

was a superb poetic craftsman and his work on the manuscript may have served to tighten its style and thus reveal even
more clearly those sensibilities unique to the narrative. Teika
admired the poetry in *Genji*, and his work on the manuscript
produced a text read by every educated person since his time
until inevitable changes in the language made colloquial translations such as Tanizaki's a necessity.

With the compilation and dissemination of the Teika text,
Genji found increased service as a sourcebook for Japanese
writers and poets. Those in each succeeding generation
viewed the work from the point of view of their own literary
ideals and artistic preoccupations. And a text so rich could
never fail to make a contribution to their own thinking, no
matter from what frame of reference it was being examined.

Genji was considered to contain the classic statements of
aware. Teika himself, who lived in a period when the role of
the court and the supremacy of its ideals seemed somehow in
doubt, could already look back on this work as containing the
embodiment of precisely those literary and aesthetic ideals
that needed to be reinterpreted and recaptured. Little in *Genji*
refers to the past; by Teika's time, however, the great statements seemed already to have been made, and art could now
achieve its highest reaches only by taking possession, to
whatever degree appropriate, of that past. Transience and
the shifting of dream and reality, both elements in Murasaki's
conception of *aware*, were remanifested again in *yūgen*, the
medieval conception of "mystery and depth" that provided
the tonality for much of *nō* and that has been recreated again
as a literary ideal in certain works of Kawabata. The work of
Teika and other later writers certainly added a richness of
lyric overtone to Lady Murasaki's aesthetic conceptions, but
Genji remains their prime source.

Many of the dozens of striking characters in Lady
Murasaki's novel served as prototypes for later writers. Few
of the direct imitations were ever successful, with the possible
exception of the Saikaku burlesques. But the categories of
personalities presented seem to have exercised considerable effect. Genji himself, the introspective hero, remained an important model; it is hard, for example, to imagine the depic-

tion given certain courtiers and military figures in *The Tale of the Heike* without reference to the earlier novel. Murasaki, his faithful, attentive, and patient wife, is the first of many Japanese heroines like her (alas, almost all less interesting). Curiously enough, the characters in the latter sections of the novel seem to have made an even greater impression on the sensibilities of later readers and writers. Kaoru, the perceptive yet weak young man, haunted by his own fragile sensibilites, has been a particular favorite, and some of his characteristics are visible in as contemporary a character as the drug-addict Naoji in Dazai's *The Setting Sun*. His companion Niou, sure of himself, and, however attractive, a shade too selfish and insensitive, might well provide the model for Shingo's son in a book like Kawabata's *The Sound of the Mountain*. Any list of convergences might be infinitely multiplied. Lady Murasaki's storehouse of personalities has provided others with endless possibilities.

Not only have the characters in *The Tale of Genji* been a source of inspiration to writers, but the nature and complexity of the interplay between them has attracted admirers and imitators. The plot of *Genji* in summary is a luxurious tangle the diffident would hesitate to penetrate. Read slowly, the novel unfolds with a masterful psychological rhythm that sustains and clarifies the various strands of the story. Lady Murasaki succeeds in her complex design because she gave herself sufficient space to show the developing inner emotions of her numerous characters. She mirrors their changing states of mind while keeping them involved with each other in intricate ways that continue the forward motion of the narrative. Such an interplay fascinated Tanizaki, for example, who attempted to use some of the same techniques in his *Thin Snow* (translated by Edward Seidensticker as *The Makioka Sisters*.)

The basic pattern of narrative movement in the novel, in which the encounters of different personalities give rise to understandings, or to misunderstandings, which in turn advance the plot, became a staple in much later fiction. Other more elaborately constructed methods of plot development occasionally gained ascendancy in the tradition (notably in the

work of Takizawa Bakin [1767-1848], a kind of Sir Walter
Scott of the Tokugawa period), but such deviations never
seem to have permanently deflected the national genius.

The kinds of influence suggested above can be categorized
as indirect; reading *The Tale of Genji* again and again developed in later writers a predilection toward that special brand
of introspective sensitivity that caused them to express themselves in certain modes of thought. But *Genji* was also used
literally as a sourcebook and was quoted directly as a means
to reveal the deeper meaning of a new situation. The technique is easily observed in a well-known poem by Fujiwara
Teika:

haru no yo no	The bridge of dreams
yume no ukihashi	Floating on the brief spring night
todae shite	Soon breaks off:
mine ni wakaruru	Now from the mountaintop a cloud
yokogumo no sora.	Takes leave into the open sky.[11]

The "bridge of dreams" is, of course, a reference to the title
of the last book of *The Tale of Genji*. The poem makes perfectly good sense without the reference, but for the reader
who knows it, the overtones are infinitely richer. Tanizaki
follows the same technique in the opening of his own story.

On reading the last chapter of *The Tale of Genji:*

> Came to sing at Heron's Nest,
> I crossed the Bridge of Dreams.
> Today when the summer thrush

This poem was written by my mother. But I have had
two mothers—the second was a stepmother—and although
I am inclined to think my real mother wrote it, I cannot be
sure.[12]

Such overt references can be satisfying to an educated
reader, as they are in any culture where literature is impor-

[11] As quoted and translated in Robert Brower and Earl Miner, *Japanese
Court Poetry* (Stanford, 1961), p. 262.

[12] See Tanizaki Junichirō, *Seven Japanese Tales*, p. 67.

tant. Japan possesses such a culture, and *Genji* was often used for such purposes.

Another use to which *The Tale of Genji* has been put, in literary terms at least, is as a source of literary landscapes for which emotional overtones have been established. *Tales of Ise* placed Suma beach on the poetic map, as was mentioned earlier, and Genji's lonely visit there, as he puts his own emotional state in consonance with those who had been exiled there before, became in turn a model for later periods. And there are so many more. Uji, the setting for the bitter romance of Ukifune, for example, or Akashi, where Genji fell in love with the daughter of a recluse, became spots which, conjured up in later works with even a brief reference, could evoke a whole emotional world. These spots became, in the phrase of *The Tale of the Heike*, "places with a history to them," and later writers who set their own narratives in these locales never failed to refer to that history. Artists too, in paintings and woodblock prints, were fond of depicting these emotionally charged landscapes, and often provided literary quotations to accompany their work.

Because *Tales of Ise* and *The Tale of Genji* served as sourcebooks for later Japanese literature, the force of their influence set certain perimeters on the etiquette of sensibility. The primacy of a lyrical response and of introspection set the tone for prose. It would be foolish to suggest that all Japanese writers merely imitated these works or even referred to them consciously. In that regard, the literary traditions of Japan stand out in some contrast to those of China, where earlier classics were continuously quoted, in and out of context, in order to provide a proper sense of artistic elevation. The use of these sourcebooks in Japanese literature suggests rather a general sense of homage to touchstones of taste and sensibility that help keep alive attitudes, insights, and ideals of great importance. Only in such a restricted way can these two books be seen as prototypes. They are complete in themselves, great classics in their own right. For that reason they discourage any but the most sophisticated, and the most circumspect, imitation.

VI

Source Books II: *The Tale of the Heike* and the *nō* Drama

THE TALE OF THE HEIKE

IF *Tales of Ise* seems an unlikely progenitor for prose fiction, another *monogatari*, the *Heike monogatari* (The Tale of the Heike) may seem an even stranger candidate. This long account of the 1185 civil war that plagued Japan serves as a chronicle of the development of the military and political power of the new warrior class which brought an end to the ascendancy of the Heian aristocracy. *Heike* is a classic of Japanese prose literature no less influential than *The Tale of Genji*. The work is certainly not a novel, although most of its episodes are constructed along the lines of narrative fiction. The Japanese in this century, at least, have been prone to making claims that *Heike* is the Japanese national epic; but without becoming embroiled in the thickets of comparative definition, I feel that the sophisticated elements of composition, as well as the tendency shown in many sections of the long tale toward a mood of lyrical introspection, make the book an unlikely candidate for that genre. In a loose sense, *Heike* seems closest to the Western historical novel, in which, although the major characters are genuine historical personages, the incidents in which they are involved are not all necessarily factual. Indeed, many modern Japanese readers who only know the *Heike* through such modern colloquial adaptions as those by Yoshikawa Eiji are no doubt justified in regarding it as such. Whatever its form, the *Heike* has become an endless sourcebook for later writers in all forms of literature—poetry, drama, and fiction. Incidents, characters, Buddhist philosophical concepts, literary quotations, all appear in diverse works that owe some part of their impetus or coloration to this classic text.

Like *Genji*, the *Heike* is classified as a *monogatari*, but the circumstances of its composition are such that it resembles

Lady Murasaki's work in no significant fashion. The textual history of the book is obscure and fascinating.[1] There are, for example, several theories as to when the work as we know it was finally assembled. Scholars seem generally agreed that the work is largely a product of the Kamakura period (1185-1333), the troubled era that followed the collapse of the court's political power. That defeat brought about the establishment of a military government outside the capital in the coastal city of Kamakura, long a stronghold of the Minamoto clan, victors in the 1185 battles. There are a whole group of these military *monogatari* that trace the origins of the war and the vicissitudes of the various factions whose machinations led to the final confrontation in which the Taira family (or Heike in Sino-Japanese) and the Minamoto family (or Genji in Sino-Japanese) fought for final supremacy. The Heike lost the war and were, for all practical purposes, exterminated. *The Tale of the Heike* thus concerns to some extent the story of the vanquished, however overweening they may have been. Basically, the story is one of loss.

The literary pedigree of the *Heike* seems to derive from two sources. One possibility includes the *rekishi monogatari* or "historical tales" popular in the late Heian period, after the composition of *Genji*. These works[2] attempt to sketch actual historical incidents, presenting them in a literary framework (breaks in chronology, flashbacks, events presented in memory, etc.) often adapted from such models as Lady Murasaki's novel. A second source of narrative model may have been the collections of tales popular at this time, such as the *Konjaku monogatari* (Tales of Modern and Ancient Times) compiled about 1050. The *Konjaku monogatari* in particular, although largely a collection of Buddhist stories from India, China, and Japan, includes in the section on Japan a few secular tales that

---

[1] For a detailed account of some of the textual problems involved in the *Heike*, see Kenneth D. Butler, "The Textual Evolution of the *Heike monogatari*," *Harvard Journal of Asiatic Studies*, 26, 1966, pp. 5-51. Most of the information concerning such problems presented in this chapter is drawn from this article.

[2] One example available in translation is *Ōkagami* (The Great Mirror), in a version by Joseph K. Yamagiwa, published in London in 1967.

in their artless way show the beginnings of an attempt to apply narrative technique to subjects dealing with military concerns. A more general contribution of collections like the *Konjaku* lay perhaps in matters of style and organization. Stories complete in themselves, and with their own titles, are here grouped in larger units with an overarching theme, however vaguely explicated. In matters of language, too, such tales, composed in a mixture of Japanese *kana* and Chinese characters, helped begin the development of the language in which later versions of the *Heike* were written, a language that became in turn the close ancestor of modern Japanese.

To speak of the literary pedigree of the *Heike*, however, is to neglect one extremely important element: the contributions of the oral tradition to its composition. The importance of these oral elements, in fact, has persuaded some critics that, like Homer, the *Heike* is a true epic. The best reference we have concerning the authorship of the work is a short paragraph in the *Essays in Idleness* of Yoshida Kenkō:

> [A former official from Shinano named] Yukinaga wrote the *Heike monogatari* and taught a blind man named Shōbutsu to recite it. That is why the temple on the mountain is described with special dignity. He wrote about Yoshitsune with a detailed knowledge, but omitted many facts about Noriyori, perhaps because he did not know much about him. Shōbutsu, a native of the Eastern Provinces, questioned the soldiers from his part of the country about military matters and feats of arms, then got Yukinaga to write them down. *Biwa* [lute] entertainers today imitate what was Shōbutsu's natural voice.[3]

The context of this passage thus puts the date of composition or compilation at about 1218. The actual *Heike* text read and studied today, however, is the so-called "Kakiuchi version," dictated by a great *biwa* entertainer in 1371, more than a hundred and fifty years later. An area of doubt remains, of course, concerning what happened in between.

[3] See Yoshida Kenkō, *Essays in Idleness*, tr. by Donald Keene (New York, 1967), p. 186.

Current scholarship suggests that Yukinaga may well have been the original author of a kind of chronicle based on the wars, drawing his information from materials made available to him by his patron, the learned Kyoto nobleman Fujiwara Kanezane (died 1207) and by Kanezane's son, well-known as a scholar. Yukinaga's version of the *Heike* was in *kambun* or classical Chinese, precisely the kind of style that would have been chosen by a man of his background and proclivities. The "Kakiuchi version" was a development of this "kernel" by generation after generation of popular entertainers, wandering Buddhist priests who used the stories as a basis for dramatic recitations performed throughout the country. A comparison between one old *kambun* text (possibly Yukinaga's) and the "Kakiuchi version" shows the older classical Chinese text contains most of the raw material in the later text. The "Kakiuchi version," however, shows the results of a long history of dramatizing and humanizing the rather dry original narrative materials. From that point of view, the present *Heike*, for all the popular elements it includes (especially a strong emphasis on the tenents of the Amida sect of Buddhism, so popular among the common people during the whole medieval period), represents a popularization of complex and sophisticated textual materials for popular consumption, not a "folk epic" at all. In particular the sections on court life in Kyoto contain a wealth of intimate detail that would hardly be available to any "local bard," no matter how assiduously he might have done his research. Japanese literary history here provides the remarkable example of a text with folk elements developing after the composition, and under the influence, of a consciously crafted work or works of high literary skill that preceded it.

Because of the diverse elements in the *Heike*, a number of critical attitudes can be taken toward the text. All are of some interest in themselves and help shed light on the importance of the text to later Japanese literature.

One significant aspect of the work concerns its overall pattern of organization. If *Genji* can be compared to a symphony, then *Heike* is surely a tone poem of the wilder Lisztian variety—diversions, exaltations, bits of tedium. The over-

reaching arch of the theme, in both its historical and philosophical aspects, is never lost, but the fact that various incidents have been added, dropped, and reconceived during the
early history of the text suggests the chameleon-nature of the
book. Again, the contributions of the oral tradition are evident. The incidents are of a length, complexity, and show a
degree of self-containment that suggest a design for oral performance. Such a structure, emphasizing discrete incidents
loosely related by a larger theme, shows a great advance over
the somewhat arbitrary arrangement of materials in the early
tale collections. Such a pattern became a familiar method of
narrative arrangement in later works of fiction. The study of
the remaining records concerning musical *biwa* performances
of the *Heike* by minstrel-priests (often blind) also helps provide clues concerning the nature of the present text. At the
least, such performances certainly contributed a certain
amount of what is termed "formula composition"[4] to the
text. The repetition of such stereotyped phrases and descriptions provides a certain rhythm to the prose. And, in general,
the dramatic language in which the text is written surely owes
much to such influences.

The content of the *Heike* reflects as well the attitudes of the
larger population of Japan at a time when the text was being
changed and elaborated through widespread oral circulation.
No matter how elaborate the incidents in the work became,
the personages presented were actual historical figures; and,
indeed, their personalities and attitudes as presented in this
work became those subsequently accepted as accurate in
much of later Japanese literature. It hardly matters that the
historical Kiyomori, the leader of the Taira clan, was evidently in many ways a shrewd and enlightened man; he has
remained a black villain in popular Japanese history. Kumagai
Naozane, after killing the young Atsumori, may not have become a monk because of any genuine remorse over the incident, but history remolded in the service of a poetic and

---

[4] For a general discussion of elements common to oral performance, see
Alfred B. Lord's *The Singer of Tales* (New York, 1967). The *Heike* contains
numerous scenes that fit into his designated categories: "naming one's
name," for example, or "dressing the hero."

philosophic image better served the national cultural imagination than any set of decaying facts. In that particular sense, the *Heike* soon became as important a sourcebook for Japanese culture as did *Genji*. Later playwrights, poets, and painters have foraged at will for characters, incidents, and attitudes to help shape and color their own work. The very fact that the *Heike* is basically a book of action rather than contemplation, like *Genji*, helped assure its continuing importance. These two great works balanced each other in polarizing two important elements in the Japanese character: introspection and military prowess.

Ultimately, however, it was the thematic content of the *Heike* that made the greatest contributions to the literary tradition. The attitudes about the meaning of life expressed there have become central to the cultural attitudes in many later periods. The juxtaposition of unresolved tensions so characteristic of the *Heike* mirrors a similar situation in all of Japanese medieval culture. The book, as was pointed out before, has no ultimate heroes or complete villains, and is basically elegiac in tone. The text shows genuine sympathy for both sides and mourns the passing of the Heian court. In the *Heike*, the past remains preferable to the present. The ideas of the inevitable movements of time and of the vanity of all human attachment are beautifully expressed in the opening and closing sections.

The first words of *The Tale of the Heike* sound out the grand themes of a Buddhist-inspired insight into the meaning of life, an insight that informs the entire work:

> The bell of the Gion temple tolls into every man's heart to warn him that all is vanity and evanescence. The faded flowers of the sāla trees by the Buddha's deathbed bear witness to the truth that all who flourish are destined to decay. Yes, pride must have its fall, for it is as unsubstantial as a dream on a spring night. The brave and the violent man—he too must die away in the end, like a whirl of dust in the wind.[5]

[5] Hiroshi Kitagawa and Bruce T. Tsuchida, trans., *The Tale of the Heike* (Tokyo, 1975), p. 5.

The beginning of the final section of the work presents another sound, also a temple bell, but a frail one, the faint ringing from the hermitage where the former Empress, Kenreimon-In, after so many unhappy incidents, now manages to live out the rest of her lonely days in solitude:

> As the evening sun was about to go down behind the mountain, the bell of the Jakkōin temple began to toll. Day was done. The cloistered emperor was reluctant to leave, but holding back his tears, he set out on his return journey. Kenreimon-In wept bitterly as thought of her past possessed her. She stood watching the imperial procession until she could see it no more. Back in her hut, she offered a prayer to the main image of Buddha: "I pray thee to save the departed spirit of my son so that he may attain perfect Buddhahood and lead the departed spirits of all the Heike to salvation as well."[6]

The theme of retribution for evil deeds done is sounded throughout the text in an infinite variety of ways. Kiyomori stands as the central example of a man who, wishing too much for himself, brings down destruction upon the whole nation. The untoward rise of Kiyomori and the Taira clan brings pain and distress to the entire court. Even the cloistered Emperor is not safe from the pressures brought to bear on the imperial establishment. His only refuge comes in reading the Buddhist sutras. For men of culture and talent, the age seemed turbulent and degenerate. Retreat into meditation or self-scrutiny seemed the only means to personal sanctity. "For men of sensitive soul, the world now seemed to be a hopeless place."[7]

The first incident of any importance in the early sections of the *Heike* provides an account of the dancer Hotoke Gozen, whose performance so excites Kiyomori that he dismisses two sisters who have faithfully served at court: Giō and Ginyō. On first reading, the incident seems to be included merely to illustrate Kiyomori's grossness of taste and his high-handedness. Then the narrative takes a new turn. The

---

[6] *Ibid.*, p. 780.   [7] *Ibid.*, p. 221.

two sisters, rejected by Kiyomori, decide to retire from the world with their old mother, and the three take vows as Buddhist nuns. One night their seclusion is interrupted by a visitor: she is Hotoke Gozen herself, who in watching the treatment they received at Kiyomori's hands has come to realize both her own responsibility in the affair and the meaninglessness of the life she has been leading. She has decided to take the vows herself and live with the sisters. This portion of the text concludes as follows:

> In this way the four nuns led secluded lives together in that place, offering flowers and incense at the house altar morning and evening. So unswervingly did they bend their gaze toward the Pure Land that we are told that all four of them, eventually, did fulfill their hopes and attain Nirvana. Therefore on the folded scroll of the dead at the Chōgō-dō temple, which was built by cloistered emperor Go-Shirakawa, all four names . . . are inscribed together as specially blessed. Truly the lives of all four are tinged with the sublime melancholy that is called *aware*.[8]

This slight incident, quite touching when read in full, serves as a microcosm, a tiny model of the larger structures of the entire text. Power serves itself and corrupts. Those involved with that power, if they have any choice (and some do not), must give it up for their own good. The final scenes of the text portray a visit by the cloistered Emperor to the Empress at the retreat of Jakkōin and serve as a more elegant variation of the same microcosm. As the *Heike* finally concludes, the former Empress, dying, prays for entrance into Paradise, something already vouchsafed for those simpler women who, in effect, could withdraw from the circle of power in time.

Kiyomori's vanity is illustrated in a number of ways, among them his moving of the imperial capital from Kyoto to Fukuhara (near the modern city of Kobe), an act also chronicled in Kamo no Chōmei's "An Account of my Hut." Kyoto, the proper seat of government, lay in ruin, a gigantic symbol of malaise in the body politic. A courtier fond of the

[8] *Ibid.*, p. 31.

Kyoto scenery, decides to return for an evening of moon-viewing (which, accompanied by the writing of poetry, was a favorite courtly pastime):

> Lord Jittei, the general of the Left, longed to see the moon above the old capital once more. On the tenth of the eighth month, he left Fukuhara and set out toward Kyoto. All was changed. The gardens of the few remaining houses were overgrown with wild, dew-heavy grasses. Birds had built their nests in the tall mugwort bushes and among the rushes. Everywhere there was the incessant hum of insects. Yellow chrysanthemums and purple orchids grew wild over the deserted land.
>
> Now that he had returned to the old capital, Lord Jittei felt that only the palace of his sister, the former empress, at Konoe-Kaware could revive in his heart the memory of the grandeur of times past. When he arrived there, he ordered his retainer to knock at the main gate. From within a woman's voice answered in a reproachful tone: "Who is there? Any who would come to this forsaken place will be soaked with the dew shaken from the weeds."[9]

The deserted capital represents one element in the degeneracy of the age. Heike pride brings corruption everywhere, through the destruction of a natural balance of political forces that has kept the society together.

Emphasizing the high moral purposes of *The Tale of the Heike* may give the mistaken impression that the book is basically a didactic one. Actually, the great strength of the chronicle lies in the power of its narrative thrust. The account of the death of Kiyomori, for example, surely ranks as one of the most powerful episodes in all medieval literature:

> From the day that Kiyomori took to his bed, he could not even drink water. He burned with fever; it was as if something within his body were on fire. Those who approached him within a distance of four or five ken found the heat unbearable. "Hot! Hot!" was all Kiyomori could say. It was not a natural illness. He ordered that water be

[9] *Ibid.*, pp. 296-297.

drawn from Senjui Spring on Mount Hiei and had a stone tub filled with it. He was lowered into the tub; the water began to bubble and soon reached the boiling point. A rain pipe was attached to a well so that running water might ease his suffering. But the water shot back from him as if it had come near a red-hot iron or stone. The water that somehow reached him turned into flames. Black smoke filled his palace, and flames roared up. . . .[10]

A sense of malaise spreads throughout the capital. Unhappy portents begin to appear.

Nii-dono, Kiyomori's wife, had a dreadful nightmare. She saw a flaming cart enter the gate of the palace. Men were standing before and behind the cart, and they had heads like those of oxen and horses. On the front of the cart was an iron tablet inscribed with the single character *mu* ["not" or "without"]. Nii-dono, still dreaming, asked: "Where has this cart come from?"

"From Emma's court [in Hell]," replied one of the cart tenders. "We have come for Kiyomori."

Nii-dono asked again: "What does this tablet mean?"

"Kiyomori burned down the sixteen-jō Buddha of Nan-Embudai. For this crime Emma's tribunal has decided to condemn him to hell-without-end. Emma wrote 'without.' He will write 'end' when Kiyomori arrives."

Nii-dono awoke in a cold sweat. Her heart was filled with terror. When she told others of her dream, their hair stood on end. She offered gold and silver and seven kinds of jewels to the temples and shrines. Saddles, armor, helmets, bows and arrows, ceremonial swords and battle swords were also gathered and given as offerings. And with these offerings, she prayed for her husband's recovery. But from the gods and buddhas there was no sign. Nobles, courtiers, and court ladies gathered by Kiyomori's bedside, but all they could do was grieve, for there was no way to save him.[11]

The purposes of the narrative require, certainly, that

---

[10] *Ibid.*, p. 368.   [11] *Ibid.*, p. 369.

Kiyomori meet a bad end. The account of his last illness and
his final death maintains a power to move the reader because
the facts are permitted to speak for themselves. Kiyomori is
treated badly by the authors of the *Heike*; but, on the whole,
sympathy is expressed for both sides. Those who suffer from
the vanities of the mighty are everywhere. Such sympathies
give the book its essential humanity, nowhere better expressed than in the famous incident between the Minamoto
warrior Kumagae Naozane and the young Taira courtier Atsumori, mentioned earlier, which exists in various versions
adapted from the *Heike* text, including dramatizations for
kabuki and *nō*. Another well-known example of deep human
sympathy can be found in the concluding section of the work,
when the cloistered Emperor arrives at the Jakkōin and meets
a nun of strange appearance:

> The cloistered emperor was unable to tell whether the
> rags that the nun wore were silk or cotton. He thought it
> strange that one in such a humble life could still uphold her
> belief in the Buddha's Way, and so he asked who she was.
>
> For some time she could not utter a word in reply, as she
> was choked with tears. Now, suppressing her tears, she an-
> swered: "Though I am hesitant to tell you, I am a daughter
> of the late priest Shinzei. In the old days I used to wait upon
> Your Majesty as a wet nurse. I am Awa-no-Naishi. At that
> time you were kind to me. Now you do not even recognize
> me. Ah, I have lost the charms of my youth. Indeed, it
> makes me miserable to admit that I am already bent under
> the weight of years." She pressed her sleeves to her face and
> wept bitterly.
>
> "You are truly Awa-no-Naishi!" exclaimed the clois-
> tered emperor. "What a shame it is that I have forgotten
> you! I feel as though I were dreaming."
>
> Tears filled his eyes. The nobles and courtiers in attend-
> ance upon him were also moved to tears and said to each
> other: "Indeed, we could sense her greatness."[12]

All have lived out this terrible dream together. They no

---

[12] *Ibid*., pp. 771-772.

longer can recognize each other after the vicissitudes they
have suffered. Such is the final elegiac and (in its context) profound comment on the terrible events to which the book
bears witness.

The *Heike*, which contains some twelve books (most containing from ten to twenty chapters) in the standard text, has
many sections juxtaposed that seem at first totally unrelated,
as though a cinema camera had been moved from spot to spot
in a battle with no explanations or transitions from scene to
scene. These accounts and events do, however, make up a
larger coherent pattern. Some of the tensions expressed cannot be resolved, and that lack of resolution in turn contributes
heavily to the somber, even tragic purposes of the work.

One important tension opposes the attitudes of the nobility
(represented by the Heike and, of course, by the court itself)
to those of the rough country warriors (represented by the
Minamoto), who, despite the fact that they represent in effect
the heroes of the book, bring with them new virtues, new
loyalties, that inevitably destroy the political, cultural, and
aesthetic balance of the great Heian state. Prince Genji himself
is often mentioned by name in the text as the embodiment of
those vanishing virtues, almost as though he had been a real
person.

The Heike courtiers are tragically conscious of the collapse
of their civilization. When the Heike forces camp at Yashima,
shortly before their final destruction, they look back to the
days they spent at Kyoto, times now gone forever, when the
courtly virtues formed an integral part of their lives:

> The chill wind blew through the bush clover. The dew
> hung heavily on the lower branches. The hum of insects
> was heard as a complaint of the arrival of autumn. The rice
> stalks rustled in the wind. Leaves began to fall from the
> trees. Even to a traveller freed from the odds and ends of
> daily life, the sky of autumn is one cause of melancholy
> thoughts. How much more so it must have been for the
> men of the Heike! In times past they had played among the
> flowers in the imperial garden, but now they lamented their
> sad fate under the autumn moon by the shore of Yashima.

They wished to compose poems, unable to forget the care-
free manner of bygone evenings in the capital. But each day
was dreary and tearful. Yukimori composed a poem of lament:

> As long as we have
> The honor of upholding
> His august presence,
> The moon is bright above us,
> And still we think of Kyoto.[13]

Poetry and the general aesthetic sensibility play an important part in the lives which the Heike courtiers find themselves forced to relinquish. Several striking scenes early in the
narrative show Taira noblemen of sensibility going off to
war. Taira Tadanori visits Shunzei, the great poet of the
time (and the father of Fujiwara Teika). Tadanori wants to
show his former teacher some of his poetry, with a hope that,
despite what might happen to him in the battles to come,
something of his best work might somehow be included in
one of the imperial anthologies. Later, Tadanori is captured in
battle:

> Tadanori had hardly finished his prayer when Tadazumi
> approached him from behind and swept off his head.
> Though he was certain of having obtained a great prize, he
> did not know whose head it was. In searching for some
> identification, however, he found fastened to Tadanori's
> quiver a piece of paper, upon which was written the follow-
> ing poem entitled "A Flower at a Traveler's Inn":
>
>> When the day is done
>> I take a tree for my lodge.
>> On my weary way,
>> Lying under its broad boughs,
>> A flower is my sole host.

Since the poet had signed his name, Tadazumi was able
to recognize Tadanori as a true Heike courtier, the gover-

[13] *Ibid.*, p. 634.

nor of Satsuma province. Sticking the head on the point of his sword, he held it high and declared in a loud voice: "The head of one of the most prominent Heike courtiers, a lord named Tadanori, governor of Satsuma province, has been obtained by Okabe no Rokuyata Tadazumi."

At this declaration, however, friends and foes alike wet their sleeves with tears and said: "What a pity! Tadanori was a great general, preeminent in the arts of both sword and poetry."[14]

Tadanori is mourned as much for his art as for his military prowess. Later, after the war is over, Shunzei, remembering his student's last wish before leaving the capital, pays him the honor of including one of Tadanori's poems in a new imperial anthology. The poem, however, could appear only without the name of the poet, since the Heike clan was in disgrace. Consolation was possible in art, if not in politics.

The Minamoto, although wishing to eradicate the Heike completely, never cease to admire the artistic cultivation of their courtier-enemies. In one telling incident, the Heike warrior Taira Shigehara is captured alive and made a prisoner by the Minamoto. One evening he sings, briefly forgetting his forlorn captivity. He is overheard by the powerful general Yoritomo. The next morning Yoritomo expresses to a retainer his considerable admiration for Shigehira's artistic gifts:

"For the last few years the men of the Heike were used to fighting all the time, and so it has been my understanding that they knew nothing but the arts of bow and sword. Yesterday, however, Shigehira sang and played the *biwa* so beautifully and skillfully that I stood all night out in the garden listening to him. He is truly a great artist," said Yoritomo.

"I too would like to have heard him," said Chikayoshi, "but unfortunately I was sick last night, and so I could not. Henceforth, however, I will not miss the chance to do so. I must admit that the Heike have produced many talented

[14] *Ibid.*, p. 558.

musicians and artists. Last year, when we talked about the Heike, comparing them to flowers, we honored Shigehira as the peony among them."

Shigehira's singing and playing on the *biwa* were so impressive that Yoritomo often remembered him and admired him long afterward.[15]

In the *Heike*, the Minamoto, on the other hand, are portrayed so as to exemplify the rougher virtues of the warrior. The chief of the Minamoto heroes is Yoritomo's younger brother Yoshitsune, the dashing young warrior who remains not only one of the central figures in the *Heike*, but one of the most important cultural heroes in Japanese history, the perfect man of action to range against Genji, the figure of cultured introspection. As such, Yoshitsune became the subject of countless plays, stories, and, more recently, films and television dramas. Many scenes in the narrative exhibit the happy relationship between Yoshitsune and his men. The qualities of loyalty his soldiers display and the willingness they show in sacrificing themselves for their lord served as models for social behavior throughout the medieval period and after. Such men would fight to an honorable death rather than surrender. Yoshitsune, for his part, is portrayed as a great leader because he has the ability, under any circumstances, to manifest his great human sympathies:

> Alighting from his horse, Yoshitsune took the wounded soldier by the hand and said: "Tsuginobu, revive yourself!"
>
> "But I am dying, my lord," replied Tsuginobu faintly.
>
> "Are there any last words you wish to say?" asked Yoshitsune.
>
> "Nothing, my lord," replied Tsuginobu. "The only thing I regret is that I shall not live to see you flourish. Except for this, I have no desires. It is the fate of a man of bow and sword to fall by the shaft of an enemy. I am content with this death, for they will say in the days to come that Tsuginobu died in place of his master at the battle on the beach of Yashima. . . . This is a great honor for a warrior,

and it is something that I will carry with me on the shaded path to the world beyond."[16]

The warriors who serve Yoshitsune revere him deeply, just as their leader holds all his loyal men in the greatest respect and affection. The mutuality of the relationship is of primary importance:

> As the valiant soldier's breath began to fail, Yoshitsune wept bitterly and ordered his men to seek a reputable priest. When they found one, Yoshitsune instructed them: "This wounded man is dying. I wish you to gather as many of your disciples as possible and let them write out a copy of a sutra within a day and pray for this soldier's better lot in the next world."
>
> With this request, Yoshitsune presented to the priest a fine black horse and a gold-studded saddle. . . . This was the horse that Yoshitsune had galloped down the precipitous slope of the Hiyodorigoe Pass behind Ichi-no-tani.
>
> Now, when all the warriors, led by Tsuginobu's brother Tadanobu, saw their master's gracious act, they were moved to tears and exclaimed: "For the sake of our lord, we shall not hesitate to risk our lives. In comparison to his, ours are as trivial as dust and dew."[17]

Another of the creative tensions found in the *Heike* is that between human affection and the necessity for force. Any love, any human intimacy, seems powerless before the onslaughts of war. Many abandon themselves completely. In one moving section, the wife of Taira Michimori, one of the Heike generals, hears of her husband's death and, despite the fact that she bears in her body their unborn child, decides to kill herself. She recounts to her companion, her former wet nurse, the sense of helplessness and despair she feels. Her husband dead, she can no longer imagine the pain of living, and of giving birth to still another life:

> ". . . if I bear a child and bring him up so that he may remind me of the form and features of my dead husband,

[16] *Ibid.*, p. 657.   [17] *Ibid.*

my every glance at him will bring back the old memories only to cause me endless grief.

"I know that death awaits me at any moment. If I could with any luck hide myself, unharassed, from this perilous world, would I be certain of escaping the fate of a woman? Can I refuse thoroughly the temptation of being entangled in another love? Such a frail vessel is a woman!

"Even to think of this is unbearable for me. When I sleep, my husband appears in my dreams. When I awake, he stands before my eyes. As long as I live in this world, I cannot set myself free from my longing for him. Now there remains nothing more for me than to drown myself in the depths of the sea. My one regret is that you will be left here alone in grief. But I pray you to take all my robes to some priests so that they will cover the expense of prayers for my husband's better lot and the Buddha's assistance to me in the world beyond. And here is a letter I have written. Send it to the capital."[18]

Later that night, she throws herself from the ship on which she has been staying and drowns.

War, and the aftermath of war, destroy the innocent on every side. After the final battles have been won by the Minamoto, the victors find it their necessary duty to eradicate all traces of the potentially traitorous Taira clan. One child named Rokudai, the charming son of Taira Koremori, lives in hiding in an obscure temple near the capital. Hōjō Tokimasa, serving as Yoritomo's deputy in Kyoto, is determined to have the boy put to death, but Rokudai is saved, after a series of hair-raising adventures involving the inscrutable monk Mongaku, who has successfully sought the intervention of Yoritomo, now undisputed head of the Minamoto clan. Rokudai later becomes a monk, hoping thus to escape forever from any further attention. Yoritomo eventually comes to realize, however, that even Rokudai is a prisoner of his own heritage, just as is Yoritomo himself. "He is the son of Koremori and the disciple of Mongaku," Yoritomo muses;

[18] *Ibid.*, pp. 570-571.

"though he has changed his appearance by adopting the tonsure, he can never really change his rebellious heart."[19] The boy's execution is reluctantly ordered and, "with the death of Rokudai, perished the Heike—for evermore."

Earlier in the narrative, Rokudai's father Koremori, perhaps the most sympathetic figure among all the Taira, also becomes a monk. Koremori is the grandson of Kiyomori, the head of the clan, and the young man soon comes to appreciate the evils of the situation in which all his family finds itself, because of his grandfather's pride and obstinacy. During the Yashima battle, Koremori decides to slip off to see his wife and children in the capital; on his way, however, he realizes that the dangers of his capture are too great and instead he seeks seclusion in the Buddhist temples of Mt. Koya. There he meets the saintly priest Tokiyori. Tokiyori had, when a young man, served as a retainer to Koremori's father. He later renounced the secular life at the age of nineteen. Koremori now puts himself under the tutelage of Tokiyori. In these sections of the narrative, still another tension, prevalent throughout the *Heike*, is revealed in all its poignant force: the pull between Buddhist detachment and withdrawal and the human attraction to ordinary life, family, and the necessary activities of the world. Such a tension was present in Japanese life earlier in the Heian period. On several occasions in Lady Murasaki's novel, Genji considers retiring to a contemplative life, but he is always restrained from doing so by a sense of the importance of his family duties. Koremori's situation, in the midst of war and destruction, is more complex and ambiguous. Eventually, filled with anxiety, he decides to take the tonsure:

> Now he could delay no longer, and so he began to recite one of the Buddhist texts: "As long as one is continuously reborn in the Three Regions, he cannot sever the bonds of affection that tie him to his wife and children. Only one who renounces his earthly affection and becomes a monk can be awakened to true affection." Thus repeating the text three times, Koremori submitted his head to the tonsure.

[19] *Ibid.*, p. 760.

"Ah, I had thought to see my loved ones but once before I took the tonsure. Had I been able to do so, I might have nothing to look back on in regret." These words revealed Koremori's lingering desire for this world, sinful enough to hinder him from salvation.[20]

His two closest attendants do the same. Koremori then makes a pilgrimage to the sacred sites at Kumano. All through the trip he cannot rid his thoughts of memories of his family; he remembers his own father's pilgrimage to the same spot, in a time of trouble, when his father had "prayed to the god to shorten his life, and grant him happiness in the after-life."[21] The pilgrimage over, Koremori takes a boat to another shrine, but suddenly decides instead to take his own life. He cannot resolve the tensions he feels between his own desire to purify himself and the warmth of the human affection he has for his missing family:

"What is the matter with me? Am I still unable to rid myself of worldly desire?"

Reproving himself, he turned to the west and joined his palms. He began to repeat the name of Amida Buddha but earthly thoughts came again to his mind: "Since my loved ones in the capital cannot know that I am now putting an end to myself, they will continue waiting for tidings of me. Even at this moment they must be hoping anxiously. Someday, however, news of my death will reach them. I have no conception of how terrible their sorrow will be!"

Having spoken these words in his heart, he ceased to invoke Amida Buddha and put down his hands. He then turned to the priest Tokiyori and said: "Ah, what a burden it is to have a wife and children! They are not only a cause of sorrows in this world but also a hindrance to enlightenment and salvation in the other world. Even at this moment my wife and children are present in my mind. As long as I still talk with such lingering affection for my loved ones, I know I shall be unable to attain Buddhahood. Tokiyori, these are sinful feelings of which I must rid myself."[22]

[20] *Ibid.*, p. 618.   [21] *Ibid.*, p. 620.   [22] *Ibid.*, pp. 623–624.

Tokiyori is shaken by the human truth in Koremori's words. Yet he does not yield:

Tokiyori was moved to compassion, but outwardly he remained impassive. He feared that Koremori would not drown himself if he showed any signs of weakness. Wiping away his tears, Tokiyori said: "What you have said is reasonable! The bonds of affection seem beyond your control. Above all, it is karma that predetermines as many as a hundred lives before a man and a woman can place their pillows together even for a single night. Deep indeed is the karma of the past. But all living creatures must die. Those who meet must part. It is the law of this fleeting world. A dewdrop on the tip of a leaf is no different from that on the trunk of a tree. One must go before the other, or one must die before the other. This is only a trivial accident of nature. All must pass away in the end."[23]

Koremori in a last burst of energy throws himself into the sea.

Those inclined to search out forms of "comedy" and "tragedy" in the literature of various cultures will surely discover elements of the latter here. Koremori's death is deeply moving, within the concepts of the Buddhist view that frames the incident. Tokiyori feels Koremori's terrible human predicament; in that way, at least, he is unable to help him. In the face of these human concerns, the law seems indeed inscrutable. Yet Koremori's death does have meaning for the living. Later in the narrative, Koremori's son Rokudai, now a priest, makes a pilgrimage, following the footsteps of his father:

Rokudai first went to Mt. Koya and visited the priest Tokiyori, who had helped his father to attain Buddhahood. From him he heard in detail how his father had become a monk and how he had died. "Kumano is an important place for me, both for learning about Buddhahood and retracing my father's steps." So saying, Rokudai went on to Kumano.

[23] *Ibid.*, p. 624.

In front of the Hama Shrine he looked across at the island of Yamanari, near which his father had drowned himself. He wished to row a boat to the island, but as the wind blew from the wrong direction and the waves rose high, he was obliged to give up the idea. He stood gazing at the offing, questioning the white foaming waves in whose waters his father had drowned. Rokudai felt affection for the sand of the shore, as though there he might find the bones of his father. All the while his sleeves were wet with tears, as wet as those of fishermen soaked with the splashes of the waves. He spent all that night on the beach, chanting "Hail Amida Buddha," and, with his fingers, drawing the image of the Buddha in the sand. When dawn came, he summoned a priest and asked him to chant a sutra for the consolation of his father's soul. He felt as though the image of the Buddha in the sand and the chanting of the sutra on the beach would reach his father in the world beyond. Having endless talks with his father in his heart, Rokudai made his return journey.[24]

As the young man's visit ends, the reader, chastened, like Rokudai, feels with him a sense of loss and of regret as he relives emotionally his father's last days.

The Tale of the Heike has contributed to the development of Japanese literature in still other ways, especially through its emphasis on the past rather than on the present as a source of moral and aesthetic excellence. The text is filled with "justification" passages, citing Chinese and older Japanese precedents for various attitudes presented in the narrative. However tedious some of them may be for a modern reader to scan (or to look up), their purport is clear: virtue lies behind us.

The Tale of the Heike is a flawed and imperfect work, certainly, and not all of its many sections can be read with the same degree of interest. But in its great scenes, of which there are many, the book shows a remarkable power to reveal the ambiguities of the human condition. The enlightened sense of resignation toward mankind that the text reveals has remained a profound statement both admired and imitated by

[24] *Ibid.*, pp. 752-753.

many later generations, for which the *Heike* seemed to provide a real and moving image, along with *Genji*, of what the polarities of Japanese literature, and Japanese culture, might be.

THE *NŌ* DRAMA

The other great contribution of the medieval period to Japanese literature was the *nō* drama, which developed rapidly from a countrified theatrical entertainment to a vehicle for spiritual and metaphysical speculation. Much of this extraordinary transition was accomplished through the genius of the dramatist and actor Zeami (1363-1443), under the patronage of the celebrated ruler Ashikaga Yoshimitsu (1358-1408). The work of Zeami and a number of others produced the first high accomplishments in Japanese drama. *Nō* is a many-sided art and so can be examined in a variety of different ways, most of which deal with concerns far removed from the present study. The text of a *nō* play, although often a work of the highest poetic excellence, forms only one element in a unified theatrical conception that embraces dance, music, masks, and costume in order to create a genuine total theatre. Spectators could enjoy any and all aspects of such presentations, and the *nō* remained, despite the difficulty of many of its texts, a popular theatre down to the Tokugawa period, when its new patrons, the Tokugawa shōguns, removed it from general circulation and turned the *nō* into virtually a private entertainment. Thus the *nō* shares much with the *Heike*. Both contain elements of great artistic subtlety and profundity. Both find roots in the popular imagination.

The very fact of the popularity of *nō* sent the writers of these dramatic texts to works of familiar Japanese literature in search of suitable materials from which to construct their dramas. Countless episodes from such works formed the nucleus of the corpus of the *nō* texts. Using literary characters and themes both gave an added dignity to the theatrical texts and in turn helped make available the classics of Japanese literature to a general population on the whole ill-prepared to read and study them in their original versions.

When writers with the artistic gifts of Zeami or Komparu Zenchiku (1405-1468) chose sections from Japanese literature as a basis for their texts, they tended to select archetypal situations with sufficient resonance to permit effective dramatization. The play *Izutsu* (The Well Curb), for example, mentioned earlier, is a dramatization and adaption of section twenty-three of *Tales of Ise*, in which the children measure their growth by the well curb. In the original poetic text, the couple marries and eventually the wife is abandoned by her faithless husband. The original passage in *Tales of Ise* appears to deal in a short space with rather many conflicting moods. In the play, however, the action is collapsed: the unhappy woman looks back to the happier time of youth. A unified means has been used to sustain one atmosphere.

The Tale of Genji provided the subjects for countless *nō* plays, among them celebrated incidents from the novel involving Yūgao, Genji's early love who dies a mysterious and romantic death (*Yūgao*), the exile of Prince Genji at Suma (*Suma Genji*), the jealousy of Lady Rokujo (*Aoi no Ue* and *Nonomiya*), and Genji's attraction to the Lady of Akashi (*Sumiyoshi-mōde*). *The Tale of the Heike* too was an endless sourcebook for the *nō*, and dramatized versions of celebrated incidents concerning many of the major figures in that chronicle form an important part of the *nō* repertoire. Shunkan, Tadanori, Tomoe, Atsumori, Kiyotsune, and many others became part of a considerable stage tradition.

Nō has another importance for later narrative fiction more significant than as a source of subject matter. The process of *nō* dramatization created a style of theatrical writing that was to have an influence on important writers of fiction from Ueda Akinari to Kawabata. The dramatic method of *nō* is a subject too complex for any extended discussion here, but at least three elements in the style of these dramas can be said to have had an influence on later techniques of narrative prose composition.

The first was a reinforcement by *nō* of poetry as a literary form of highest excellence. Poetry takes pride of place in a *nō* text just as it did in the *monogatari* and *uta monogatari*. Usually the central conception of a *nō* play is contained in a poem that serves as a kind of kernel or seed around which the play is built. In the case of *The Well Curb*, mentioned above, that kernel is provided by a poem (quoted twice in earlier chapters) by Narihira himself. At the climax of the play, the protagonist (originally disguised as a young girl) reveals herself as the Daughter of Ki no Aritsune, now abandoned by the poet Narihira:

Daughter:	Hither returned I call back time past
Chorus:	And on the ancient well
	Of the Ariwara Temple
	The moon shines brightly as of old,
	The moon shines brightly as of old.
Daughter:	"Is not the moon in heaven the same?
	Is not the springtime as it was?"
	Thus did he sing, long, long ago.
	"Standing against the well curb,
Chorus:	Standing against the well curb,
	As children we compared our heights.
Daughter:	But I
Chorus:	Have grown much taller."
Daughter:	And much older.[25]

The text, in mixed poetry and prose, builds steadily to this lyric outburst, in a pattern already familiar from the *uta monogatari* and other forms. Ueda Akinari in particular adopts a similar pattern in his *Tales of Moonlight and Rain*, and Mori Ōgai creates a somewhat similar effect in his *Sanshō Dayū*.

The second contribution of *nō* to later literature represents part of a related phenomenon: the stress on interiority. The lyric thrust of a poem, usually accompanied by a dance, that crowns many *nō* plays arrives most often at the moment when the protagonist comes closest to revealing the most inward emotions that he or she is capable of feeling. The usual form of a *nō* drama contains dramatic movement but of a very special type. A typical play may begin with the appearance of a priest, or traveller, who acts as a point of objectivity for the spectator. The priest will then perhaps encounter some per-

---

[25] *Izutsu*, in Nippon Gakujutsu Shinkōkai, ed., *Japanese Noh Drama*, Vol. I (Tokyo, 1955), p. 104.

son (in *The Well Curb*, a young woman) who seems to have some hidden dimension to his or her character that is not visible at once. In the second part of the play, the priest or traveller, perhaps in meditation or sleep, learns the reality behind the person he has met earlier. (In *The Well Curb*, the girl reveals herself as the ghost of the daughter of Ki no Aritsune.) The apparition reveals its innermost feelings, then disappears, leaving the traveller to awaken and bring himself back, and his audience, to the real world.

Such a structure, a journey from the exterior to the psychic interior and back, permits great dramatic intensity. Usually little conflict in the Western theatrical sense is provided. Rather, the spectator is moved closer and closer to the inner truth of the protagonist, until all the tensions within that protagonist's soul are laid bare (again, in *The Well Curb*, the woman's longing for her philandering husband). The tension represented lies within the central character, not between two characters, and a *nō* play is in some ways closer to a powerful portrait than it is to a Western drama. The structure of *nō* represents a highly satisfactory means to achieve such results, and the mechanism has been taken over by a number of prose writers. The technique of moving closer and closer to the reality of a character is one basis for the narrative structure of *Kusamakura*; and Kawabata has suggested a similar technique is at work in *Snow Country*. The artistic dangers of using the *nō* scheme in a work of fiction are many. The movement in and out of a character's psychology may not provide sufficient plot interest, for example. Those who insist that *Snow Country* is defective because "nothing happens" may find part of their explanation in the fact that the construction of the novel owes something to *nō*. Those who admire the work, as I do, will find instead solace in the intensity and superbly formal qualities of many of its episodes.

Still another contribution of the *nō* to the techniques of narrative fiction lies in a general rhythm in terms of which the plays are constructed. A *nō* drama is normally divided into three musical sections, *jo*, *ha*, and *kyū*, or, in a very rough translation, introduction (during which some of the objective circumstances of the play are set down), exposition, and climax. The pace of the play goes from slow to fast, from a slow and stately introduction through an ever-quickening exposition to a final burst of energy, when the tensions of the protagonist are most openly revealed just before a final resolution. Such a pattern of increasing speed, coupled with increasing tension, which builds with the rising expectations of the spectators, is invariably effective. This device has also been taken over consciously by some writers, in particular Ueda Akinari, and perhaps unconsciously by others (Dazai is a good possibility) as a means to provide forward impetus in prose narrative. Such an emotional and rhythmical pattern often serves as a kind of "microstructure" for many writers. In the case of Ueda Akinari, Leon Zolbrod would see such a pattern as a "macrostructure" as well, for he finds the total rhythm of the arrangement of the various stories that make up *Tales of Moonlight and Rain* follows in the same ascending pattern.[26]

Nō, like *The Tale of the Heike*, was composed by those with a new cognizance of the past, and a new self-consciousness about how the past, both historical and literary, might help create a new literature appropriate for one's own time. The *nō* succeeded so well in that task that it, in turn, in what may seem still another "confusion of genres," influenced the composition of later fiction.

[26] See his introduction to his translation of *Tales of Moonlight and Rain* (Vancouver, 1974), pp. 74–76, for a discussion of this influence of the *nō*.

VII

Ueda Akinari: The Past as Art
Tales of Moonlight and Rain

THE rich literary heritage of the Tokugawa period
(1600-1868) presents for the Western reader another
higher level of complexity than does the literature written
during the preceding medieval era. The "Tokugawa peace"
brought a new audience for literature, new philosophical
modes of thought, and, perhaps most importantly of all, the
development of a new historical self-consciousness. Such social and intellectual changes occurred slowly and brought
diverse and sometimes contradictory influences to bear on all
the Japanese arts. The literary monuments from this period all
manifest the responses of their authors to shifts in ideas and
attitudes to which their society exposed them.

The unification of the country in 1600 by Tokugawa Ieyasu
brought stability and peace. Political stability was strengthened in turn after 1637, when most significant contacts with
the outside world were limited by law for over two hundred
years. Peace brought increasing commerce, the development
of urban life, and eventually, the rise of a merchant class, a
nascent *bourgeoisie* whose financial resources, tastes in entertainment, and increasing leisure were to bring about vast
changes in the arts. The introduction of printing, plus greater
opportunities for education outside the aristocratic classes,
created a whole new public with different expectations and
different linguistic abilities. The forces of democratization
that began by creating an oral public for *The Tale of the Heike*
now expanded to provide a generous portion of this same
general audience with an ability to read, as well as to listen to,
works that dealt more closely with the realities of their own
lives. Tokugawa realities were, of course, very different from
those of the medieval period: the mirror held up to Tokugawa
life produced not images of Buddhist transcendence but
rather earthy and witty views of urban life, notably in the entertaining novels and stories of Ihara Saikaku (1642-1693) and

the tragedies (some would say melodramas) of the townsmen in the puppet dramas of Chikamatsu Monzaemon (1653-1724). In particular, the writing of Saikaku put the Japanese literary tradition firmly back in touch with the present, and the effectiveness of his bawdy and evocative descriptions of life in the large cities has assigned to him the role of the first Japanese realist, another Defoe whose London was Edo.

To leave Saikaku (or Chikamatsu, for that matter) in such a context, however, limits an appreciation of certain aspects of their larger artistic purposes. Those purposes were to entertain, of course, but at least part of the meaning of entertainment in the period involved an attempt to broaden the participation of ordinary citizens in those higher forms of culture from which they had formerly been excluded. This culture, no matter what its ultimate redefinition in the Tokugawa period, remained basically the culture of the aristocrats, the culture of the past. If the new middle class amateur poets of Osaka and Edo did not have sufficient time to master the arcane rules of *waka*, the thirty-one syllable poetic form favored by the court since Heian times, then they could learn to master the simpler *haiku*. They could learn to relive great moments in the Japanese past by watching the historical dramas of Chikamatsu and his contemporaries, plays that on the whole were more popular at the time than the plebeian domestic tragedies so much admired in our day. Saikaku's *Kōshoku ichidai onna* (The Life of an Amorous Woman) (1686), for example, an unsentimental and vastly entertaining account of the rise and fall of a woman who loves the pleasures of the flesh, contains in its brief and witty introduction references to the Chinese Chou Dynasty *Wen Hsün* poetry anthology, *The Tale of Genji*, the twelfth-century *waka* anthology, the *Senzaishū*, and mention of a favorite subject for traditional poetry, the Rapids of the Yellow Rose. Those who have read Saikaku in English know the heavy baggage of footnotes required to understand those references and many others even more obscure; but they also know that Saikaku's narratives usually make excellent sense without a knowledge of many of them. His aim was certainly to entertain, and his own early training as a comic *haiku* poet helped school him in the comic possibilities of the glancing reference, or the sly juxtaposition. Such references, however, and such a continuing consciousness of the past on Saikaku's part, helped establish his pedigree of learning and his relationship to the larger concerns of Japanese culture. Western readers appreciate Saikaku for his wit and for his sly observations concerning a vast range of foibles he found in the society of his time. Yet his contemporary readers took equal pleasure in his learning, in the skill with which he could blend the literary past with the observed present. To fully grasp the accomplishments of Saikaku, we must, as it were, come to enjoy the footnotes as much as the text. Intellectual as well as emotional response is required of those who would truly experience his art. If the Western reader can grasp the significance of such an amalgam, he will be that much better prepared to appreciate the eclectic and peculiar virtues of the greatest intellectual accomplishments of the period.

There are three such areas, at least, that present such a combination of art and learning: the philosophical and historical writings of the National Studies Movement, the accomplishments of the great *haiku* poets, in particular Bashō, and, in serious narrative fiction, the work of Ueda Akinari.[1] The National Studies Movement and the poetry of Bashō have received a certain amount of attention from Western scholars. The outlines, at least, of their accomplishments are visible. Now that the major works of Akinari are becoming available in modern, annotated translations,[2] we may better come to understand how the complex cultural attitudes of the Tokugawa period were manifested in the art of fiction.

The development of the National Studies Movement illustrates the means by which a shift in ideas can produce a complex synthesis resulting in new cultural attitudes. The long Tokugawa peace brought time for necessary reflection, in

---

[1] In the visual arts, the work of the witty and learned *nanga* painters shows a similar interpenetration of intuition and learning. A strong parallel between the attitudes of these painters and of writers like Bashō, Buson, or Akinari can be posited. Such a study, however, is outside the scope of the present chapter.

[2] Notably in the 1974 Leon Zolbrod translation of *Tales of Moonlight and Rain* and in the 1975 Barry Jackman translation of *Tales of Spring Rain*.

particular for the study of the Confucian doctrines stressing self-cultivation and the importance of the social order. These Chinese importations found encouragement from the government, and such texts were memorized by many generations of students, whose own unconscious cultural sensibilities had been formed by the kind of Buddhist conceptions inherent in the view of the world propounded in *The Tale of the Heike*. The admixture of the two led not only to a better understanding of China but to a firmer awareness of the crucial pecularities of the Japanese character as well. Such a comprehension in turn led to the development of the National Studies Movement, which took its proponents in the field of literature all the way back to the ninth-century *Manyōshū*, that great collection of early poetry written without significant reference to the Chinese canons of taste popular later in the Heian period. The writers and thinkers who participated in the movement were on balance the most prodigiously equipped intellectuals of their time. Their learning, in Chinese and Japanese history, literature, and philosophy, was certainly sufficient for the difficult task they set themselves: that of attempting a synthesis of all that was unique in their own civilization. A study of the past provided the basis for all their efforts.

The past was of central importance, too, to a poet like Matsuo Bashō, who, more than any other poet of his time, invested the *haiku* with a philosophical profundity. Bashō saw his duty not merely to uphold the classical virtues and transmit them but to transmute them as well into terms comprehensible to himself and to his contemporaries. "Do not seek to follow in the footsteps of the men of old," he wrote, "seek what they sought."[3] The past was not only to serve a source of precedent and insight (any past can provide those); rather, an understanding of the past might help put the ever-shifting present into some fruitful relationship with the deepest elements in the Japanese character, elements that, under vastly different social circumstances, had been clearly defined. Bashō copied nothing. Yet he seemed conscious of

[3] Quoted in Wm. Theodore de Bary, *et al.*, *Sources of Japanese Tradition* (New York, 1958), pp. 455-456.

everything. His *haiku* and *haibun* diaries bore a recognizable relation to the literary past, just as the central preoccupations of his texts reveal his attempt to relate his own sensibility and his personal concerns to a larger field of reference. His homage to the past in both literary style and areas of philosophical concern seems always to represent a free, genuine, and compelling choice on his part; and indeed such choices allowed him to turn the *haiku* into the kind of metaphysical vehicle for speculation that it was to become. Arguably the *haiku* did become a great poetic form precisely because of the extent to which poets writing in the form came to take cognizance of the past and its meaning. The past provided no ultimate meaning and no final sanctions for them (as the past sometimes seemed to do for Chinese writers), but it did provide certain paradigms worthy of emulation.

Like Bashō, Ueda Akinari (1734–1809), in his major work, the *Ugetsu monogatari* (Tales of Moonlight and Rain), written in 1776, succeeded in combining in technique and subject matter alike his intellectual and emotional perceptions of the Japanese literary tradition with his own creative intuitions as a writer. Akinari, again like Bashō, was highly conscious of the extremely disparate nature of the materials he chose to use. This consciousness permitted him to assemble and adapt surprisingly eclectic sources to his own artistic ends.

Akinari is a figure who might fascinate readers with any interest in Japanese history, culture, or literature.[4] An adopted child, he rose from humble beginnings and eventually practiced medicine, although he gave up the profession when he allowed a patient to die. The practice of medicine in his time was nothing whatsoever what it was to become after the introduction of Western science to Japan; still, he seems in certain facets of his artistic personality to prefigure attitudes of mind later expressed by Mori Ōgai, another famous Japanese doctor attracted to literature a hundred years or so later. Both had a strong sense of history, plus an objective eye for significant detail that, despite the disparity in many other elements of their artistic personalities, gave certain similar di-

---

[4] For biographical details on Akinari, see Leon Zolbrod's Introduction to his translation of *Tales of Moonlight and Rain* (Vancouver, 1974), pp. 22–28.

rections to their concerns with the Japanese cultural past. Akinari's researches in early Japanese history were connected with the work of the National Studies Movement. Eventually he became friends for a time with Motoori Norinaga (1730–1801), the great figure in that effort. Such influences were important in developing Akinari's attitudes concerning the nature of artistic creation. *Tales of Moonlight and Rain* exhibits the skills of a writer who can synthesize and harmonize intuition and knowledge to a degree seldom matched among his contemporaries. The appeal of the past represents the principal assumption on which all nine stories in the collection depend. In each, the literature of the past serves as the source of Akinari's art.

The nine stories are of varying lengths. All deal with the supernatural; even those that are not, strictly speaking, ghost stories, have some elements of the supernatural central to them. The stories show all the elements already observed in early Japanese tales, and they reveal at the same time Akinari's skill in exhibiting the fanciful in a structure more tightly organized than normally employed in more realistic fiction of the period. (In that regard, the "realist" Saikaku's plots, if indeed they can be called that, are scarcely held together at all.) Ueda has taken the form of the tale he inherited and, by making use of his own considerable literary skill, has transformed the genre from fanciful entertainment into an eloquent vehicle to convey his own sophisticated sense of the real mysteries of his world.

All the stories show various ties with the literature of the past. One can ascertain three levels of homage paid by Akinari to the Japanese and Chinese literary heritage that made up his intellectual world. The first concerns his appropriation of older stories or narrative sequences on which he imposes his own particular vision. None of the plots of the stories in the collection is wholly original. Akinari has borrowed widely and self-consciously, secure in his assumption that his readers would take pleasure in the sophistication with which he reshaped his models. His art was one of transformation. Plots are borrowed but not copied. "The Chrysanthemum Tryst," for example, is a retelling of a well-known Chinese story, written in the colloquial language, recorded in the Ming Dynasty (1368-1644). In that account, two young men pledge eternal friendship. One is killed, but his ghost returns for a reunion the two had planned, shocking his live friend into visiting the site of his friend's death. In "The Lust of the White Serpent," a snake disguised as a beautiful woman haunts a young man in a fashion resembling certain incidents in a story from the eleventh-century collection *Konjaku monogatari*, also the source of elements in the medieval *nō* play *Dōjōji*. A tale from the *Uji shūi monogatari*, a collection of tales from a century or so after the *Konjaku monogatari*, provides the outlines for the plot of "The Blue Hood," in which a Zen priest saves a depraved monk from his final destruction. In all these examples, Akinari's methods follow a certain general pattern. Little is ever taken over whole. Even in "The Chrysanthemum Tryst," which bears the closest resemblance to any of the stories to its original version, he has filled out the plot, recast its motivations, and established his own unique and compelling sense of atmosphere wholly appropriate to his personal vision.[5]

Without exception, the original narratives are much enhanced through Akinari's retelling. Encounters, attitudes, atmospheres, outcomes experienced through the double memories of writer and reader create a newly suggestive poetic profundity. Akinari's new treatments often make characters and situations seem archetypal. This weight, in turn, gives greater impetus to the reader's "willing suspension of disbelief," reinforced as it is by a literary example of high quality. Many of the stories in the collection involve historical personages who lend significance to the tales by their very presence there. Plots from earlier works of literature are cast in the same role; they add grandeur and depth to the narratives.

A second level of homage paid by Akinari to his literary past concerns his many overt references to the texts of the

[5] For those who wish to compare the two versions, a translation of the Chinese original entitled "Fan Chu-Ch'ing's Eternal Friendship" can be found in John Lyman Bishop, *The Colloquial Short Story in China*, Harvard-Yenching Institute Series xiv, Cambridge, 1965, pp. 88-103.

Chinese and Japanese classics. Akinari shares with Bashō—
and with Saikaku, for that matter—an ability to strengthen
the evocative power of his own text by creating reverberations to earlier works he admires. Akinari's contemporary
readers would be expected as well to take genuine pleasure in
recognizing them. Scarcely a paragraph in any of these stories
fails to echo some trace of another, earlier text. Here, by way
of example, is a short section from "The House amid the
Thickets." Katsushirō, the protagonist, has returned home
after an absence of seven years, to find his wife still waiting
for him in his old home. Delighted beyond measure, he prepares to take up his old life again:

> Katsushirō took her in his arms and comforted her, say-
> ing, "These nights are the shortest of all," and they lay
> down together. In the cool darkness the window paper rus-
> tled as the breeze whispered through the pines. Exhausted
> from his travel, Katsushirō fell into a sound sleep. Around
> the fifth watch, however, when the sky began to grow
> light, he suddenly became partially aware of the world of
> the senses. He vaguely knew that he was cold, and groping
> with his hands, he tried to pull up the covers. But to his
> surprise leaves rustled beneath his touch, and as he opened
> his eyes a cold drop of something fell on his face.
>
> He wondered if it were rain coming in, and then he
> noticed that the roof was gone, as though torn away by the
> wind, and that it was daybreak, and the pale shining moon
> of dawn still remained in the sky. All of the shutters to the
> house were gone, and through spaces in the dilapidated lat-
> ticework bed there grew high grass and weeds. The morn-
> ing dew had fallen and soaked his sleeves wringing wet.
> The walls were covered with ivy and vines, and the garden
> was buried in tall madder weed. The season was still late
> summer, but the desolation of the house reminded him of
> autumn moors.[6]

Looking around, Katsushirō realizes that somehow he has
been bewitched:

[6] *Tales*, p. 128.

Although it had been long deserted, the dwelling was without a doubt his old home. He recognized its spacious interior, its walls, and even the storehouse—all of which he had built to suit his own particular tastes. Bewildered and uncertain and scarcely knowing where he stood, he slowly realized that Miyagi was surely dead and that this was now the home of foxes and badgers—and perhaps, too, of fearsome spirits who had entered this desolate place and taken the form of his wife. "Or was it her ghost," he thought, "her ghost yearning for love that came back to meet me? It was just as I remembered her," and in an excess of grief, he began to weep.

"It is only I, I alone who remain unchanged," he muttered, as he searched—first here, then there. Finally, in what had been the sleeping quarters he saw her grave, a heaped-up mound of earth, which someone had covered by boards removed from the verandah in order to give protection from rain and dew. "Is this where her ghost came from last night?" he wondered, horrified and yet entranced.[7]

The text reads perfectly smoothly. The thrust of the narrative remains clear without the literary references. Two in particular, however, carry important freight. The image of summer desolation that suggests the atmosphere of fall derives from a poem in the *Kokinshū*:

Sato wa arete	The place is desolate,
hito wa furi ni shi	And mother is growing old
yado nare ya	In my poor cottage,
niwa mo magaki mo	And both the garden and the hedge
aki no nora naru	Will remind you of autumn moors.[8]

Katsushirō's own background would hardly prepare him to quote such elegant poetry; yet the atmosphere of the moment pulls him, as it were, into a mental realm where his natural reactions will mirror those expressed in the classical poem. Later, his realization that he alone remains unchanged echoes the poem of Ariwara no Narihira quoted several times earlier.

[7] *Ibid.*, p. 129.   [8] *Ibid.*, p. 228.

Tsuki ya aranu	Is not that the moon?
haru ya mukashi no	And is not the spring the same
haru naranu	Spring of the old days?
wa ga mi hitotsu wa	My body is the same body—
moto no mi ni shite	Yet everything seems different.[9]

Just as that poem provided the kernel for the narrative of
Narihira's lost love, so the poem is used here by Ueda Akinari
to underline the emotional message of his own tale, which,
although constructed from vastly different materials, remains
still another treatment of the *Ise monogatari* theme of the transcience of time. The poetic reference attaches the story to that
earlier work and connects both worlds together. In a sense,
then, all of "The House amid the Thickets" becomes a reference to *Tales of Ise*.

Akinari's use of literary references in this organic fashion is
important in many of the narratives. In "The Lust of the
White Serpent," for example, the protagonist Toyoo (a pen-
niless scholar who seems in some ways a satirical portrait of
Ueda himself) meets a beautiful young woman named
Manago, who, after making herself attractive to him, suddenly disappears. After various vicissitudes, Toyoo marries,
then finds to his horror that his innocent bride Tomiko is possessed by the spirit of his earlier temptress. At first, Toyoo had
been delighted to find himself such an accomplished bride;
after all, Tomiko had served at court:

> Accustomed to serving in the great palace, where she had
> spent several years, Tomiko's manners were impeccable,
> her appearance splendid to behold, and when Toyoo
> moved to the Shibas' home and saw her, he felt satisfied in
> every way with her remarkable charm. But there was
> something about her that reminded him of his previous
> love for Manago. The first night passed without any event.
> On the second night, however, after Toyoo became
> slightly intoxicated, he said, "Now that you have spent
> several years in service at the palace, we country folk must
> strike you as decidedly boorish. While you were in the capi-

[9] See Keene, *Anthology of Japanese Literature*, p. 71.

tal what captains, imperial advisors, and the like did you sleep with? It's very disconcerting to think about!"

Although Toyoo had spoken playfully, Tomiko suddenly straightened up and replied, "You, who have forgotten your old promises and have stooped to toy with a worthless common creature! It is your behavior, on the contrary, that's disgusting." Her appearance changed. The voice was unmistakably that of Manago.[10]

Toyoo is horrified to find his past literally catching up with him. Manago tries to reconcile him to the fact:

> "My dear, you mustn't be afraid. We have vowed to the oceans. We have pledged to the mountains. How can you forget so quickly, when it was ordained by fate that we should meet again. If you believe what other people say and recklessly try to abandon me, I shall seek vengeance, and tall though the peaks of the mountains of the Kii High Road may be, your blood will drain from the ridges into the valleys. You must not be so rash as to throw away your life in vain."
>
> Toyoo trembled uncontrollably, as a man confronted with the prospect of immediate death.[11]

Tomiko's words, or rather, the words spoken through her by Manago, echo those of Lady Rokujo, who, in *The Tale of Genji*, haunts Genji's wife, Lady Aoi, until her untimely death. By repeating a variation on this well-known paradigm, Akinari quickly identifies for the reader the real nature of Manago's power and, using the example of Lady Rokujo as a literary "proof," gives additional substance to the fabric of his own story. Similar techniques are used with great effectiveness in certain passages of "The Cauldron of Kibisu."

Many of Ueda Akinari's references are more formal and may strike a modern reader as pedantic; yet they are no more so than, say, the classical references in Milton, which most modern readers must look up as well. The more familiar a reader becomes with Japanese literature in general and with

[10] *Tales*, p. 179.   [11] *Ibid*.

Akinari's techniques in particular, the more apparent becomes the powerfully suggestive quality of his citations.

The third, and perhaps the most sophisticated level of homage paid by Akinari to his literary past, involves his adaptation of older literary structures as a means to shape his narratives. He finds great significance in these older forms which succeeded for him in manifesting certain profound realities of human life. By reusing such older forms (but always in his own fashion), Akinari attempts to add some of that force to his own stories. He seeks to search out reality by passing through the narrative rhythms created in the art of the past. Many such examples can be provided. Poetic techniques of linkage from the *waka* and *renga* traditions,[12] or the narrative modes from the diary tradition merit extended comment, but I would prefer here to choose by way of example Akinari's use of certain principles in the structure of the *nō* drama in constructing his narratives. At least four elements of that tradition are involved. The first concerns the paradigm of dramatic movement peculiar to the *nō* that was described in the previous chapter. In such a sequence, a visitor going to a spot of a sacred or magical character witnesses the revelation of the inner emotions of a character closely associated with that place. In "White Peak," the poet Saigyō (1118-1190) visits the tomb of the Emperor Sutoku (1119-1164); the ghost of the Emperor appears and predicts the holocausts that will result in a civil war, the same civil war that forms the subject of *The Tale of the Heike*. "Bird of Paradise" shows the reader a man and his son on a visit to Mount Koya to view the tomb of the great Shingon Buddhist cleric Kūkai (774-835). The two meet the ghost of Toyotomi Hidetsugu (1568-1595), the nephew of the famed general Toyotomi Hideyoshi. Hidetsugu was

---

[12] For example, Akinari creates a series of situations that link the various stories together. Illness, and the curing of illness, appear in various guises in "The Blue Hood," "The Chrysanthemum Tryst," "The Cauldron of Kibisu," "The House amid the Thickets," and, in a metaphysical sense, in "The Lust of the White Serpent." The setting of a ruined house reoccurs in "The House amid the Thickets," "The Cauldron of Kibisu," "The Lust of the White Serpent," and "The Blue Hood." A promised tryst is an important element in the plots of "The Blue Hood," "The Chrysanthemum Tryst," "The House amid the Thickets," and several others.

ordered to commit suicide by his own uncle, and his thirst for vengeance permeates the emotional atmosphere of the text. In both stories the ghosts become involved with chance emissaries from the ordinary world. The contact is made through the medium of poetry. Both Saigyō and Hayashi, the father in "Bird of Paradise," have written poems that attract the attention of the spirits. Both narratives use the rhythms of *nō*: the explanatory opening, the first encounter with the personality of the ghostly protagonist, the final revelation, climax, and poetic conclusion.

Secondly, many of Akinari's characters seem to represent a personification of the powerful emotions they manifest. In this respect such figures closely resemble the protagonists of the *nō* drama who, as was pointed out earlier, epitomize certain powerful psychic states. Manago, for example, represents a manifestation of lustful passion, just as the warrior Akana Soēmon, who returns from the dead to keep his appointment in "The Chrysanthemum Tryst," seems the embodiment of fraternal affection. Kōgi, the painter-priest in "The Carp that Came to My Dream," so identifies himself with those resplendent fish that he becomes one himself in the course of the narrative, fulfilling all too literally Bashō's dictum that "your poetry issues of its own accord when you and the object have become one."

Thirdly, the pacing of the *nō* drama, moving slowly as it does from a quiet beginning to a powerful climax, provides the rhythm of several stories in the collection, notably "The Cauldron of Kibisu." In that tale, the protagonist Shōtarō, a young man with a roving eye, marries Isora but is unfaithful to her. She dies of grief. Her ghost comes to haunt the unfortunate philanderer, whose final demise comes after a series of hair-raising climaxes that build up a faster and faster narrative rhythm. Such an ever-increasingly rapid tempo represents an important structural device in a novel like *Kusamakura*. Sōseki, like Akinari, refers to the *nō* throughout his text.

Lastly, the use of a poem to provide a kernel or seed around which a *nō* play is constructed finds reflection not only in Akinari's two stories closely patterned on the *nō*, "White Peak" and "Bird of Paradise," but in others as well, notably

"Blue Hood" and "The House amid the Thickets." In the latter, a poem from the *Manyōshū* concerning the suicide of the
maiden Tegona provides a model for certain concerns in Akinari's tale. A section of the original poem reads as follows:

> Many suitors came
> And pleaded for Tegona's love,
> And she in time grew sad
> That she could not give her heart
> In the way she wished,
> And she threw herself
> Into the surf
> That pounds the shore,
> And found a watery grave.
> Though it was long ago
> When Tegona
> Laid herself to rest,
> It seems like yesterday
> That I gazed
> Upon her lovely face.[13]

Katsuhiro comes to realize the real significance of his adventure with the ghost of his wife, not at the time of his actual
experience, but later, when he is presented with the appropriate literary paradigm by Grandfather Uruma, who tells him
this *Manyōshū* poem. Poetry informs Katsuhiro just as it
exorcises his pain, for he gains release by composing a crude
verse of his own:

inishie no	No matter how much
Mama no Tegona wo	They loved Tegona
kaku bakari	In that bygone age,
koite shi aran	I loved my dear wife
Mama no Tegona wo	Every bit as much.[14]

These poetic clusters focus the prose narrative in Akinari's
stories in a fashion analagous to the *waka* quoted in the *nō*
plays of Zeami.

Akinari's art, in sum, defines itself through a profound

[13] *Ibid.*, pp. 229-230.   [14] *Ibid.*, p. 132.

homage to the past. And the result of such an effort yields him new accomplishment, uniquely his own. He has managed to combine the elements of the tale (tight structure, fanciful plot) with the attributes of the *monogatari* and the essay (introspection, an emphasis on poetic virtues, and a certain psychological realism) into a highly wrought form of narrative that represents a synthesis of many varied traditions in Japanese literature. The past, in particular the literary past, has become the source of art. Individual perceptions of the realities of life become sharpened as they come closer to literature, just as the preoccupations of literature help explain the meaning and significance of life.

For many contemporary readers, a retreat from the life of one's time into the past may suggest merely a needless classicism, a psychological necessity to refer, and to defer, to traditions that have outlived their real usefulness. Akinari escapes this stricture, however, not only because of his genius as a storyteller, but because of the nature of the period in which he lived. Tokugawa Japan was relatively stable in its political structures, yet its cultural values were in a state of flux. Akinari himself, through his own research on the *Manyōshū* and in early Japanese history, sought throughout his intellectual life, like many others at the time, to locate some larger perenniality in Japanese culture. His own preferences, his own passions, may represent metaphysical and even political statements on his part as to what the effective elements in such a perenniality might be. Like Bashō, Ueda Akinari explored for himself in his own stories those metaphysical spots where "the footsteps of the men of old had trod," and thus, paradoxically, *Tales of Moonlight and Rain* expands the past into something altogether new. Seen in this fashion, his classical references seem to provide a series of reassuring signposts as the author, like those priests who begin the *nō* plays, leads his readers into a wholly mysterious world. The literary arts in the Tokugawa period have no more poetic universe to reveal.

VIII

Nagai Kafū and Mori Ōgai: The Past
versus the Present
The River Sumida and *Sanshō the Steward*

THE beginning of the Meiji Period, in 1868, brought as radical changes to Japan as any society has possibly ever undergone. The arrival of ideas from the West, and the government's decision to encourage study abroad, sent a significant number of Japanese, often young people at the beginning of their careers, to Europe and America. Their purpose in travelling was to carry out the challenge set down in the words of the Charter Oath of 1868: "knowledge shall be sought throughout the world so as to strengthen the foundations of imperial rule." Along with banking, railroad construction, school administration, and countless other Western subjects that caught the attention of these willing pupils were the arts. Although Western conceptions of painting, theater, poetry, and fiction were slower to attract attention in Japan than more immediately practical subjects in that very usefully minded age, their Japanese advocates managed, through translations and enthusiastic paraphrase, to introduce these new concepts to the educated public. In the field of fiction, the first powerful stimulus came with the publication of Tsubouchi Shōyō's *Essence of the Novel* in 1885. As mentioned previously, the introduction of Western aesthetic views brought an immediate conflict with the moralistic literary values inherited from the late Tokugawa period. In the realm of serious writing, at least, the Westernizers won, possibly because many of their new "Western" literary ideals bore a considerable, if largely unrecognized, resemblance to certain traditional Japanese literary values prevalent before the Confucianizing Tokugawa period.

Nevertheless, young writers could no longer look merely to Japanese models. Tolstoy, Turgenev, Ibsen, the French Symbolists, and Zola became as important and as influential in Japan as they were elsewhere. Of the Japanese writers of the first rank active during the Meiji period, almost all went abroad during an important period in their intellectual and artistic formation. Nagai Kafū (1879-1959) spent four years in the United States and a year in France; he was out of Japan from 1903 to 1908. Mori Ōgai (1862-1922) was in Germany from 1884 to 1888. Natsume Sōseki's visit to England from 1900 to 1903 has been mentioned earlier, and Shimazaki Tōson (1872-1943), another leading novelist and poet, was in France from 1913 to 1916. Through the work of such men, a wide variety of literary attitudes and ideas entered into the mainstream of modern Japanese literature.

In one sense, the infiltration of Western literary ideas into Japan produced a less drastic confrontation than might have been expected. In the first place, the Japanese literary tradition was always significantly eclectic to permit a positive response. In particular, the Chinese tradition, linquistically and conceptually so different from the Japanese, had always provided a continuous point of reference, to be appealed to or rejected in turn, depending on the circumstances. The work of a writer like Ueda Akinari shows the stability of the native tradition even when most involved with an outside aesthetic. The combination produced poise and balance.

By the 1890s, however, balance seemed a virtue impossible to sustain. Japanese visitors to Europe were overwhelmed at the differences they found; any underlying sense of a shared similarity was to take much more time to develop. Indeed, the shock of the European experience turned both Kafū and Ōgai into creative writers. Like Sōseki (and Lu Hsun, the greatest figure in modern Chinese literature), Kafū and Ōgai were both placed in the position of having to interpret their own feelings and understand their own traditions in a way that would have been incomprehensible to their parents' generation. Both were young men at the time of their European experience. Both were relatively unspoiled and open as to the nature of their expectations. Both, faced with the shock of living and working in a foreign culture they admired, reached a heightened level of self-consciousness about themselves and, in returning, about their own society, then undergoing such a drastic set of social and spiritual changes. Each responded quite differently, according to his own temperament, as the natures of the two men's writing will immediately attest. Yet, despite the vast differences between the two men, the similarity of the process through which they went made it inevitable that both of them, in their own way, should address themselves to the task of examining their own traditions and the meaning of the past for the present. Nor should it be any surprise that the two men became good friends. Perhaps, beneath their genuine differences in character, they felt a basic sympathy in each other's outlook. Certainly Kafū, the younger of the two, admired and looked up to Ōgai almost as a son might regard a father.

KAFŪ AND "THE RIVER SUMIDA"

Nagai Kafū's *Sumidagawa* ("The River Sumida"), written in 1909, the year after his return from France, represents the first sustained piece of writing that helped him maintain his enduring reputation. The work seems more an impressionistic novelette than a sustained work of fiction, but its relatively brief text sustains superbly the kind of atmosphere Kafū set out to create. Many of the hallmarks of his later style are already in evidence here. Chief among those, certainly, is the author's consciousness of the passing of time and, with it, of the erosion of traditions that lay at the roots of the culture that had formerly sustained the nation.

Kafū's visit to the West, and to France in particular, allowed him to grasp what he termed the wholeness and beauty of that culture; his return to Japan showed him that, although Japan too had possessed such a wholeness, it was vanishing under the impetus of a mindless desire for change, which, in Kafū's mind, could only destroy. Much of his writing at this time articulates such a point of view. In an early story, *Sneers*, the protagonist reflects on the appositeness of European and Japanese architectures to their respective civilizations:

> Within six months or a year, as he began casually looking back over his youth, he found himself feeling a strong nostalgia for the relics of a vanished day, and seeing much that was admirable in the special qualities of his race. . . .

The first suspicion of this new mood came one day when he was walking through Shiba Park. He could see nothing in the bronze statue of Count Gotō that struck him as in any way beautiful, but asleep behind it, solitary and forgotten, lay the mortuary shrines of the Shoguns. He stepped into the grounds and his astonishment grew. The memory had quite faded of days when his parents had brought him to this same park to see the cherry blossoms, and the surprise, as he found in a corner of the vulgar, ugly, accursed city a place yet reserved for art, was as if he had unearthed Pompeii.[1]

As he observes the details of the architecture, the appositeness of proportion in the structures, and the harmony between the buildings and their natural surroundings, he is filled with admiration. The shrines fulfill their function magnificently:

> The design, in sum, was such as to raise to the highest possible intensity the sense of reverence and worshipfulness. It succeeded magnificently, the place was a masterpiece. As he sought to compare the complex with Parisian buildings he had believed to be the supreme aesthetic experiences of his life, he felt that the Shiba mausoleum, whether their superior or not, was in no way their inferior. Just as the acute angles of Gothic architecture communicated perfectly the spirit of the people that had created it, he thought in the intensity of his delight, so the rectangular lines of this shrine and the richness of its colors gave perfect expression to the proud and lonely and aloofly aristocratic bent of the East. . . .[2]

Yet, he muses further, Japan is no longer at ease with this culture. A restless spirit of change obscures the natural relationship men had heretofore found with their environment:

> When we think of the relationship between the left bank of the Sumida and Edo literature, we see that the men of

---

[1] Quoted in Edwin Seidensticker, *Kafū the Scribbler* (Stanford, 1965), p. 37.
[2] *Ibid.*, p. 38.

Edo were even quicker than the Parisians to find beauties
on the outskirts of their city. . . .

Even now the people of Paris take their families to the
suburbs on Sundays, and sit on the grass and drink wine.
We, by contrast, seem driven by an urgent need to destroy
the picture-like beauties of tradition in the interests of the
new age.[3]

Progress, for the protagonist (and for Kafū), creates an im-
balance that endangers that balance of harmony and poise that
Japanese life, to judge from the traces that remain, surely
must have possessed.

Kafū's skepticism over the qualities of modern life later
turned into a kind of aristocratic disdain; by 1911, he was able
to give up his important position as Professor of French Literature at Keio University and retire from the active, distasteful
world altogether. He became an observer of society. He
studied it closely, with the objectivity of an outsider, coupled
with a species of fatigued impatience for the quality of life he
saw being lived around him. In this aspect of his personality
Kafū strongly resembles Ōgai. Ironic objectivity had always
been an important element in Japanese fiction, as Sōseki was
at pains to point out in *Three-Cornered World*. Kafū used his
profound knowledge of the Japanese past plus what he gained
from his European experiences to flail the pallid and unsatisfactory present.

"The River Sumida" shows off Kafū's ironic objectivity to
good advantage. The story pays homage to the past both in
its subject matter and in its literary structure. The plot, if such
it is, can be quickly described. Ragetsu, a *haiku* poet, is asked
by his widowed sister Otoyo to help her in her attempt to
turn her son Chōkichi into a model young student and bu-
reaucrat. Chōkichi, on the other hand, is in love with Oito, a
young girl who becomes a geisha, and he is all too anxious to
give up his studies for his real interests in traditional Japanese
music. Eventually, a victim of his own indecision, he falls ill
and, at the end of the story, lies on the verge of death; now his
uncle, ruefully reflecting on the boy's unhappy life, deter-

---

[3] *Ibid.*, pp. 27-28.

mines to help him after all. "No matter how ill you may be, you are not to die. I am with you," he concludes, as the story ends.

As Edward Seidensticker remarks in his superb *Kafū the Scribbler*, the evocative descriptions that make up much of the text of "The River Sumida" seem to indicate that Kafū actually set his story at an earlier time, a fact Kafū himself denied. Nevertheless, the elegiac atmosphere, the suggestion that the world portrayed is a world already gone, is strongly conveyed. The successful creation of that world, however, lies in Kafū's remove from his surroundings, not in time but in artistic attitude. His European experience had given him a psychological distance from his own culture sufficient to permit him to identify the elements in that culture he admired and, indeed, to mourn their neglect at a time when many of his countrymen were still unable to identify for themselves what those very elements might have been.

The means chosen by Kafū to evoke this atmosphere are wholly in accord with his artistic purposes. He chose to place the focus of his story not on his characters but on the setting. The narrative moves along through the contrasting atmospheres of various cityscapes, conditioned by them and by the presence of the river Sumida, which gives the story its title. The Sumida, which flows through the center of Tokyo, appears as an important locale in a number of celebrated works of Japanese literature, from the *Manyōshū* onwards. In Kafū's narrative, the river appears in some fashion in each section, even in a scene from *kabuki* that Chōkichi watches in Section VI; he, naturally, is quick-witted enough to identify with his own problems both the locale and the dramatic situation in the play he is watching. In the final section of the narrative, Chōkichi, who wants to go to watch the river in flood, wades into the "mud and ooze" and catches what is diagnosed as typhoid fever. Ragetsu wonders if Chōkichi, without the courage necessary to resolve his own problems, may have tried to commit suicide. The protagonist has, in effect, immersed himself in the symbol that unites the whole story.

The choice of such a central symbolic device to organize his story may reflect Kafū's profound involvement with the

French literary tradition. His interests in French literature were extensive. He was a fine translator of Baudelaire, Verlaine, and other Symbolist poets and was widely read in the best of nineteenth- and earlier twentieth-century French literature. Again, his command of another language and literature gave him a particular sense of discrimination concerning his own literary tradition. "The River Sumida" shows a new psychological acumen peculiar to Kafū and other contemporary Japanese writers who were affected by Western modes of fiction. Nevertheless, his overall plan for his narrative shows a felicitous regard for traditional patterns of structure. In particular, Kafū's use of the movements of his characters through the seasons is strongly reminiscent of the patterns of traditional fiction. The story, divided into ten sections, moves evenly from August, in Section I, through the new year, ending in the summer of the year following. The cyclical motion of the narrative flows naturally and provides an appropriate temporal structure to parallel the flow of the river itself. Both suggest the slow, natural passage of time, the movement that brings inevitable change to the city and to the characters in the story.

In each of the ten sections, Chōkichi finds his own moods shifting, one emotion succeeding another as he ponders the difficulties of making a decision concerning his own future. Kafū uses the settings of his story to project on his lightly sketched characters an objective rendering of their emotional states. Setting and character cannot be separated: one defines the other. The progression of the plot in "The River Sumida" serves essentially as a vehicle for the controlled, precise, and steady progression of emotional states portrayed in scene after scene.

A few examples may suffice to indicate the care with which each scene is planned in relation to the emotional state Kafū wishes to create. In Section II, which takes place in early autumn, Chōkichi has a last interview with Oito before she begins her training as a geisha. Chōkichi waits for her by a bridge overlooking the river. The passage that follows illustrates both Kafū's trenchant powers of observation and his ability to create and sustain a mood as well. His description is precise, never merely generalized, and the final effect created is an atmosphere of melancholy yearning, precisely what is necessary to advance the larger purposes of the story:

> From a new two-story house with willows at its gate came the sound of a samisen, and the masters of the low houses along the canal were beginning to emerge half naked from latticed doors to enjoy the evening cool. Chōkichi gazed intently across the bridge. It would be time for her to come.
>
> The first figure to cross the bridge was a priest in a dark hempen robe. Then, in tights, a hitched-up kimono, and rubber shoes, came a man who might have been the head of a building gang, and, after him, some minutes later, a rather shabby housewife carrying an umbrella and a small cloth bundle, inelegantly kicking up gravel with her high clogs as she walked along in great strides. There was no one else. He turned his tired eyes toward the river. The surface was brighter than before, and the threatening bank of clouds had quite disappeared. Then he saw, rising over the embankment and the grove of the Chōmeiji Temple across the river, a red moon, probably the seventh full moon of the lunar calendar. The sky shone like a mirror, and the embankment and the trees against the moon were ever blacker. Only the evening star was in the sky, all the others having been blotted out in the too-bright moonlight. The wisps of cloud stretching along the horizon were silver, and as the moon rose above the trees everything took on its white glow—the tiled roofs in the evening dew along the river bank, the wet stakes in the water, the bits of seaweed coming under the bridge on the flood tide, the hulls of boats, the bamboo poles. His own shadow was clearer on the bridge. A pair of strolling singers paused for a moment to admire the moon, and hurried down the canal, to sing coaxingly before the houses that fronted on it:
>
> The young man waits at the railing of the bridge.
>
> But seeing that their efforts were not likely to bring money, they hurried off again, scarcely finishing their song, in the direction of the Yoshiwara.[4]

[4] *Ibid.*, pp. 188-189.

Chōkichi's emotions are not described. Rather, the reader is presented directly with the same series of images that came to his "tired eyes": cool after heat, the beauty of the moonlight, the singers who take up a song that well might have the young man as its subject. Such a juxtaposition of specific images (as in Bashō's *haibun*), by evoking a response directly in the reader, creates a powerful manifestation of Chōkichi's emotional state beyond the means of purely exterior description. The reader is provided similar materials with which to construct a sense of identification with each important character in the story.

In Section III, Chōkichi suddenly sets off, "pursuing the image of Oito, so vivid in his mind and his alone." He hurries to the place where she now lives. The energy of the bright morning scene he witnesses provides a precise objectification of the hope, the anticipation he now feels:

> With the morning sun pouring into it, the lane was bright to its deepest recesses. It was lined by more than little houses with latticed fronts: now, in the daylight, he saw that there were also high-roofed warehouses. There were board fences topped by spikes, and above the spikes the branches of pine trees. There were lime-sprinkled bathroom doors, lines of garbage boxes, cats slinking about. And there were remarkable numbers of people, turning sideways as they passed one another on the narrow walks. The strains of samisen practice mixed with the sound of voices, and laundry water was splashing busily. Girls with hitched-up kimonos and red underskirts were sweeping the boards, and others were polishing away at the latticework, strip by strip. Chōkichi felt a bit shy that there should be so many eyes to see him, and it came to him for the first time that, having arrived, he did not know what to do next. He had thought that he might slip past the Matsubaya and perhaps catch a glimpse of Oito, but the street was altogether too bright. Should he then stand at the entrance to the lane and wait for her to come out on some errand or another? But it seemed to him that all the eyes up and down the street were fixed on him alone, and he could not bring himself to stand there for even five minutes. He would have

to reconsider. He started off into the alley opposite, where an old candy vender had come up clapping a pair of sticks to attract children.[5]

Light and energy replace the melancholy darkness of the preceding section. The episode by the bridge was sparsely populated; now the scene bursts with people, animals, children. Chōkichi still shows his diffidence, but the coloration of his mental state is more vivid. Each succeeding section thus helps by contrasting means to define Chōkichi's evolving state of mind, through a direct appeal to the emotional state such a profusion of carefully selected and vivid detail can create in the reader.

Kafū makes use of such contrasts in an ironic way as well, setting the emotional states of his characters at variance with the mood of the scene around them. In Section VIII, for example, Chōkichi's mother Otoyo, preoccupied with her son's situation and her attempts to earn enough money to live, falls out of touch with the real life of the passing seasons. Self-absorbed, she has withdrawn from life:

> Otoyo had gone as far as Imado Bridge before she realized that it was high April—and spring. The sky was blue and the sun poured through the window, and the willow by the door of the shop across the street put out its threads of green, to make even Otoyo, a woman alone and sorely pressed, notice the change of seasons. But now, from the low ground in the outer reaches of the city, with the view blocked off by shabby tiled roofs on either side, she came out on the bridge, and an uninterrupted view of the Sumida in April. She left her own street no more than two or three times a year, and she wondered whether her aging eyes might not be deceiving her. The shining flow of water, the green grass on the embankment, the line above it of cherries in bloom, the university boathouse with its banner flying, the shouts of people and the roar of guns, all of these under a cloudless sky. And the confusion of blossom viewers, getting on and off the ferries. This sudden flood of color was too much for the weary Otoyo. She started

[5] *Ibid.*, p. 195.

down toward the ferry landing, and then, as if in fright, she turned back and hurried south, in the shade of Matchi Hill.[6]

The freshness and vigor of the spring demand too much of a woman too weary to renew herself, without the hope of any change in her own existence. She can no longer be sustained by these fresh rhythms. Kafū often permits such moments to suggest their own meanings; here, however, he provides an analysis of Otoyo's feelings:

> She was in no mood for looking at cherry blossoms. She did not know where to turn. Not only had the son upon whom she had pinned all her hopes failed his examinations, but he said he no longer wanted to go to school. He was finished with lessons and learning. Otoyo had no recourse other than to go consult with her brother Ragetsu.[7]

In the final section of "The River Sumida," Kafū makes use of still another setting to evoke the sense of despair felt by the family over Chōkichi. Otoyo's brother Ragetsu, left alone after Chōkichi is taken to the hospital, feels emptied of emotion. He is tired, bored. The setting of the empty house defines his mood precisely:

> Ragetsu found himself left behind to watch the house.

> The ward office had disinfected it with sulphur and carbolic acid. The silence, added to a disorder like that of spring-cleaning or a moving day, made him think of a house after the funeral is over and the coffin has gone. Outside, beyond shutters that had been closed from before dark as a sign of deference and withdrawal, a sharp wind seemed to have come up. All through the house shutters and doors were rattling. There was an unpleasant chill in the air. Occasionally, as a gust of wind came through the battered kitchen door, the dim light of the ceiling lamp would threaten to go out, a cloud of oily smoke would darken its chimney, and the shadows of the disordered furniture would move across the scarred floor and up the peeling walls. In a nearby house a voice was chanting a Buddhist invocation, the sound of it dark and oppressive.[8]

[6] *Ibid.*, p. 209.   [7] *Ibid.*   [8] *Ibid.*, p. 216.

After such a passage of descriptive juxtaposition, Kafū (in a transformation analogous to that of Bashō when he moves from the poetic *haiku* to the prose *haibun*) introduces a series of statements explicating directly Ragetsu's emotional state, to sum up the significance of the state of mind just engendered in the reader and so reinforcing a close identification with the mood of the character portrayed:

> Time passed slowly for Ragetsu, left all alone. He was bored, and he was dejected. At times like these, he said to himself, a man needed a drink. He went for a look around the kitchen, but of course it was a household run by a woman, and he could not find even a wine glass.[9]

The mood explicated, Kafū returns again to a new *collage* of specific, evocative detail, to further refine the emotional state he has just described. And so the rhythm continues:

> Going back to the window, he pulled a shutter partly open and looked out. He did not see, among the lights on the other side of the street, the mark of a single wine merchant. Although it was still early, most of the shutters were already closed in this unflourishing neighborhood. The chanting voice, dark and gloomy, sounded out the more clearly. A violent wind from the river set the electric wires above the house to singing, and the stars seemed to have been swept cleaner; and the windy night, as windy nights will, brought a feeling that winter had suddenly returned.[10]

In a sense all these descriptions serve something of the function of prose *haiku*, providing highly selected and juxtaposed objects that help create a flash of emotional insight in the reader. If Kafū had written in the eighteenth century, he might have turned them into poetry; as a prose novelist, however, he linked them instead in a relationship with the characters he created. The effects of the changing perceptible world (in this case, the landscape of a huge city) on the emotional state of a writer, or of his characters, goes back in the Japanese tradition at least to the poem of Ariwara no Narihira in *Tales of Ise* quoted earlier. Kafū understood the workings

[9] *Ibid.*   [10] *Ibid.*

of this traditional aesthetic mechanism very well, and he admired it. In many scenes in "The River Sumida," he creates a
mood from his setting so powerful that its effect on the reader
is often stronger than on the character involved. The reader is
doubly influenced, moved, both by the setting itself, plus by
the reaction of the character to that setting and situation. The
effect is richly poetic.

In each of these individual scenes, whatever their particular
purposes in the narrative framework, Kafū posits the processes of nature as the ultimate referent: time, and the movement of nature in time constitute the theme of "The River
Sumida." Time, like the river itself, links the various sections
of the narrative together. In Ragetsu, the *haiku* poet, Kafū has
created a character admirably suited to serve as a means to
begin and end the story. After all, the art he practices, and the
importance of which he signals, offers many of the techniques
Kafū himself has used. In a prose context, however, these juxtapositions based on traditional poetic techniques strike many
readers as surprisingly fresh, something like methods of cut-
ting used in contemporary film. Kafū has used these techniques from the literary past to reflect his own sense of the
present. The theme of his narrative is doubtless very modern,
in terms of his characters and their emotional concerns: "To
thine own self be true," he urges, even if that truth may lead
to possible poverty and decadence. The force of that message,
however, is carried through to the reader by a series of literary techniques, newly ordered though they may be, that owe
their effectiveness almost entirely to the Japanese literary past.

ŌGAI AND "SANSHŌ THE STEWARD"

Mori Ōgai's career, on the surface of things, could scarcely
have been more different from that of Nagai Kafū. Born a
generation earlier, he was one of the first young intellectuals
to go abroad. His years spent in Germany, from 1884 to 1888,
had a profound effect on him, but his personal circumstances
were considerably different from those of Kafū. Ōgai was the
son of a distinguished doctor (whose training was, of course,
in traditional Japanese medicine). Ōgai learned German as a
young student in Tokyo as a means to help him in his study of

Western medicine, then largely taught by German professors resident in Japan. After completing his studies, Ōgai joined the army as a physician and was shortly sent by the Japanese government on a scholarship to study new methods of European hygiene. Unlike Kafū, who visited France as a private citizen, Ōgai's strong sense of duty to the government for the opportunity given him became the obligation of a lifetime, whatever the ambiguities he felt in his private and artistic life. Ōgai remained in the army and eventually, by the time of the Russo-Japanese War in 1904, became Surgeon-General. Ōgai maintained precisely the kind of public career that Kafū was at considerable pains to shun.

While in Germany, Ōgai began reading German literature, especially Goethe and the Romantics, and his enthusiastic avowal of their accomplishments was manifested in a number of excellent translations into Japanese, an effort that soon brought to the intelligentsia of Japan a consciousness of the high level of German civilization. In a later phase of his career as an advocate and translator of European literature, Ōgai translated contemporary writers who, for whom, seemed to better reflect the realities of his own time; and again, he created a considerable enthusiasm among his contemporaries for Ibsen, Strindberg, Rilke, and other important twentieth-century writers. In terms of an enthusiasm for European civilization, at least, Ōgai and Kafū resembled each other closely. Each found something in that civilization corresponding to powerful elements already latent in their own personalities. For Ōgai his hero was doubtless Goethe; for Kafū it was Baudelaire. The translations of these two European writers by Ōgai and Kafū remain as monuments in the history of modern translated literature in Japan.

Like Kafū too, Ōgai felt some tensions, a desire to be free. In his first story "Maihime" (The Girl Who Danced), written in 1890, two years after his return from Germany, Ōgai had his protagonist express himself as follows:

> While I was repudiating authority, something still troubled me. I was now annoyed that I had been following a road others had mapped out for me. But I was still afraid of failing to meet their expectations. I now despised them for

driving me, but the thought of displeasing them still
frightened me. I could not stop oscillating between free-
dom and subservience. While I was trying to assert myself
in Berlin and break free of the tradition that has bound me,
I kept thinking of something that happened to me when I
set sail for Yokohama. I walked up the gangplank as
though I were a shining hero, knowing that my superiors
were watching me and that my mother was among them.
But once the ship got underway, I wept like a child. And
while I was in Berlin, I began to realize that I lacked as
much courage as my convictions demanded of me.[11]

Unlike Kafū, Ōgai could not kick over the traces. Despite
his wishes to somehow break away from the restraints imposed upon him by his military career, he kept his profes-
sional commitments to the end of his career. Critical speculation as to why he continued has produced no convincing
arguments. Some superficial reasons seem apparent. He loved
scientific research; his generation was much closer than Kafū's
to the Confucian ideology of the Tokugawa period, where
service to one's superiors was a supreme virtue; his own personality was certainly more attracted to participation in society than was Kafū's who had much of the recluse in his
general makeup.

Nevertheless, the disparity between Ōgai's official duties
(and with the political attitudes his colleagues presumed must
go along with them) and the demands of his artistic life set up
in him a tension that ultimately could not be resolved. That
tension in turn provided him with a sense of detachment, an
ironic objectivity, that separated him from any particular activity in which he found himself engaged. In one story, written in 1911, Ōgai tried to express this particular quality of
mind that formed such an important part of his whole outlook on the world. The protagonist, invited to a party, witnesses the air of abstraction shown by his host, Shikayama,
then reflects on his own similar predilections:

[11] Translation by Leon Zolbrod, from "The Girl Who Danced," in M. A.
Martin, ed., *The Language of Love* (Bantam Books, 1964), p. 3.

I have thought often, and deeply, about those born to be
bystanders. I myself have no incurable disease. Yet I, too,
am inherently a bystander. From the time I first began to
play with other children, and even when I grew to adulthood and made my way in the world, and with every kind
of person in society, I have never been able to throw myself
into the whirlpool and enjoy myself to the depths of my
being, no matter what kind of excitement may have been
stirred up in me. Even though I have made my appearance
on the stage of human activity, I have never played a role
worthy of the name. The most I have achieved has been the
position of a supernumerary. And indeed I have felt most
like myself when I had no need to mount that stage and,
like a fish in water, could remain at ease among the bystanders. With these feelings, I watched Shikamaya, and,
as I did so, I realized that I felt as though I had met an old
friend in a foreign country. I felt as though one bystander
had discovered another.[12]

Kafū's distaste for society caused him to turn to the past;
Ōgai too, by 1914, had done the same. While in his forties,
Ōgai began to realize the necessity for understanding the past
as a crucial means to grasp the real significance of the present.
Examination of his own past began in a series of short stories
and a short novel *Vita Sexualis* (1909). In his next novel *Gan*
(Wild Goose) (1911), he placed the setting during the time of
his childhood, in the early Meiji period. In that novel Ōgai
attempted, among other things, to capture the social attitudes
of that time in his narrative. In the course of a long story-
essay written the following year, "Ka no yo ni" (As If), Ōgai
first expresses the larger purposes to which history might be
put. The protagonist Hidemaro insists that a study of history
can make clear the divisions between myth and fact. Fiction,
like myth, he continues, represents a kind of belief:

For example, a novel represents an untruth insofar as its
purpose is regarded as presenting facts. But a novel is not

[12] From "Hyaku monogatari" (The Tale of a Hundred Candles). See *Mori
Ōgai zenshū* (Tokyo, 1971), Vol. II, p. 170.

accountable for this sort of truth but is indeed conceived of precisely in terms of such fabrication. Its very life exists in those fabrications. And its value. Sacred myths were conceived of in the same fashion; the only difference lies in the fact that the primal events of myth were considered to be true.[13]

Such attitudes in Ōgai were further strengthened by the death of the Emperor Meiji in 1912. The ruler who had served as a symbol of progress and unity to his countrymen through the difficult decades since the opening of the country was gone. Many others followed their leader by committing ritual suicide. Eminent among them was General Nogi, the hero of the Russo-Japanese War. Ōgai, like Natsume Sōseki and other writers at the time, was moved and troubled by the ambiguous nature of Nogi's act. In Sōseki's case, the suicide formed the setting for perhaps his most celebrated novel, *Kokoro*. For Ōgai, the incident provided an impetus to re-examine Japanese history in an attempt to reach some understanding of the larger moral principles guiding that earlier society. These explorations resulted in a series of historical stories and novellas that for many Japanese readers constitute Ōgai's finest achievement.

Ōgai turned to the past to find something quite different from what Kafū sought. Given Ōgai's position in the military hierarchy and his desire to participate in his contemporary artistic world, his attitude toward the past was conditioned by an intellectual desire to grasp certain moral threads and lines of tension. For Kafū the past seemed something more of a retreat; for Ōgai, the past served as a kind of laboratory in which he could gather evidence to continue his philosophical experiments. Concerning his writings on historical themes and subjects Ōgai insisted that "if contemporary authors can write about life 'just as it is' and find it satisfactory, then they ought to appreciate a similar treatment of the past."[14] He then commented as follows:

A number of my friends say that other writers choose their material and treat it on an emotional basis, while I do

---

[13] *Ibid.*, p. 247.   [14] *Ōgai zenshū*, Vol. VII, p. 105.

so on a rational one. Yet I hold this to be true of all my literary work, not merely of the stories based on historical characters. In general, I would say that my works are not "Dionysian" but rather "Apollonian." I have never exerted the kind of effort required to make a story "Dionysian." And indeed, if I were able to expend a comparable effort, it would be an effort to make my creation all the more contemplative.[15]

On the other hand, Kafū's stories of decaying Tokyo may come as close to the "Dionysian" as anything in recent Japanese literature. He not only made use of the past in his subject matter but, as was pointed out above, in his narrative style as well. Ōgai, however, continued to write in a contemporary colloquial style he himself helped to perfect. With a few significant exceptions, his historical works showed both in their narrative structures and linguistic usages little concern for the past. Ōgai had other outlets for these predilections. He was an excellent poet in classical Chinese and showed some real talent for writing 31-syllable *waka* as well. His prose style, however, was as "Apollonian" as was his attitude toward his subject matter.

One of Ōgai's most attractive longer historical stories is his tale *Sanshō Dayū* (Sanshō the Steward), written in 1914. The story may be familiar to those who have seen the celebrated 1954 film of Mizoguchi, by the same title, although that director has changed certain details in the original.

Ōgai took his story from a medieval legend. He first thought to write a drama on the theme, then chose instead to write a prose narrative. The legend concerns two children of a noble family whose father has been exiled. When the children grow to an age when they are able to travel long distances, they set out on a journey with their mother and a servant woman, in order to try to locate their father. On the road they are waylaid by an unscrupulous slave dealer named Yamaoka, who sells them to two boatmen. One takes away the mother as well as her serving woman (who later commits suicide). The other takes the two children and eventually sells them to a terrifying man named Sanshō the Steward, who

[15] *Ibid.*

puts them to work as the young members in a kind of slave labor camp deep in the country, far from any source of help. The main sections of the narrative concern the life of the two children in the camp. At the time of their capture, Anju, the girl, is roughly twelve and her younger brother Zushiō is several years younger. After a long period of hardship, the children plan an escape. Anju sacrifices herself, committing suicide so that her brother might flee unharmed. The boy eludes his captors and eventually reaches Kyoto, the capital, where, in accordance with the legend, his titles and fortunes are restored to him. At the end of the narrative, Ōgai created an especially poignant scene in which the young man is reunited with his mother.

The literary construction of the story seems at first glance to owe little to the fanciful tale tradition from which the original account was taken. Ōgai, in his way, acknowledges the fact himself:

> Following the general account of the original, I wrote my own version according to my own imagination. The basic language of my story was composed in the kind of modern colloquial style I have long been accustomed to; the conversations take place in contemporary Tokyo language, and only in the works spoken by Sanshō and Yamaoka did I add a certain archaic element. Yet, accustomed to dealing with actual historical figures as I am, I could not write the story in complete disregard for the period in which it took place. In choosing names for the various objects used at the time, I employed words I found recorded in a dictionary of old Japanese I had close at hand. I also used the old forms of such things as court titles. Eventually, a certain number of classical nouns were inserted into the modern colloquial structure. Not wishing to slight the particular period itself, I constructed a chronology for the story.[16]

Nevertheless, in a more subtle way, "Sanshō the Steward" does owe a considerable debt to the past. The subject matter, of course, is traditional. Ōgai's art in retelling the story lies in his understanding of the psychological and philosophical significance of the legend, as well in his ability to translate that

[16] *Ibid.*, pp. 106-107.

significance to his readers. The task he set himself was not dissimilar from the efforts he made to make Goethe and Ibsen comprehensible to his contemporaries, although the source in this case was classical Japanese rather than modern German. Ōgai's attempt to make the atmosphere of the story intelligible to his audience resembles the much more sophisticated attempt of Tanizaki to recreate the world of *Genji* in "The Bridge of Dreams."

Some of Ōgai's techniques involve selection. By his own account, he removed a certain brutality he found in the original version. In that account, the girl Anju is tortured and killed by her captors. Ōgai allows her to drown herself. In the original, the children are branded on their foreheads for attempting to escape; in Ōgai's version, they merely dream the experience, although it is a terrifying dream. In the original, Zushiō returns to wreak vengeance on Sanshō and has him killed with a bamboo saw. Ōgai, on the other hand, has Zushiō send his former master to free all the slaves. Sanshō then hires them and pays them properly for their labors. By removing the violence from the story, Ōgai chose to concentrate on those elements in the original that strongly attracted him: the profound love between parents and children that the legend reveals. He retained certain miraculous events in the narrative, in particular the incident, near the end of the story, when Zushiō is adopted by a Fujiwara courtier because of a small statue of a Boddhisatva found in the boy's possession. Ōgai sets a level of psychological reality close enough to our own to permit both a series of realistic conversations between the two children, while still encompassing without strain a number of fanciful happenings. To say that Ōgai merely recreated the medieval tale in terms of modern sensibilities is to miss the delicacy of artistic observation that lies at the root of his accomplishment.

The areas of Ōgai's main concern in "Sanshō the Steward" lie primarily in the nature of the relationship between the two children. Japanese literature presents many precedents for this subject matter, beginning, as noted earlier, with *Tales of Ise*. Ōgai portrays the two at that brief moment between childhood and adulthood, when the whole world seems to open, and just before it closes in again. There are many poignant

episodes in the story that can provide examples, but none is
more moving than the scene when Anju, "now fifteen, adopting an adult's manner, as wise as if possessed by some higher
power," convinces Zushiō that he must escape. She says
nothing about herself. He finally agrees, without understanding fully the implications of what she is about:

> When they got down as far as the grove of trees, the two
> put down their sickles and baskets on the fallen leaves.
> Anju took out her amulet and pressed it in her brother's
> hand. "You know how much I prize this. I want you to
> keep it for me until we meet again. Think that the image is
> me and take good care of it, just like your guardian
> sword."
>   "But Anju, what will you do without it?"
>   "I want you to have it. You will face greater dangers
> than I. When you don't come back this evening, they will
> send a party to search you out. No matter how fast you go,
> if you simply run off without a plan, you're sure to be
> caught. Go along the upper reaches of the river we saw just
> now, until you get to Wae. If you are lucky enough not to
> be seen and can manage to get to the opposite bank,
> Nakayama can't be much further. Go there, to the
> temple—we saw the pagoda sticking up through the
> trees—and ask for asylum. Stay there for awhile, until your
> pursuers have given up and gone away. Then run away
> from the temple."
>   "But do you think the priest in the temple will give me
> shelter?"
>   "It's all a question of chance. If your luck is good, the
> priest will hide you."[17]

Zushiō, in awe of the wisdom and foresight shown by his
older sister, acquiesces to her wishes and puts his entire trust
in her. Anju is deeply moved:

> "I'm so happy. You've understood everything I told
> you. The priest is surely a fine man. I know he will take
> care of you."

[17] "Sanshō Dayū," tr. by J. Thomas Rimer, in Mori Ōgai, *The Incident at
Sakai and other stories*, Honolulu, 1977, pp. 142-143.

"Yes. I've come to believe that myself. I'll get away and go to the capital. I'll find father and mother too. And I'll come back for you." Zushiō's eyes took on the same sparkle as his sister's.

"I'll go down to the bottom with you, so let's hurry." The pair quickly clambered down the hillside. Their whole manner of walking now changed, for Anju's intensity had been transferred to Zushiō as well.

They passed the spot where the spring gushed up from the rocks. Anju took out the wooden bowl in her provision box and dipped into the cool water. "Let us drink together to celebrate your departure," she said, as she took a draft and passed the bowl to her brother.

Zushiō emptied the bowl completely. "Goodbye then, my dear sister. Please take care of yourself. I will get to the temple in Nakayama without being seen by anyone."[18]

The ceremony of parting concluded. Zushiō takes his leave. The family, although now completely separated, is still bound together in the strongest psychological and emotional terms. Anju, secure in the knowledge of this fact, now is able to await her end with dignity:

Zushiō rushed down the bit of path remaining on the hillside and took the main road running along the swampy sea. He hurried off in the direction of the Okumo river.

Anju stood by the spring and watched the figure of her brother grow smaller as he appeared, then disappeared behind rows of pine trees. The sun was almost at its highest point, yet she made no effort to climb the mountain again. Fortunately there seemed no other woodcutters at work nearby, so no one questioned Anju, who stood idling away her time at the foot of the mountain path.

Later the search party sent out by Sanshō to catch the pair picked up a pair of straw sandals at the end of the swamp at the bottom of the hill. They belonged to Anju.[19]

Zushiō's own growth to maturity comes partially through his experiences with a wise and courageous Buddhist priest who rescues him, partially through his adventures in Kyoto

18 *Ibid.*, p. 143.   19 *Ibid.*, pp. 143-144.

when his wealth is restored to him. Zushiō's entrance into the adult world sends him on a quest to find again all that he loved in the past. His father, he discovers, is dead. He learns of his sister's suicide. Finally, despondent, he sets off to find some trace of his mother. He travels to Sado, a remote island of exile, where he thinks she may have been taken. Psychology, poetic imagination, and a deep sense of pathos, of the classical *mono no aware*, give the final scene, in which figure a sense of time, transcience, and reconciliation, a powerful atmosphere:

> By chance, Zushiō noticed a rather large farm house. Looking through the sparse hedge that grew on the south side of the building, he saw an open area where the earth had been pounded flat. Straw mats were spread there on which cut grains of millet had been spread to dry. In the midst of the drying grain sat a woman dressed in rags, who carried a long pole in her hand to chase the sparrows coming to peck at the grain. She seemed to murmur what sounded like a song.
>
> Without knowing precisely why, Zushiō was attracted to something in the woman. He stopped and looked inside the hedge. The woman's unkempt hair was clotted with dust. When he looked at her face, he saw she was blind, and a strong surge of pity for her went through him. As the moments passed, he began to understand the words of the little song she was muttering to herself. His body trembled as if he had a fever, and tears welled up in his eyes. For these were the words the woman was repeating over and over to herself:

> My Anju, I yearn for you.
>   Fly away!
> My Zushiō, I yearn for you.
>   Fly away!
> Little birds, if you are living still,
>   Fly, fly far away!
> I will not chase you.

He stood transfixed, enraptured by her words. Suddenly his whole body seemed on fire; he had to grit his teeth to

hold back the animal scream welling up within him. As
though freed from invisible chains, he rushed through the
hedge. Tramping on the millet grains, he threw himself at
the feet of the woman. The amulet, which he had been
holding up in his right hand, pushed against his forehead
when he threw himself on the ground.

The woman realized that something bigger than a spar-
row had come storming into the millet. She stopped her
endless song and stared ahead of her with her blind eyes.
Then, like dried seashells swelling open in water, her eyes
began to moisten and to open.

"Zushiō!" she called out. They rushed into each other's
arms.[20]

Reconciliation with the past, with its beauties and its horrors, remains the ultimate theme of "Sanshō the Steward,"
and this same urge for reconciliation lies behind much of
Ōgai's last work. In this regard, his temper of mind remained
different from that of Kafū, who seldom abandoned his aristocratic disdain sufficiently to transcend his distaste for the
present. Kafū did, of course, pay homage to *mono no aware* in
his own work, and in this regard at least "The River Sumida"
and "Sanshō the Steward" have much in common. In technique, however, the two show few similarities. Ōgai's
story builds to a series of climaxes, carefully prepared, much
like those in the kinds of Western fiction he so much admired.
"The River Sumida" seems to have a modest beginning, a
lengthy middle, and no real ending at all. Yet in the end both
writers were true to the Japanese literary tradition. Ōgai in-
fused the old form of the tale with narrative consistency and
sustained lyricism; and the tale, as was pointed out earlier, has
always shown a greater emphasis on structural elements than
other narrative prose forms. Kafū, on the other hand, went to
poetry, especially to the narrative patterns established in *haiku*
and in the poetic diary, for his organizing principles. Ōgai's
energy is moral, Kafū's lyrical. Both, estranged from the
past, used their new and painfully gained sense of objectivity
to look back, searching for a means to come to terms with
what they felt they had lost.

[20] *Ibid.*, p. 148.

IX

Kawabata Yasunari: Eastern Approaches
Snow Country

KAWABATA YASUNARI (1899-1972) was perhaps the most respected of the modern Japanese novelists who made manifest both in his fiction and in his critical writings an enthusiastic debt to the past. His choice as the recipient of the 1968 Nobel Prize for Literature indicates that foreign readers as well as his Japanese public continued to respond to the kind of evocative style of which Kawabata was capable. The increasing number of translations of his work available suggest further that his popularity continues unabated. Among those works known outside Japan, *Yukiguni* (Snow Country), written in 1937, has attracted the most comment and seems to have gained the largest readership. Much has already been written about the themes and structures of this novel, and further discussion of its merits may seem unnecessary. Nevertheless, *Snow Country* still holds the potential to shed considerable light not only on the larger purposes of Kawabata's work but on the techniques of Japanese narrative fiction in general. In this regard, *Snow Country* is a mirror, reflecting both backwards and forwards.

Kawabata's own views on literature help to show the kind of role that *Snow Country* may be expected to play in the larger design of his work. His Nobel Prize acceptance speech is perhaps the best place to begin, since there he attempted to sum up the basic principles of his art as he saw them. The talk dealt little with Kawabata personally. He spent considerable time, however, on the traditional Japanese aesthetic views that he continued to admire. The lecture was not, on the other hand, a thorough discussion of those values, but rather provided a selection of certain principles especially important to him, many of them related in turn to Zen Buddhism.

The first of these is asymmetry. Kawabata cites flower arranging and gardening as the two artistic activities that best reveal the uses of suggestiveness:

The Western garden tends to be symmetrical, the Japanese garden asymmetrical, and this is because the asymmetrical has the greater power to symbolize multiplicity and vastness. The asymmetry, of course, rests upon a balance imposed by delicate sensibilities.[1]

Asymmetry and a resulting suggestiveness provide the means by which one small thing can evoke a whole world. Closed structures, harmoniously arranged, merely define themselves. Kawabata is careful to point out, however, that the asymmetry is not naturally evoked but comes from a discipline created through "a balance imposed by delicate sensibilities" that have in turn been rigorously formed and refined.

The suggestiveness prized by Kawabata bears a close family resemblance to the traditional literary virtue of *yūgen*. At the end of his lecture, he quotes the remarks of a medieval Japanese poet on his great contemporary Saigyō (1118-1190), one of the finest in a long line of poets, including Bashō, whose literary and poetic ideals were transcendental and, by some definitions at least, religious:

> Saigyō frequently came and talked of poetry. His own attitude towards poetry, he said, was far from the ordinary. Cherry blossoms, the cuckoo, the moon, snow: confronted with all the manifold forms of nature, his eyes and his ears were filled with emptiness. And were not all the words that came forth true words. When he sang of the blossoms the blossoms were not on his mind. When he sang of the moon he did not think of the moon. As the occasion presented itself, as the urge arose, he wrote poetry. The red rainbow across the sky was as the sky taking on color. The white sunlight was as the sky growing bright. It was not something to take on color. With a spirit like the empty sky he gave color to all the manifold scenes, but not a trace remained. In such poetry was the Buddha, the manifestation of the ultiamte truth.[2]

[1] Kawabata Yasunari, *Japan, the Beautiful, and Myself* (tr. by Edward Seidensticker), Tokyo and Palo Alto, 1969, p. 53.
[2] *Ibid.*, pp. 41-42.

Saigyō's art consisted of suggesting, not stating, a general truth. Kawabata's own sensibilities led him to adopt the same mentality, and many of the same methods, in his own composition of fiction. Such sensibilities, however, are the result of rigorous training. Kawabata's admiration for the classic literary texts of the past, and the fact of their continuing importance to him as literary models, are clear from statements made elsewhere in the lecture.

In poetry there came, early in the tenth century, the first of the imperially commissioned anthologies, the *Kokinshū*, and in fiction the *Tales of Ise*, followed by the supreme masterpieces of classical Japanese prose, the *Tale of Genji* of Lady Murasaki and the *Pillow Book* of Sei Shōnagon, both of whom lived from the later tenth century into the early eleventh. So was established a tradition which influenced and even controlled Japanese literature for eight hundred years. The *Tale of Genji* in particular is the highest pinnacle of Japanese literature. Even down to our day there has not been a piece of fiction to compare with it. That such a modern work should have been written in the eleventh century is a miracle, and as a miracle the work is widely known abroad. Although my grasp of classical Japanese was uncertain, the Heian classics were my principal boyhood reading, and it is the *Genji*, I think, that has meant the most to me. For centuries after it was written, fascination with the *Genji* persisted, and imitations and reworkings did homage to it. The *Genji* was a wide and deep source of nourishment for poetry, of course, and for the fine arts and handicrafts as well, and even for landscape gardening.[3]

A desire to pay homage to the nourishment provided by the past seems to put Kawabata in the role of advocate for traditional styles and roles of literature in Japanese culture. In assuming this stance, he was as self-conscious about his own distance from the past as were, for different reasons, Kafū and Ōgai. Kawabata's very distance from his tradition gave him a self-conscious awareness of the workings of the traditions

---

[3] *Ibid.*, pp. 46-47.

necessary to permit him to adapt them for his own particular purposes. Indeed, what now strikes the readers of Kawabata (including those who have no knowledge of traditional Japanese aesthetics) is his ability to capture with startling freshness the psychology of his characters and the atmosphere that surrounds, and indeed helps define, that psychology. His remarkable skill certainly attests to the continuing vitality in the older traditions, but it shows as well his uncanny agility in recasting the traditional literary techniques into a modern narrative form so compelling that the results seem not only agreeable but inevitable.

Kawabata's concerns often extend over more than one particular novel. More revealing than the relatively few remarks he himself has made about *Snow Country* are the more general propositions he voiced in a 1969 lecture at the University of Hawaii, entitled "The Existence and Discovery of Beauty." There he quoted a *haiku* by the Tokugawa poet Kobayashi Issa (1763–1827):

utsukushi ya	How beautiful!
toshi kurekitta	The sky on the night
yoru no sora	When the year has ended completely.

I learned this *haiku* of Kobayashi Issa upon finding it in an antique shop in Kamakura on a *kakemono* written by Issa himself. I have not yet investigated when and where this *haiku* was composed, but if it was written after his return to his home in Kashiwabara on the shore of Lake Nojiri, which is on the border between snowy Echigo and Shinano, and at the foot of such mountains as Togakushi, Īzuna, and Myōkō, then the night sky was high and extremely clear, as if frozen over, and we can think that it had a vast number of stars which seemed to be showering down in brilliance. We must also remember that this would be his home which he has described in a famous *haiku*:

kore ga maa	Is this after all
tsui no sumika ka	My final dwelling-place?
yuki goshaku	Five feet of snow.

Furthermore, it was in the very middle of the night on the last day of the year. Therefore, in the commonplace words "utsukushi ya" (how beautiful!) Issa discovered and created great beauty.[4]

Kawabata's remarks reveal a necessary and close connection postulated between the poetic impulse and the atmosphere of the place that gives rise to that impulse. The aptness and simplicity of Issa's response represent the outcome of his attunement to what might be termed the poetry of place. His reactions are personal and precise. Later in the same lecture, Kawabata cites Bashō's similar attitudes, quoting a well-known incident when that poet praised Kyorai, one of his followers, who told him that "how true it is that a certain scene at a certain time will move the emotions of men."[5] Commenting on Kyorai's belief that "the elegant is that which arises in particular circumstances," Kawabata concludes as follows:

> In discovering the elegant, that is, beauty which exists, in sensing the beauty one has discovered, and even in creating the beauty one has sensed, the particular circumstances of that which exists naturally in those circumstances are truly important, and we may say that they are the grace of Heaven; moreover, if we can know those particular circumstances as being actually those circumstances, then we may say that this is a gift of the god of beauty.[6]

The particular place and the poetic implications of that place form one element in the delicate balance that produces the narrative style of Kawabata in *Snow Country*. The concept of the poetry of place may provide a useful way to open a discussion of the book itself. In the first place, Kawabata's ability to evoke a natural scene represents one of his strongest talents as a writer. Whatever the larger purposes of his descriptions, his sensibilities (like those of the great *haiku* writers) are invariably particular, sharp, and precise:

---

[4] Kawabata Yasunari, *The Existence and Discovery of Beauty*, tr. by V. H. Viglielmo, bilingual edition (Tokyo, 1969), pp. 35-37.

[5] *Ibid.*, p. 71.   [6] *Ibid.*, pp. 72-73.

From behind the rock, the cedars threw up their trunks in perfectly straight lines, so high that he could see the tops only by arching his back. The dark needles blocked out the sky, and the stillness seemed to be singing quietly. The trunk against which Shimamura leaned was the oldest of all. For some reason all the branches on the north side had withered and, their tips broken and fallen, they looked like stakes driven into the trunk with their sharp ends out, to make a terrible weapon for some god.[7]

A few brief sentences of this sort suffice to create an atmosphere for the whole environment of the novel. Precision creates suggestiveness, as in a good *haiku*:

Probably to keep snow from piling up, the water from the baths was led around the walls of the inn by a makeshift ditch, and in front of the entrance it spread out like a shallow spring. A powerful black dog stood on the stones by the doorway lapping at the water. Skis for the hotel guests, probably brought out from a storeroom, were lined up to dry, and the faint smell of mildew was sweetened by the steam. The snow that had fallen from the cedar branches to the roof of the public bath was breaking down into something warm and shapeless.[8]

Above and beyond Kawabata's skill in the technique of nature description, however, rests his ability to construct his whole novel on an extended metaphor of travel. Shimamura, the male protagonist of *Snow Country*, leaves his home and family in Tokyo for occasional visits to the cold and remote area of northern Japan that Kawabata names in the title of his book. When the narrative opens, the reader soon learns that the protagonist has been there previously and has established a liaison with Komako, a young girl who becomes a geisha. The novel proper chronicles his relationship with her and concludes when he makes his final decision to leave his "snow country" for good. Reduced to the level of plot, Kawabata's

[7] Kawabata Yasunari, *Snow Country*, tr. by Edward Seidensticker (New York, 1956), p. 30.
[8] *Ibid.*, p. 48.

seems to have a number of precedents, including Sōseki's *Kusamakura*, Bashō's travel diaries, and even the *Tosa Diary* of Heian times. Like the travellers described in these earlier accounts, Shimamura too is in search of something. A modern man, and a somewhat weak and self-preoccupied one at that, his purposes are rather more modest than those of his literary predecessors. "Shimamura," writes Kawabata, "who lived a life of idleness, found that he tended to lose his honesty with himself, and he frequently went out alone into the mountains to recover something of it."[9] The family resemblance to Sōseki's traveller, and to Bashō, is strong.

Shimamura moves in and out of the "snow country," and, as Kawabata shows us in his dazzling opening chapter, that world is a special one, every bit as special as the village encountered by the painter in Sōseki's novel. Like the painter, Shimamura encounters a woman concerning whom he can achieve only a partial understanding. Komako and Onami, different as they are in temperament and personality, bear a similar relationship to their respective male protagonists in the structures of the two novels: different views of them at different times produce varying, indeed conflicting, impressions.

Kawabata's narrative technique is, of course, more sophisticated, and more self-conscious, than that of Sōseki. Kawabata is able to carry through certain implications of this basic paradigm common to both novels, implications that were not among the central concerns of Sōseki. Kawabata, for example, often blends the character and the geography of his story together, until Shimamura finds it difficult to distinguish in himself any distinction between his attraction to Komako and his attraction to the "snow country." Fresh from days of hiking in the mountains, Shimamura, remembering his pleasure in talking with Komako on a previous visit, summons her again:

> She said she was nineteen. Shimamura had taken her to be twenty-one or twenty-two, and, since he had assumed that she was not lying, the knowledge that she had aged

beyond her years gave him for the first time a little of the ease he expected to feel with a geisha. When they began talking of the Kabuki, he found that she knew more about actors and styles than he did. She talked on feverishly, as though she had been starved for someone who would listen to her, and presently began to show an ease and abandon that revealed her to be at heart a woman of the pleasure quarters after all. And she seemed in general to know what there was to know about men. Shimamura, however, had labeled her an amateur, and, after a week in the mountains during which he had spoken to almost no one, he found himself longing for a companion. It was therefore friendship more than anything else that he felt for the woman. His response to the mountains had extended itself to cover her.[10]

Looking at her again, early in the morning, Shimamura cannot separate his vision of her from his vision of nature.

Presently the room was so light that he could see the red of her cheeks. His eye was fastened on that extraordinarily bright red.

"Your cheeks are flaming. That's how cold it is."

"It's not from the cold. It's because I've taken off my powder. I only have to get into bed and in a minute I'm warm as an oven. All the way to my feet." She knelt at the mirror by the bed.

"It's daylight. I'm going home."

Shimamura glanced up at her, and immediately lowered his head. The white in the depths of the mirror was the snow, and floating in the middle of it were the woman's bright red cheeks. There was an indescribably fresh beauty in the contrast.

Was the sun already up? The brightness of the snow was more intense, it seemed to be burning icily. Against it, the woman's hair became a clearer black, touched with a purple sheen.[11]

Such blurring and blending produces the suggestiveness so

---

[10] *Ibid.*, p. 19.   [11] *Ibid.*, p. 48.

important to Kawabata in setting up the larger evocative purposes of his novel, purposes that lie behind any given set of
narrative particulars.

Kawabata is careful to make this blending of character and
setting a source of self-conscious pleasure to Shimamura, just
as the protagonist in *Kusamakura* takes satisfaction in his own
"non-human tour." Sōseki's artist is interested in Western
painting, Kawabata's in Western ballet. Shimamura, however, is a dilettante, who has no serious purpose in life. He
treats the ballet as a fantasy world toward which he bears no
responsibility. Komako for him seems to fill a similar function; and like Sōseki's hero, Shimamura wishes to remain uninvolved.

> . . . Shimamura, with no real occupation, took some
> satisfaction from the fact that his occasional introductions
> to the occidental dance put him on the edge of the literary
> world—even while he was laughing at himself and his
> work.
> It might be said that his knowledge was now for the first
> time in a very great while being put to use, since talk of the
> dance helped bring the woman nearer to him; and yet it was
> also possible that, hardly knowing it, he was treating the
> woman exactly as he treated the occidental dance.[12]

All the other characters in the book are seen through the
eyes of Shimamura, and the reader's basic sense of confusion
over their various relationships mirrors Shimamura's own. In
particular, Komako's relationship with her friend Yoko puz-
zles Shimamura. Both women seem to have been in love with
the same young man, Yukio, who dies of tuberculosis early in
the novel. The tensions between the two women seem at
times to be intense, yet Shimamura, glimpsing both women
only from time to time, cannot grasp the precise nature of
their feelings for each other. Again, like Sōseki's painter,
Shimamura finds himself in a world he has no wish to penetrate fully and thus destroy. Watching the passengers in the
train window beside him that reflects their images as if in a

[12] *Ibid.*, pp. 25-26.

mirror, Shimamura muses on the distance and separation he feels.

> For Shimamura there was none of the pain that the sight of something truly sad can bring. Rather it was as if he were watching a tableau in a dream—and that was no doubt the working of his strange mirror.
> In the depths of the mirror the evening landscape moved by, the mirror and the reflected figures like motion pictures superimposed one on the other. The figures and the background were unrelated, and yet the figures, transparent and intangible, and the background, dim in the gathering darkness, melted together into a sort of symbolic world not of this world. Particularly when a light out in the mountains shone in the center of the girl's face, Shimamura felt his chest rise at the inexpressible beauty of it.[13]

Dream and reality feed upon each other. Sōseki's protagonist only separates them when he sees Onami out of her poetic environment. Shimamura is never provided with that opportunity.

Kawabata's own narrative structure helps create the necessary dream-like quality. Edward Seidensticker, in his apt introduction to his fine English translation of the novel, writes of Kawabata's *haiku*-like construction of the novel, producing a style ". . . notable for its terseness and austerity . . . rather like flashes in a void."[14] The movement of the novel is often oblique. In the opening chapter, for example, the reader is provided with the suggestion that some important events have happened before, yet the nature or meaning of the events is never clearly stated. Again, the novel has no clearly defined ending at all: the final episode presents Shimamura with a last unsettling vision of the "snow country" just as he decides to leave it, probably forever. While Sōseki's novel is rounded off nicely by the final trip to the city, Kawabata manages to make the reader accept his more open aesthetic structure by changing the reader's expectations, who is slowly led to see that, in its totality, the novel makes a surprisingly unified whole.

---

13 *Ibid.*, p. 9.   14 *Ibid.*, p. viii.

Kawabata's unusual structuring of *Snow Country* has been studied by Nakamura Mitsuo, one of the leading contemporary critics of Japanese fiction, and his observations provide a most suitable means to come to terms with Kawabata's techniques. Nakamura suggests that Kawabata has constructed his novel along the lines of a *nō* drama. Komako, the focus of attention in the novel, functions something like the *shite* in *nō*, the character whose personality the spectator must penetrate as the drama proceeds. Shimamura is the modern equivalent of the *waki*, or subsidary character, often a priest travelling in search of enlightenment.[15] Kawabata himself has suggested such a focus for the novel:

> Shimamura, of course, is not myself. He is nothing but a foil to the geisha, Komako. This is at once the failure as well as the success of the novel. I entered deeply into the character of Komako and only very shallowly into Shimamura. In that sense it is truer to say that in many ways I am Komako rather than Shimamura. I consciously tried to keep Shimamura at a distance from me as I wrote. Also, the events and feelings expressed are the products of my imagination rather than of any lived experiences. The feelings of Komako in particular are the embodiment of my own sadness.[16]

Kawabata has used other traditional literary techniques in constructing his novels, notably the *haiku* in his long and ambitious work *Yama no oto* (The Sound of the Mountain). Nakamura's suggestion is by no means implausible, as an examination of the narrative progress of the book will serve to indicate.

A typical *nō* play, as was indicated in Chapter VI, involves a traveller, often a priest, who meets a person who manifests some attractive, alluring quality, a quality that remains at first unexplained. After the first meeting, there often follows an interlude during which the priest or traveller learns more

[15] See Nakamura Mitsuo, *Contemporary Japanese Fiction 1926-1968* (Tokyo, 1969), p. 27.

[16] Quoted in Francis Mathy, "Kawabata Yasunari, Bridge-builder to the West," *Monumenta Nipponica* XXIV, #3 (1969), p. 212.

mundane information about the person he has met, or about the place he is visiting. In the second and more intense section of the play, that mysterious person returns and reveals his or her real identity (often the ghost of a famous figure in poetry or in history), then relives some powerful emotional crisis, the climax culminating in a dance. This moment of highest tension is often followed by a postlude in which the priest awakens to find his whole experience has been a dream.

Nakamura is certainly correct in finding this pattern in the plan of the novel. The traveller, of course, is Shimamura, moving out of his ordinary life into his special world, "to recover something" of the honesty he felt he had lost. His first meetings with Komako leave him puzzled at his own incomplete picture of her, a puzzlement shared as well by the reader. As in the *nō*, the real name of the central character remains unrevealed until well into the narrative. At first, Komako is merely "the woman." After Shimamura's initial encounters, he asks others about her and manages to learn certain mundane details about her life (notably the fact of her relations with Yukio, the young man ill with tuberculosis). Shimamura's own status as a visitor in the "snow country" shields him from the realities of her difficult existence, from the fact that she has sold herself and her talents to help pay Yukio's medical bills. Komako tells Shimamura, in fact, that he cannot understand her, just as the *shite* in a *nō* play often hints that what the visitor can glimpse and the actual reality are not the same:

"... Do you understand how I feel?"

"I understand."

"If you understand, then tell me. Tell me, if you see how I feel." Again that tense, urgent note came into her voice. "See, you can't. Lying again. You have plenty of money, and you're not much of a person. You don't understand at all." She lowered her voice. "I'm very lonely sometimes. But I'm a fool. Go back to Tokyo, tomorrow."[17]

Finally, towards the end of the novel, Shimamura does

[17] *Snow Country*, pp. 102-103.

begin to form a more precise picture of Komako; yet even here, Kawabata uses images rather than statements:

> All of Komako came to him, but it seemed that nothing went out from him to her. He heard in his chest, like snow piling up, the sound of Komako, an echo beating against empty walls. And he knew that he could not go on pampering himself forever.
>
> He leaned against the brazier, provided against the coming of the snowy season, and thought how unlikely it was that he would come again once he had left. The innkeeper had lent him an old Kyoto teakettle, skillfully inlaid in silver with flowers and birds, and from it came the sound of wind in the pines. He could make out two pine breezes, as a matter of fact, a near one and a far one. Just beyond the far breeze he heard faintly the tinkling of a bell. He put his ear to the kettle and listened. Far away, where the bell tinkled on, he suddenly saw Komako's feet, tripping in time with the bell. He drew back. The time had come to leave.[18]

Shimamura's decision to leave comes at the time of the fire that burns the village warehouse, the incident that provides a final rapid scene not unlike the climactic dance in *nō*. The vision of the distraught Komako rushing to embrace the body of Yoko, burned in the fire, has all the power, and all the intensity, of a powerful *nō* drama. And, as in the *nō*, such a final moment of intensity serves to show the innermost layer of emotion that makes up the character of the personage portrayed, a summation of the dramatic purposes of the whole. And, like the *nō*, Kawabata's structure serves to emphasize the deepest roots of personality in the central character rather than to increase tension between characters in the narrative: the tension remains internal.

Snow Country can by no means be reduced to any mere schema; on the other hand, some appreciation of the novel's design helps clarify the author's purposes. If we examine it from the point of view of its general structure, the strengths of the novel seem even greater and the weaknesses found by

---

[18] *Ibid.*, p. 155.

those readers who examine the text with a Western, conflict-centered aesthetic expectation in mind, seem to disappear almost completely. Again, Kawabata's supreme skill lures most readers into an acceptance of his aesthetic framework. As the reader progresses through the text, he is slowly led to a natural sense of satisfaction with the presentation of the world of the novel.

An examination of the text of *Snow Country* in terms of the *nō* drama reveals not only the structural similarities pointed out previously, but a series of consistent references to the *nō*. Many of the earlier references are elliptical or casual; in the climactic chapters, the references become increasingly explicit. On what Shimamura decides will be his last morning in the "Snow Country," he awakens to the sound of a *nō* recitation, chanting and drums. Komako reminds him that he heard a similar recitation when they first met. He then remembers the Chijimi linen he admires so much, that fabric for which the thread is "spun in the snow . . . woven in the snow, washed in the snow, and bleached in the snow."[19] Shimamura had searched for such cloth; "through acquaintances in the dance world, he had found a shop that specialized in old *nō* robes, and he had a standing order that when a good piece of Chijimi came in, he was to see it."[20] These associations between Komako, the "snow country," and *nō* are continued in the imagery chosen by Kawabata to describe Shimamura's last glimpse of Komako as she races off in the dark towards the burning warehouse:

> The shape of her slightly aquiline nose was not clear, and the color was gone from her small lips. Was it so dim, then, the light that cut across the sky and overflowed it? Shimamura found that hard to believe. The light was dimmer even than on the night of the new moon, and yet the Milky Way was brighter than the brightest full moon. In the faint light that left no shadows on the earth, Komako's face floated up like an old mask. It was strange that even in the mask there should be the scent of the woman.[21]

[19] *Ibid.*, p. 151. [20] *Ibid.* [21] *Ibid.*, pp. 167-168.

All these considerations touch, but do not explain, the theme of the novel. Mr. Seidensticker writes in his Introduction that Kawabata "has found in Shimamura's love affair the perfect symbol for a denial of love, and he has in the woman Komako and in the shadowy beauty of the snow country fit subjects for the *haiku*-like flashes that bring the denial forth."[22] If the relationship between the two is taken as the central focus of the novel, the observation is just; yet, if we look at the novel in terms of Kawabata's own statement about the importance of Komako, the themes seem more extended, still more profound. *Snow Country* enlarges an evocation of the poetry of place to a general comment on the human condition, specifically on the sadness, and on the beauty, of human dedication. Kawabata's particular method of manifesting these larger themes comes through his constant reference to the beauty that lies in wasted effort, a beauty that ultimately justifies that effort. The references are explicit and cumulative.

In Part One of the narrative, Kawabata establishes certain parallels between the "wasted efforts" of both Shimamura and Komako. For him, it is the ballet:

> He gathered pictures and descriptions of the occidental ballet, and began laboriously collecting programs and posters from abroad. This was more than simple fascination with the exotic and the unknown. The pleasure he found in his new hobby came in fact from his inability to see with his own eyes occidentals in occidental ballets. There was proof of this in his deliberate refusal to study the ballet as performed by Japanese. Nothing could be more comfortable than writing about the ballet from books. A ballet he had never seen was an art in another world. It was an unrivaled armchair reverie, a lyric from some paradise. He called his work research, but it was actually free, uncontrolled fantasy. He preferred not to savor the ballet in the flesh; rather he savored the phantasms of his own dancing imagination, called up by Western books and pictures. It was like being in love with someone he had never seen.[23]

[22] *Ibid.*, p. xix.   [23] *Ibid.*, pp. 24-25.

For Komako, her first "wasted effort" revealed to the reader is her naive interest in literature. Komako reads everything and anything she can find:

> Shimamura was surprised at her statement that she had carefully catalogued every novel and short story she had read since she was fifteen or sixteen. The record already filled ten notebooks.
> "You write down your criticisms, do you?"
> "I could never do anything like that. I just write down the author and the characters and how they are related to each other. That is about all."
> "But what good does it do?"
> "None at all."
> "A waste of effort."
> "A complete waste of effort," she answered brightly, as though the admission meant little to her. She gazed solemly at Shimamura, however.
> A complete waste of effort. For some reason Shimamura wanted to stress the point. But, drawn to her at that moment, he felt a quiet like the voice of the rain flow over him. He knew well enough that for her it was in fact no waste of effort, but somehow the final determination that it was had the effect of distilling and purifying the woman's existence.[24]

Shimamura is astute enough to see at once a parallel between himself and the girl, and intelligent enough to sense the crucial difference as well. In the end, he realizes that behind her indiscriminate enthusiasm lies a sadness that attracts him to her:

> Not a few of the new novelists whose names came to her meant nothing to Shimamura. Her manner was as though she were talking of a foreign literature. There was something lonely, something sad in it, something that rather suggested a beggar who has lost all desire. It occurred to Shimamura that his own distant fantasy on the occidental ballet, built up from words and photographs in foreign

[24] *Ibid.*, p. 41.

books, was not in its way dissimilar. . . . She did not seem
to find herself especially sad, but in Shimamura's eyes there
was something strangely touching about her. Were he to
give himself quite up to that consciousness of wasted effort,
Shimamura felt, he would be drawn into a remote
emotionalism that would like his own life be a waste.[25]

As Shimamura learns more about Komako, and comes to
realize the great lengths to which she has gone to help the
dying Yukio, his thoughts about her "wasted effort" grow
more precise:

> If Komako were the man's fiancée, and Yoko was his
> new lover, and the man was going to die—the expression
> "wasted effort" again came to Shimamura's mind. For
> Komako thus to guard her promise to the end, for her even
> to sell herself to pay doctors' bills—what was it if not
> wasted effort?
> He would accost her with this fact, he would drive it
> home, when he saw her again, he said to himself; and yet
> her existence seemed to have become purer and cleaner for
> this new bit of knowledge.[26]

Still later, when he hears the beauty and dexterity of
Komako's playing on the samisen, his feelings are reinforced
still further:

> Practicing alone, not aware herself of what was happen-
> ing, perhaps, but with all the wideness of nature in this
> mountain valley for her companion, she had come quite as
> a part of nature to take on this special power. Her very
> loneliness beat down sorrow and fostered a wild strength of
> will. There was no doubt that it had been a great victory of
> the will, even granted that she had had an amount of pre-
> paratory training, for her to learn complicated airs from
> only a score, and presently to go through them from mem-
> ory.
> To Shimamura it was wasted effort, this way of living.
> He sensed in it too a longing that called out to him for

[25] *Ibid.*, pp. 42-43.   [26] *Ibid.*, pp. 61-62.

sympathy. But the life and way of living no doubt flowed thus grandly from the samisen with a new worth for Komako herself.[27]

Shimamura comes to feel that his whole relationship with her is a wasted effort. Komako, of course, has difficulty in accepting such a situation (earlier in the novel she tells him, "You lost. You're the weak one. Not I."),[28] but Shimamura finds beauty in the waste itself.

In Part Two, the theme continues to develop, and in a more complex fashion, as Kawabata, through the guise of Shimamura, begins to create an inevitable connection between the poetry of the unreal and the idea of wasted effort. Shimamura first makes the connection concerning himself:

> Shimamura had come down from these mountains, as the new green was making its way through the last of the snow, to meet Komako for the first time; and now, in the autumn climbing season, he found himself drawn again to the mountains he had left his tracks in. Though he was an idler who might as well spend his time in the mountains as anywhere, he looked upon mountain climbing as almost a model of wasted effort. For that very reason it pulled at him with the attraction of the unreal.[29]

Later, he extends his understanding to his relationship with Komako:

> He was conscious of an emptiness that made him see Komako's life as beautiful but wasted, even though he himself was the object of her love; and yet the woman's existence, her straining to live, came touching him like naked skin. He pitied her, and he pitied himself.[30]

Shimamura's fascination with the Chijimi linen woven in the "snow country" leads to a passage in which all the related images are combined. The infinite care and labor required to produce the cloth can perhaps be justified, despite the wasted effort involved, because of the love that went into its making:

[27] *Ibid.*, p. 72.   [28] *Ibid.*, p. 37.
[29] *Ibid.*, pp. 111-112.   [30] *Ibid.*, pp. 105-106.

The thread of the grass-linen, finer than animal hair, is difficult to work except in the humidity of the snow, it is said, and the dark, cold season is therefore ideal for weaving. The ancients used to add that the way this product of the cold has of feeling cool to the skin in the hottest weather is a play of the principles of light and darkness. This Komako too, who had so fastened herself to him, seemed at center cool, and the remarkable, concentrated warmth was for that fact all the more touching.

But this love would leave behind it nothing so definite as a piece of Chijimi. Though cloth to be worn is among the most short-lived of craftworks, a good piece of Chijimi, if it has been taken care of, can be worn quite unfaded a half-century and more after weaving. As Shimamura thought absently how human intimacies have not even so long a life, the image of Komako as the mother of another man's children suddenly floated into his mind.[31]

Here Kawabata binds together the characters (Shimamura, Komako), the plot (Shimamura's realization that he must leave for good), the images recurrent throughout the text (the cloth, the "snow country" itself), and the thematic concern of wasted beauty, a concept that in turn evokes those characters, images, and plot. Such linking, such reinforcement, becomes impossible to unravel. The poetry of place becomes the poetry of self-realization and, as in a *nō* drama, the dream then comes to an end. The image of the Chijimi cloth, like the *waka* poem embedded in the climax of many a *nō* play, serves as a kernel from which all the other images can be seen to have sprouted and grown.

Kawabata's achievement in *Snow Country* shows the strength of the earlier traditions to which he remained so attracted; and his achievement reveals the pliancy of those traditions as well. For many writers in the earlier generations of writers like Sōseki, Ōgai, and Kafū, any choice of the literary past was a self-conscious one. For Kawabata, who never imagined abandoning the best of that tradition, his advocacy produced a body of work that, for all its homage to tech-

[31] *Ibid.*, p. 154.

niques and values of the past, remains in many ways the most
contemporary among the work of all twentieth-century
writers. His inner poetic world, like that of Lady Murasaki's,
moves quickly across the spaces of time, out of its own culture and into our own, remaining both accessible and suggestive at the same time. Kawabata's genuine success with
readers everywhere is thus not difficult to understand.

X

Dazai Osamu: The Death of the Past
The Setting Sun

DAZAI, who was born in 1909 and who committed suicide in 1948, reveals in his life and writings all the tensions felt by Japanese intellectuals in those difficult years before, during, and just after the Pacific War. While attending Tokyo University, where he took courses in French literature, Dazai joined a coterie of young people interested in pursuing a Marxist analysis of society. Much of his work shows a consciousness of social realities at a time when economic hardship made life in his urban environment increasingly difficult. Dazai's first works were published in the mid 1930s; during the war, he wrote on traditional themes and experimented with a fictionalized account of the great modern Chinese novelist Lu Hsun (1881-1936) during that writer's years of residence in Japan as a medical student from 1902 to 1909. At the end of the war, Dazai reached a new level of achievement with his two major novels *Shayō* (The Setting Sun) and *Ningen shikaku* (No Longer Human) (1948). Both earned him an enormous reputation with his contemporaries. That reputation has, on the whole, been maintained.

Dazai's education was Western in orientation and highly intellectual. In that sense, Dazai's generation differed from those of Kafū, Tanizaki, Kawabata, and others, whose attachments to the past formed part of their early education. On first reading, he seems a novelist more conscious of Western methods of composition than those who precede him. His knowledge of Western art and literature is, in general, sure and relatively sophisticated, and the characters in *The Setting Sun* move gracefully from one intellectual frame of reference to another.

The phenomenon of Dazai's continued popularity in Japan indicates the astonishing degree to which he touched on concerns of importance to his countrymen in the years directly after the war. The word *shayō* itself became a trademark for those who lost their money and their place in society at the end of the war, and *shayōzoku* (literally, "setting sun tribe") has become a noun now included in current Japanese language dictionaries. Some critics have likened his importance in postwar Japanese culture to that of Camus in France. Both bore witness to the terrible incertitudes facing their respective generations in works that could be admired and understood by a segment of their societies far larger than might normally take an interest in serious literature. In the case of Dazai, the despair and romantic nihilism expressed in a book like *The Setting Sun* was quickly recognized as authentic. The plot of the novel concerns two young people, both of aristocratic birth, the girl Kazuko and her brother Naoji. Kazuko is already divorced and lives in the country with her widowed mother, who falls ill and dies partway through the novel. Naoji has returned from the war an opium addict and proceeds to consume the pitiful remainder of the family fortunes in wild drinking bouts in Tokyo with his dissolute friend, the novelist Uehara. After her mother's death, Kazuko goes to Tokyo to seek out Uehara, for whom she has developed a strange longing, and she briefly becomes his lover. Naoji commits suicide, but Kazuko, at the novel's end, manages to find the strength to go on. The story, told in a series of diaries, memoirs, and other documents, creates brilliantly the degraded and spent atmosphere prevalent in Japan at the time.

The Setting Sun, however, is no mere sociological account. At the end of the novel, Kazuko writes to Uehara, who has quickly deserted her. "Victims. Victims of a transitional period of morality. That is what we both certainly are."[1] The status of victim, and the need to escape that status, provide the thematic focus of the novel. Dazai's conception of "victim" goes far beyond the economic situation created by the war. Kazuko's cry is one of existential despair, and her courage in the midst of the blackness of her own life gives evidence of a strength that is as much metaphysical as literal. In this limited way, perhaps, Camus and Dazai do share certain concerns.

[1] Dazai Osamu, *The Setting Sun*, tr. by Donald Keene (New York, 1956), p. 173.

The existential anguish Dazai portrays gains spiritual depth from the fact that, for many Japanese of his generation, even the best in the values of the past remained impotent in the face of militarism. Kazuko's mother is meant to serve as the embodiment of those positive forces which heretofore had managed to hold the culture together, qualities now destroyed by the coming of the war. Kazuko's mother can only die. Her death represents for her children, and for the reader alike, the death of continuity, the disappearance of the past. The moment of her death is touchingly portrayed:

> Three hours later she passed away . . . in the still autumn twilight, as her pulse was being taken by the nurse, watched over by Naoji and myself, her two children, my beautiful mother, who was the last lady in Japan.
> Her face in death was almost unaltered. When my father died his expression had suddenly changed, but Mother's was exactly the same as in life. Only her breathing had stopped. And even that had happened so quietly that we did not know exactly when she had ceased to breathe. The swelling in her face had gone down the previous day, and her cheeks were now smooth as wax. Her pale lips were faintly curved, as though she were smiling. Mother seemed more captivating even than she was in life. The thought that she looked like Mary in a *Pietà* flickered across my mind.[2]

The death of the mother reflects the death of a culture, and Kazuko and Naoji both become victims of the void that follows. Kazuko, in order to escape, tries to create for herself a new set of values. The manifesto Dazai created for her seems an inevitable one for a writer of his generation and intellectual inclinations:

> What in the world have I been doing all this time? I have never felt myself drawn toward revolution, and I have not even known love. The older and wiser heads of the world have always described revolution and love to us as the two most foolish and loathsome of human activities. Before the

[2] *Ibid.*, pp. 127-128.

war, even during the war, we were convinced of it. Since
the defeat, however, we no longer trust the older and wiser
heads and have come to feel that the opposite of whatever
they say is the real truth about life. Revolution and love are
in fact the best, most pleasurable, things in the world, and
we realize it precisely because they are so good that the
older and wiser heads have spitefully fobbed off on us their
sour grapes of a lie. This I want to believe implicitly: Man
was born for love and revolution.[3]

Dazai, however, is no orthodox Marxist. In a slightly earlier passage, when Kazuko reads a book on economics she
finds in her brother's study, Dazai is careful to portray not the
substance of the ideas (of no importance in the context), but
Kazuko's emotional attitude toward them:

> Even I found some things rather objectionable when I
> read Rosa Luxembourg's book, but, given the sort of per-
> son I am, the experience on the whole was one of profound
> interest. The subject matter of her book is generally consid-
> ered to be economics, but if it is read as economics it is bor-
> ing beyond belief. It contains nothing but exceedingly ob-
> vious platitudes. It may be, of course, that I have no under-
> standing of economics. Be that as it may, the subject holds
> not the slightest interest for me. A science which is postu-
> lated on the assumption that human beings are avaricious
> and will remain avaricious through all eternity is utterly
> devoid of point (whether in problems of distribution or any
> other aspect) to a person who is not avaricious. And yet as I
> read this book, I felt a strange excitement for quite another
> reason—the sheer courage the author demonstrated in tear-
> ing apart without any hesitation all manner of conventional
> ideas. . . . Destruction is tragic and piteous and beautiful.
> The dream of destroying, building anew, perfecting.
> Perhaps even, once one has destroyed, the day of perfecting
> may never come, but in the passion of love I must destroy.
> I must start a revolution. Rosa gave tragically her undi-
> vided love to Marxism.[4]

[4] *Ibid.*, pp. 111-112.

Dazai shows here an admirable skill in rendering the psychological impetus behind an intellectual attitude. Using his intuition that radical ideas, like any ideas, are conceived of by human beings with their own emotional identities, he was able to create in Kazuko a paradigm of the sort of romantic revolutionary increasingly familiar to contemporary readers. Few Japanese writers have succeeded as well in portraying the thrust of such a personality. For Dazai, the emotional coloration of the ideas, rather than their intellectual content, was the element of significance to capture.

In the case of Kazuko, the conflicts between optimism and despair, death and rebirth, sustain a tension resolved only at the end of the novel, when she realizes she has found the strength to go on living. She writes of this fact to the novelist Uehara, before his child which she bears is born:

> The revolution must be taking place somewhere, but the old morality persists unchanged in the world around us and lies athwart our way. However much the waves on the surface of the sea may rage, the water at the bottom, far from experiencing a revolution, lies motionless, awake but feigning sleep.
>
> But I think that in this first engagement, I have been able to push back the old morality, however little. And I intend to fight a second and a third engagement together with the child who will be born.
>
> To give birth to the child of the man I love, and to raise him, will be the accomplishment of my moral revolution.[5]

The emotional hunger expressed in the last pages of the novel exemplifies a need still felt in Japan today. Dazai's cry echoes from his own heart; its genuineness has never been in dispute. Indeed many Japanese readers assume that his characters are merely ill-disguised manifestations of his own personality. In terms of the author's entire *oeuvre*, perhaps the charge can be sustained. But in *The Setting Sun*, at least, Kazuko, Naoji, and their mother present themselves as distinct figures who complement each other in producing a cumulative poignancy central to Dazai's concerns.

[5] *Ibid.*, p. 173.

The contemporary quality of the anguish expressed in the novel is reinforced by certain techniques used by Dazai in the construction of his text. It is doubtless natural that this should be so—how difficult it would be to mirror such anxieties using only traditional aesthetic means. Dazai's literary strategies grow naturally out of his concerns. Many of them will put a Western reader at ease immediately. The narrative has been assembled with enormous care, its shifting moods rigorously arranged to build toward the climax sought. Dazai has unified the atmosphere of the novel in a manner familiar to contemporary readers everywhere. In particular, his use of repeated symbolic images adds an enormously resonant layer to the text; even when the meaning of the images remains obscure, their unconscious, Jungian significance is real, their presence authentic. There are, for example, repeated references to flowers, and constant allusions to death in summer. Most powerful are the images of snakes. Early in the novel, Kazuko sees a snake in the garden; she feels nervous but nevertheless finds the snake somehow beautiful. She makes the association between the snake and her mother; suddenly she has the feeling that "the ugly snake dwelling in my breast might one day end by devouring this beautiful, grief-stricken mother snake."[6] She then tries to burn the eggs the snake has laid. Later, as her mother grows more ill, Kazuko reflects that ". . . Mother pretends to be happy, but she grows thinner by the day. And in my breast a viper lodges which fattens by sacrificing Mother, which fattens however much I try to suppress it."[7] Kazuko's mother also associates snakes with her own death. In her last illness, she suddenly calls for Kazuko:

Mother remained silent, but I could tell that she wished to say something.
"Water?"
She shook her head faintly. After a while she said in a small voice, "I had a dream."
"What kind of dream?"
"About a snake."
I was startled.

[6] *Ibid.*, p. 21.   [7] *Ibid.*, p. 27.

"I believe you'll find a female snake with red stripes on the step in front of the porch. Please go and look."

I stood up with a feeling of growing cold all over. I went to the porch and looked through the glass door. On the step a snake was stretched out full length in the autumn sun. I felt dizzy.

I know who you are. You are a little bigger and older than when I saw you last, but you are the snake whose eggs I burned. I have already felt your vengeance. Go away at once.[8]

Kazuko then remembers the death of her father.

There was no hope, none. Resignation first began to germinate in my heart after I saw the snake. I had heard that when my Father died there was a small black snake by his bed, and I myself had seen a snake twisted around every tree in the garden.[9]

Kazuko, associating herself with "that snake dwelling in my breast," takes as her motto the words of Christ, "wise as serpents and harmless as doves" in order to give herself the courage to continue her own life. The serpent is still with her when she finally meets Mr. Uehara:

"I don't suppose you have anywhere to spend the night, have you?" Mr. Uehara asked half under his breath.

"I?" I was conscious of the snake with its head lifted against itself. Hostility. It was an emotion close to hatred which stiffened my body.[10]

Whatever the meaning of the snakes (death and renewal have been suggested as one possibility), they represent a set of troubling images that evoke a strange beauty whenever they appear in the narrative. The emotional states they suggest are more powerful than the images themselves. On this level, Dazai's appeal touches a Western reader with as much force as it does a Japanese one. We all share a culture that recognizes the symbolic significance of the unconscious. Dazai too inhabits that shared present. In many ways, he is the first author

[8] *Ibid*., pp. 120–121.   [9] *Ibid*., p. 121.   [10] *Ibid*., p. 143.

treated in this book who can be said to share fully in the painful world we have all made together.

THE PAST IN THE PRESENT

Yet *The Setting Sun*, even while chronicling the death of the
past, remains impregnated with it. Indeed, neither the structure nor the theme of the novel could find adequate expression without constant reference to the culture and literature of
the past. The presence of such traditions pervades the text,
giving the novel a peculiar power to move even those who do
not share those inherited ideas or attitudes.

The Setting Sun, like *A Portrait of Shunkin*, is comprised
of a series of documents juxtaposed together. Like the Heian
diaries and the Bashō travel diaries, these documents are written in the first person. The bulk of the narrative, through the
sixth chapter, is in the form of a memoir written by Kazuko
herself, who recalls the various experiences that have led her
to her present state. The final two chapters provide the most
penetrating glimpses of the two young people given the
reader. Chapter Seven is the suicide letter written by Naoji to
Kazuko. Chapter Eight is a final letter written by Kazuko to
Uehara. These two sections in many ways form the kernel of
the novel. The sections preceding them prepare the reader to
understand the nuances and implications of the statements
that the two young people make about themselves and about
each other. Interspersed with Kazuko's memoir are other
documents as well. In Chapter Three, for example, sections
of a diary kept by Naoji, the "Moonflower Journal," are inserted as a means to illustrate the growing apprehensions of
Kazuko concerning the family's desperate situation. Chapter
Four gives the text of three letters written by Kazuko to Uehara in her attempt to help her brother and, even more importantly, as a means of making her own appeal to him. The
reader is always given narrative information by means of a
document, never directly. The various sources of information
provided tend to reinforce each other; the same truths come
from different angles, and the truth becomes that much more
inexorable. Use of the letters and the journal helps to pace the

flow of the narrative and gives a satisfying rhythm to the whole. In *Shunkin*, Tanizaki used his narrator to raise questions about the materials being presented. Dazai makes no use of speculation, preferring to reinforce his central theme from several directions.

The use of the first person narration, as discussed elsewhere, has a heritage in Japanese literature going back to the early diary writers and essayists. Like many of these writers, Dazai can, through the economy possible in such a restricted narrative environment, quickly sketch a mood or render an emotional attitude. In particular, he has in Kazuko created a character of such sensitivity that the briefest of her observations manages to remain both precise and evocative at the same time. The novel opens with a description of Kazuko's mother, couched in terms of table manners:

Take the matter of eating soup. We are trained to lean slightly over the plate, to take up a little soup with the spoon held sideways, and then to bring it to our mouth, still holding the spoon sideways. Mother, on the other hand, lightly rests the fingers of her left hand on the edge of the table and sits perfectly erect, with her head held high and scarcely so much as a glance at the plate. She darts the spoon into the soup and like a swallow—so gracefully and cleanly one can really use the simile—brings the spoon to her mouth at a right angle, and pours the soup between her lips from the point. Then, with innocent glances around her, she flutters the spoon exactly like a little wing, never spilling a drop of soup or making the least sound of sipping or clinking the plate. This may not be the way of eating soup that etiquette dictates, but to me it is most appealing and somehow really genuine. As a matter of fact, it is amazing how much better soup tastes when you eat it as Mother does, sitting serenely erect, than when you look down into it.[11]

Even such a seemingly ingenuous passage, based as it is on a nicety of observation, carries considerable freight, suggesting at the same time important elements both in the mother's

[11] *Ibid.*, pp. 4–5.

character (delicate, other-worldly, slightly gauche, fastidious) and in Kazuko's (loving, highly observant, introspective). The use of the diary form permits such a double image, in which subject and object alike reveal themselves. Dazai exploits to the full the possibilities inherent in the form.

In terms of the three major characters in the novel, Dazai's use of the diary form permits him to stress the reticence that all show concerning any direct and human contact. Faced with others, they are mute. The briefest examination of the text reveals how little the characters actually say to each other and how little their conversations suggest of the larger emotional significance of the moment portrayed. This very reticence is, in Kazuko's eyes, a virtue. At one point she confides this sentiment to her mother:

> "Mother, recently I have discovered the one way in which human beings differ completely from other animals. Man has, I know, language, knowledge, principles, and social order, but don't all the other animals have them too, granted the difference of degree? Perhaps the animals even have religions. Man boasts of being the lord of all creation, but it would seem as if essentially he does not differ in the least from other animals. But, Mother, there is one way I thought of. Perhaps you won't understand this. It's a faculty absolutely unique to man—having secrets. Can you see what I mean?"
>
> Mother blushed faintly and gave a charming smile. "If your secrets only bear good fruit, it will be all I could ask. . . ."[12]

The deepest emotional responses of Kazuko and Naoji, their "secrets," are revealed only in the written word, never in conversation. But Kazuko can confide her secret to her memoir and so to the reader:

> We climbed up the dark stairs from the basement. Mr. Uehara, who was one step ahead of me, turned around suddenly and gave me a quick kiss. I took his kiss with my lips tightly shut. I felt no special attraction for him, but all

[12] *Ibid.*, p. 51.

the same, from that moment on my "secret" came into being. Mr. Uehara clattered up the stairs, and I slowly followed, with a strangely transparent feeling. When I stepped
outside, the wind from the river felt wonderful against my
cheek.[13]

Naoji too has a secret, which is revealed to the reader only
in his final suicide letter:

> Kazuko.
> I have a secret.
> I have concealed it for a long, long time. Even when I
> was on the battlefield, I brooded over it and dreamed of
> her. I can't tell you how many times I awoke only to find I
> had wept in my sleep.
> I shall never be able to reveal her name to anyone, but I
> thought that I would at least tell you, my sister, everything
> about her, since I am now on the point of death. I discover,
> however, that I am still so terribly afraid that I dare not
> speak her name.[14]

Dazai can so create a reticence in his characters and overcome that same reticence through his use of the diary form.
Such a narrative structure thus serves a double purpose.

The diaries and letters of Kazuko and Naoji reveal with
great force the torment of their inner worlds. No such direct
exposure toward the inner life of their mother is given the
reader. She is portrayed through the responses of her children; and as she represents the last manifestation of a dying
culture, her slight air of remoteness is altogether appropriate.
Her own reticence and her own patience sustain both young
people. Without her, and the values she stands for, the two
feel abandoned. No matter that her world remains at too
great a distance from the children, beyond the range of
efficacy—her effect on them remains powerful. Kazuko com-
prehends with terrible clarity what the significance of her
mother's death will represent for her:

> I must go on living. And, though it may be childish of
> me, I can't go on in simple compliance. From now on I

[13] *Ibid.*, p. 75.   [14] *Ibid.*, pp. 160-161.

must struggle with the world. I thought that Mother might well be the last of those who can end their lives beautifully and sadly, struggling with no one, neither hating nor betraying anyone. In the world to come there will be no room for such people. The dying are beautiful, but to live, to survive—those things somehow seem hideous and contaminated with blood. . . . Now that it was clear that Mother would soon die, my romanticism and sentimentality were gradually vanishing, and I felt as though I were turning into a calculating, unprincipled creature.[15]

Naoji too feels keenly the power that his mother (and her values) has maintained over him:

I should have died sooner. But there was one thing: Mama's love. When I thought of that I couldn't die. It's true, as I have said, that just as man has the right to live as he chooses, he has the right to die when he pleases, and yet as long as my mother remained alive, I felt that the right to death would have to be left in abeyance, for to exercise it would have meant killing her too.[16]

Naoji's mother dead, the restraint vanishes. He closes his suicide note with the words, "Kazuko. I am, after all, an aristocrat." Those words are, among other things, a final tribute to his mother.

The stress on the private layers of anguish in the minds and souls of his characters suggests an atmosphere of emotional intimacy redolent of that found in many Heian works of literature, notably in *The Tale of Genji*, where the social and political life outside the secluded women's quarters is seldom mentioned. In the Heian diaries too, the exterior lives of the figures portrayed are seldom sketched in any detail. We know much about how they responded to the circumstances of their lives, but little about what they actually did. Our knowledge concerning Naoji and Kazuko is often of the same order. None of the political turmoil of the early postwar period finds mention in the text. Kazuko's rebellion remains throughout an intense interior state of mind.

Overt references to such diary literature in *The Setting Sun*

---

[15] *Ibid.*, pp. 124-125.   [16] *Ibid.*, p. 158.

indicates that Dazai sensed the importance of the parallels between such atmospheres and made good use of them. In
many ways, Kazuko herself seems a Heian sensibility transplanted, or rather thrust, into the contemporary world. In
this regard, Dazai's references to the Heian period *Sarashina
Diary* are particularly significant. That diary chronicles certain responses and attitudes of a delicate and reticent woman
from a minor branch of the Fujiwara family who finds difficulties in adapting to her life in court. She shows as well a
certain spiritual restlessness that gives her diary continuing
significance as a psychological document. Indeed, Lady
Sarashina, as she has come to be known, serves as an appropriate model for Kazuko. At one point, Dazai establishes the
connection directly:

> It was a winter twelve years ago.
> "You're just like that spineless girl in the *Sarashina Diary*
> who can never open her mouth. It's impossible to talk to
> you."
> My friend, so saying, walked away. I had just returned
> to her, unread, a book by Lenin.
> "Have you read it?"
> "I'm sorry. I haven't."
> It was on the bridge from which you could see the
> Tokyo Russian Orthodox Cathedral.
> "Why? What was the trouble?"
> My friend was about an inch taller than I and very gifted
> in languages. Her red beret became her. She was a beautiful
> girl with a face which was reputed to look like the Mona
> Lisa's.
> "I hated the color of the jacket."
> "You *are* strange. That wasn't the real reason, I'm sure.
> Wasn't it because you've become afraid of me?"
> "I am not afraid of you. I couldn't stand the color of the
> jacket."
> "I see." She spoke sadly. It was then that she compared
> me to the girl in the *Sarashina Diary* and decided that it was
> no use talking to me.[17]

For Kazuko, to be a "Lady Sarashina" is to be a victim.

[17] *Ibid.*, pp. 112-113.

Nevertheless for Dazai, and for his readers, the passing of that which is beautiful is profoundly moving.

Kazuko's sensibility and reticence remain her most attractive qualities. Perhaps the most celebrated passage in the *Sarashina Diary* concerns a romantic infatuation Lady Sarashina develops for a nobleman she meets only once, while serving at court, a position that merely increases her nervousness and timidity. The meeting takes place almost by accident. The two discuss poetry and seem to discover a common sensibility. "He talked in a quiet and gentle way and I could tell that he was a man of perfect qualities," wrote Lady Sarashina. "Then he started to speak about the sadness of the world and other such matters, and there was something so sensitive about his manner that, for all my usual shyness, I found it hard to remain stiff and aloof."[18] Dazai creates a similar encounter for Kazuko, based on this incident, early in *The Setting Sun*. Just as Lady Sarashina must go to court and leave the quiet of her own home, Kazuko is forced to do manual labor in the fields just at the end of the war. She feels insecure, nervous, altogether out of place:

> One fine morning which I had spent hauling logs along with the men, the young officer suddenly frowned and pointed at me. "Hey you. You, come here."
>
> He walked quickly toward the pine forest, and I followed him, my heart pounding with nervousness and fear. He stopped by a pile of timber just brought from the saw mill, and turned around to me. "It must be very hard working that way every day. Today please just watch over this lumber." He spoke with a smile, flashing his white teeth.
>
> "You mean I should stand here?"
>
> "It's cool and quiet, and you can take a nap on top of the pile. If you get bored, perhaps you'd like to read this." He took a small volume from his pocket and tossed it shyly on the boards. "It isn't much of a book, but please read it if you like."[19]

Kazuko takes the book, reads it, then falls asleep.

[18] Ivan Morris, tr., *As I Crossed a Bridge of Dreams* (New York, 1971), p. 91.
[19] *The Setting Sun*, pp. 39-40.

I woke after three with the sudden impression that I had seen the young officer before, but where I could not recall. I clambered down from the pile and was just smoothing down my hair when I heard the crunching of his boots again.

"Thank you very much for having come today. You may leave now if you wish."

I ran up to him and held out the book. I wanted to express my thanks, but the words did not come. In silence I looked at his face, and when our eyes met, mine filled with tears. Then tears shone also in his.

We parted without words, just like that, and the young officer never again appeared at the place where I worked.[20]

Like Lady Sarashina, Kazuko has a glimpse of the possibility of a shared sensibility never to be repeated. Her later liaison with Uehara remains, whatever its meaning in terms of the development of Kazuko's existential courage, a grotesque parody of that earlier scene. Lady Sarashina, Dazai seems to suggest, can perhaps afford to retire in her dreams. Kazuko cannot.

The corrosive pressures of contemporary society on these retiring aristocrats provide a major source of creative tension in the novel. The reader is continuously forced to witness their anguish as they are obliged to take cognizance of the world around them. Dazai is careful to show not only their malaise and their gaucheness in facing that society. By his use of the diary form, he can also show their self-consciousness of that awkwardness, which in turn gives both Kazuko and Naoji a certain peculiar strength. Both can sense falsehood in others. Naoji harbors a particular disdain for those of Marxist persuasion who have not thought through the implications of their doctrines; Kazuko sees through the postures struck by the novelist Uehara and can cut him down with a single remark.

In emphasizing the interior world of his characters, Dazai insists that such a world be complete: thus he records all the pressures from the relentless, alien world in a fashion quite

[20] *Ibid.*, p. 41.

unnecessary for those characters created by Lady Murasaki. The harmony between the interior and the exterior world has been broken decisively. In one compelling incident, Kazuko records her own shock of awareness at her own otherworldliness. Early in the novel, through inadvertence, she neglects to put out a fire. Sparks set the woodshed afire, and only a great deal of hard work on the part of the villagers prevents the destruction of her home. Kazuko is ashamed of her carelessness and makes her apologies to various people who live nearby:

> Wherever I went the people sympathized and attempted to console me. Mr. Nishiyama's young wife—I say young but she's already about forty—was the only one who rebuked me. "Please be careful in the future. You may belong to the nobility, for all I know, but I've been watching with my heart in my mouth the way you two have been living, like children playing house. It's only a miracle you haven't had a fire before, considering the reckless way you live. Please be sure to take the utmost care from now on. If there had been a strong wind last night, the whole village would have gone up in flames."[21]

Through Kazuko's own words the reader is jolted, like her, into an awareness of how dangerous such otherworldliness can be. By the occasional insertion of such scenes, Dazai "objectifies" the emotional world inhabited by his characters, making their plight all the more poignant. Society now penetrates into the most sensitive layers of the human soul. Kazuko has the will to take new strength from the intrusion. Naoji her brother does not.

For this reader at least, the compelling power of *The Setting Sun* derives from the relentless will shown by Naoji and Kazuko in confronting their own realities, their own destinies. Kazuko feels able to proceed because, in her own terms, she possesses what she calls "a clear conscience." In this emphasis on triumphant sincerity, Dazai pays a profound homage to the Japanese traditional literary virtue of *makoto*, the same trait that made Ariwara no Narihira such an appeal-

---

[21] *Ibid.*, p. 35.

ing figure in *Tales of Ise*. Now, however, that search for sincerity perforce takes on a restless, nervous quality that marks contemporary life. Still, the traditional concept remains flexible enough to persist as a virtue in a novel of contemporary concerns. Naoji and his sister both exhibit this quality. Kazuko searches for a new order. Naoji has searched but has found nothing:

> I wanted to become coarse, to be strong—no, brutal. I thought that was the only way I could qualify myself as a "friend of the people." Liquor was not enough. I was perpetually prey to a terrible dizziness. That was why I had no choice but to take to drugs. I had to forget my family. I had to oppose my father's blood. I had to reject my mother's gentleness. I had to be cold to my sister. I thought that otherwise I would not be able to secure an admission ticket for the rooms of the people.[22]

Looking at the world he terms "out of joint," Naoji finds his self-realization must end in self-destruction:

> Just as a man has the right to live, he ought also to have the right to die.
>
> There is nothing new in what I am thinking: it is simply that people have the most inexplicable aversion to this obvious—not to say primitive—idea and refuse to come out with it plainly.
>
> Those who wish to go on living can always manage to survive whatever obstacles there may be. That is splendid of them, and I daresay that what people call the glory of mankind is comprised of just such a thing. But I am convinced that dying is not a sin.
>
> It is painful for the plant which is myself to live in the atmosphere and light of this world. Somewhere an element is lacking which would permit me to continue. I am wanting. It has been all I could do to stay alive up to now.[23]

In his suicide note, Naoji examines his own weaknesses, his social insecurity, and his own consciousness of the failure of

[22] *Ibid.*, pp. 154-155.   [23] *Ibid.*, pp. 153-154.

any political philosophy or system to fully sustain him in his understanding of life:

> All men are alike.
>
> What a servile remark that is. An utterance that degrades itself at the same time that it degrades men, lacking in all pride, seeking to bring about the abandonment of all effort. Marxism proclaims the superiority of the workers. It does not say that they are all the same. Democracy proclaims the dignity of the individual. It does not say that they are all the same. Only the lout will assert, "Yes, no matter how much he puts on, he's just a human being, same as the rest of us."
>
> Why does he say "same." Can't he say "superior"? The vengeance of the slave mentality!
>
> That statement is obscene and loathsome. I believe that all the so-called "anxiety of the age"—men frightened by one another, every known principle violated, effort mocked, happiness denied, beauty defiled, honor dragged down—originates in this one incredible expression.[24]

Naoji, knowing his own weaknesses, is powerless before them. He searches for answers to his terrible questions, and his relentlessness cannot fail to leave a profound impression on a sympathetic reader. In "Burnt Norton" of his *Four Quartets*, T. S. Eliot has reminded several generations that "Human kind/ Cannot bear very much reality." Naoji and Kazuko, in the view of Dazai at least, must be seen as sympathetic because they are trying to find, and bear, as much of their reality as possible. In describing their search, Dazai does not hesitate to make use of the past even as he shows us its dissolution.

[24] *Ibid.*, pp. 156-157.

XI

The Tale of Genji as a Modern Novel

NOTHING prepares us for a masterpiece. All the other novels so far discussed in this study were created, consciously or unconsciously, under the shade of this great tree, *The Tale of Genji*. Lady Murasaki's novel made possible, very early in the long Japanese tradition, a degree of psychological introspection and a concern for aesthetic and, by implication, philosophical truths that set high standards for Japanese narrative. Indeed, some critics have suggested that the long and sophisticated history of Japanese fiction owes its very existence to the presence of a text of this quality, created toward the very beginnings. Traditions, of course, may exist only to be broken; yet even at moments of greatest change in the Japanese cultural and literary scene, Lady Murasaki's novel reasserts itself. Tsubouchi Shōyō, for example, in his 1885 literary manifesto *The Essence of the Novel*, cited the values of *Genji* as consonant with the values of nineteenth-century English literature.

The Tale of Genji became a work of world literature when the remarkable complete translation by Arthur Waley first became available in 1935. Edward Seidensticker, Ivan Morris, Earl Miner, and others have pointed out the discrepancies and omissions in Waley's English text and have warned readers of the problems of translating a book written in Heian Japanese into far more flexible modern English. Nevertheless, Waley's enormous achievements permit a foreign reader a full and satisfying view of the greatest monument of Japanese letters. And, as a means of showing the significance of that monument, it seems best to discuss it here, toward the end of this book, so that certain literary preoccupations and techniques now familiar to the reader can be reexamined in the context of Lady Murasaki's masterpiece.

Many years ago Donald Keene suggested the affinities between *Genji* and Marcel Proust's *The Remembrance of Things Past*. Certainly the affinities exist. Yet it seems unnecessary to praise (or dismiss) Lady Murasaki as an ancient oriental Proust; the discrepancies in time, language, and literary tradition are too great to permit many concrete comparisons. *Genji* is unique, and any comparisons made must begin from that assumption.

The sudden appearance in Heian Japan of *The Tale of Genji* seems almost as startling in terms of the history of Japanese literature as it does in terms of world literature. No work of fiction of this quality, or of this appeal to the modern sensibility, existed anywhere else in the world at that time; and nothing very much like it existed in Japan either. On first examination, *Genji* seems to have sprung from nowhere. A closer examination shows at once, however, that Lady Murasaki's work had a considerable number of precedents; and, indeed, an examination of those precedents confirms the prodigality of Lady Murasaki's accomplishments. A Western reader who begins *Genji* with no background in Japanese literature may not always distinguish which sensibilities are unique to Lady Murasaki and which belong to her tradition.

First of all, much of the literary subject matter of the novel draws on themes known to the author and her original readers, whose responses were thus at least partially anticipated. A wide variety of citations might be provided. In terms of plot, for example, a paradigm for the general events that take place in the last book of *Genji* is provided in a well-known poem credited to Takahashi Mushimaro (early Nara period) in the *Manyōshū*, concerning the legend of Unai, mentioned in several poems in that collection. The long poem begins as follows:

> The Maiden Unai of Ashinoya,
> From her half-grown eighth year,
> Until her loose-hung hair was done up,
> Dwelt in safe seclusion,
> Unseen by neighbouring folk.
>
> Then many wooers gathered round,
> Eager to see this lovely girl;
> But two among them, Chinu and Unai,
> Vied with each other for her smile.

> They met, grasping their sword-hilts,
> And with their quivers and bows of spindle-wood
> Slung from their shoulders;
> Each swearing in hot rivalry
> To plunge through flood and fire.
>
> Helpless she sought her mother:
> "When I see their deadly strife
> Because of simple me,
> How can I marry him I love?
> I will wait in Yomi, the Nether World."
> So telling of her secret love for one
> She killed herself in grief.[1]

In *Genji*, the young girl Ukifune, raised in seclusion, is pursued by two courtiers, Kaoru and Niou. She too decides to kill herself. Lady Murasaki's treatment of the theme is infinitely more complex than what is suggested by the simple poem. But a model had been provided her.

There are precedents too for the settings often employed by Lady Murasaki. The importance of Suma, the site of Genji's exile, has been discussed elsewhere. She chose to set the last books of the novel at Uji, a lovely area now a suburb of Kyoto but in the Heian period a remote and wild area. Uji too had certain literary associations by Lady Murasaki's time. Kakimoto Hitomaro's poem in the *Manyōshū* concerning the Uji river suggests some of the thematic concerns Lady Murasaki will later take up in her narrative:

> The waves lingering about the fish-weir stakes
> In the Uji, the river of eighty clans of warriors—
> Whither they are drifting away
> Who knows?[2]

Ukifune, attempting to drown herself, drifts away, and, until the end of the novel, few of the other characters in the novel realize what has happened to her. Another well-known poem in the *Manyōshū* by the priest Manzei (early Nara peri-

---

[1] *The Manyōshū*, tr. by Nippon Gakujutsu Shinkōkai (New York, 1969), p. 242.

[2] *Ibid.*, p. 50.

od) is commonly associated with Uji and suggests even more forcefully the themes to be taken up in Lady Murasaki's novel:

> To what shall I liken this life?
> It is like a boat,
> Which, unmoored at morn,
> Drops out of sight
> And leaves no trace behind.[3]

Uji is thus already a "place with a history" by the Heian period. Lady Murasaki integrates that history with her own concerns to produce the most evocative portions of her long narrative. She is able to take the literary conventions of her day, even those stale from repetition, and breathe new life into them. One of these customs involved the inevitable poetic comparison between the beauties of spring and autumn. Again, the *Manyōshū* contains the paradigm:

When the Emperor Tenji commanded Fujiwara Kamatari, Prime Minister, to judge between the luxuriance of the blossoms on the spring hills and the glory of the tinted leaves on the autumn hills, Princess Nukada decided the question with this poem.

> When loosened from the winter's bonds,
> The spring appears,
> The birds that were silent
> Come out and sing,
> The flowers that were prisoned
> Come out and bloom;
> But the hills are so rank with trees
> We cannot seek the flowers,
> And the flowers are so tangled with weeds
> We cannot take them in our hands.
>
> But when on the autumn hill-side
> We see the foliage,
> We prize the yellow leaves,
> Taking them in our hands,
> We sigh over the green ones,

---

[3] *Ibid.*, p. 237.

> Leaving them on the branches;
> Ah, that is my only regret—
> For me, the autumn hills![4]

Such "judgments" or "contests" were part of the Heian social scene, and poets vied with each other in writing evocative comparisons of the two seasons. Often the results were merely formal or, worse, hackneyed. Lady Murasaki, however, has Genji, speaking to a consort of the Emperor, express his feelings on the subject in such a fresh and thoughtful way that the whole subject becomes possible again:

> "And when all these weighty matters are off my hands," said Genji at last, "I hope I shall have a little time left for things which I really enjoy—flowers, autumn leaves, the sky, all those day-to-day changes and wonders that a single year brings forth; that is what I look forward to. Forests of flowering trees in spring, the open country in autumn. . . . Which do you prefer? It is of course useless to argue on such a subject, as has so often been done. It is a question of temperament. Each person is born with 'his season' and is bound to prefer it. No one, you may be sure, has ever yet succeeded in convincing anyone else on such a subject. In China it has always been the springtime with its 'broidery of flowers' that has won the highest praise; here however the brooding melancholy of autumn seems always to have moved our poets more deeply. For my own part I find it impossible to reach a decision; for much as I enjoy the music of birds and the beauty of flowers, I confess I seldom remember at what season I have seen a particular flower, heard this or that bird sing. But in this I am to blame; for even within the narrow compass of my own walls, I might well have learnt what sights and sounds distinguish each season of the year, having as you see not only provided for the springtime by a profusion of flowering trees, but also planted in my garden many varieties of autumn grass and shrub, brought in, root and all, from the countryside. Why, I have even carried hither whole tribes of insects that

[4] *Ibid.*, p. 10.

were wasting their shrill song in the solitude of lanes and fields. All this I did that I might be able to enjoy these things in the company of my friends, among whom you are one. Pray tell me then, to which season do you find that your preference inclines?"[5]

Lady Murasaki's modes of thought and speculation also belong to her time. Modern readers have been struck with her preoccupation with time and the changes it brings (in this regard her work does bear some comparisons with Proust), yet she was by no means the first to take up such subject matter in literature. The poem of Ariwara no Narihira, quoted several times previously, suggests precisely such a concern. Indeed the whole cluster of attitudes concerning transience, death, and beauty that go into a definition of *mono no aware* were the common property of Lady Murasaki's generation. Yoshida Kenkō, writing of such attitudes about three hundred years later, sums up the whole tradition:

> Were we to live on forever—were the dews of Adashino never to vanish, the smoke on Toribeyama never to fade away—then indeed would men not feel the pity of things.
> Truly the beauty of life is its uncertainty. Of all living things, none lives so long as man. Consider how the ephemera awaits the fall of evening, and the summer cicada knows neither spring nor autumn. Even a year of life lived peacefully seems long and happy beyond compare; but for such as never weary of this world and are loath to die, a thousand years pass away like the dream of a single night.
> What shall it avail a man to drag out till he becomes decrepit and unsightly a life which some day needs must end? Long life brings many shames. At most before his fortieth year is full, it is seemly for a man to die. . . .[6]

Aware (here translated as "the pity of things") arises from

---

[5] Lady Murasaki, *The Tale of Genji*, tr. by Arthur Waley (London, 1957), pp. 380-381. I have, incidentally, observed Waley's spellings of the names of all the characters in the novel, even though some of his versions do not follow the standard procedures for romanization.

[6] From Yoshida Kenkō, "Essays in Idleness," tr. by G. B. Sansom, in Donald Keene, ed., *Anthology of Japanese Literature* (New York, 1955), p. 232.

the self-consciousness of transience. Lady Murasaki expresses
the theme with every nuance at her command in the text of
Genji. But she did not create that theme herself; rather, she
refined and harmonized a sensibility shared with her readers
from the beginning.

Lady Murasaki's real accomplishments thus lie in a slightly
different sphere, one uniquely appropriate for literature.
Anyone who has read even a small portion of the novel
realizes that she is a beguiling, often brilliant, storyteller. She
creates dozens of intriguing characters, some in quick
sketches, some in full portrait; and she manages to involve
many of them in narrative complexities that never fail to pull
the reader on and on.

Most astonishing of all is Lady Murasaki's skill in creating
an evocation of reality for the reader through her observations, in exquisite detail, of the subjective responses of her
characters; and those responses in turn alter and redefine the
reader's perception of that reality. Such a concentration on the
inner life gives her novel a curiously contemporary tone.
However strange the appurtenances of the society in which
her characters live, they quickly reveal their humanity at this
inner level. The reader is soon one with them.

Lady Murasaki's ability to create this inner world is obvious from the very beginning of the novel. The second chapter
of *Genji* is largely devoted to a celebrated scene in which Genji's companions discuss the nature of women. One, the young
man Uji no Kami, tells of an entanglement he suffered
through. At one point, he recalls, the girl he admired suddenly vanished:

"The fact that she had till now sent no poem or concilia-
tory message seemed to show some hardening of heart, and
had already disquieted me. Now I began to fear that her
accursed suspiciousness and jealousy had but been a
stratagem to make me grow weary of her, and though I
could recall no further proof of this I fell into great despair.
And to show her that, though we no longer met, I still
thought of her and planned for her, I got her some stuff for
a dress, choosing a most delightful and unusual shade of

colour, and a material that I knew she would be glad to have. 'For after all,' I thought, 'she cannot want to put me altogether out of her head.' When I informed her of this purchase she did not rebuff me nor make any attempt to hide from me, but to all my questions she answered quietly and composedly, without any sign that she was ashamed of herself."[7]

The passage shows Lady Murasaki's skill in creating a character who possesses a full self-awareness not only of his partner's attitudes but of his own as well. Such acute observation concerning the workings of psychology no doubt seem unexceptional to a contemporary Western reader. One must remind oneself that the text dates from the eleventh century.

Lady Murasaki's interest in focusing on the inner lives of her characters is nowhere better observed than in the long and rich relationship between Genji and Murasaki, his principal consort. Here is a passage in which Genji tells Murasaki (who cannot bear him any children) that he has fathered a descendant by another woman:

"I had far rather that this had not happened. It is all the more irritating because I have for so long been hoping that you would have a child; and that, now that the child has come, it should be someone else's is very provoking. It is only a girl, you know, which really makes it rather a different matter. It would perhaps have been better from every point of view if I had left things as they were, but this new complication makes that quite impossible. I think, indeed, of sending for the child. I hope that when it arrives you will not feel ill-disposed towards it." She flushed: "That is just the sort of thing you always used to say," she answered. "It seems to me to show a very strange state of mind. Of course I ought to put up with it, but there are certain things which I do not see how I can be expected to get used to. . . ." "Softly, softly," he answered, laughing at her unwonted asperity, "who is asking you to get used to anything? I will tell you what you are doing. You are inventing

all sorts of feelings for me such as I have never really had at
all, and then getting cross with me for having them. That is
not a very amiable proceeding, is it?" And having gone on
in this strain for some time, he became quite cheerful.[8]

Genji's playful analysis of Murasaki's wounded feelings
serves several purposes, including that of blunting her wrath
or disappointment: again, Lady Murasaki concentrates on the
inner layers of personality in order to produce for the reader
examples of self-awareness. Characters possessed with this
facility can articulate their own feelings in a remarkably
sophisticated way.

Lady Murasaki's powers of observation often remind a
Western reader of certain elements in the art of Jane Austen:
both possess, for example, a keen eye for the often incongru-
ously imagined demands of society on the individual. Here is
one amusing example: To no Chujo (Genji's confidant and
closest friend) goes to visit his mother after his sudden rise in
court:

> Only two days later To no Chujo came to his mother's
> rooms again. The princess was extremely flattered and
> pleased; it was seldom that he honoured her with two visits
> in such rapid succession. Before receiving him she had her
> hair set to rights and sent for her best gown; for though he
> was her own child he had become so important that she
> never felt quite sure of herself in his presence, and was as
> anxious to make a good impression as if he had been a
> complete stranger.[9]

Image and self-image remain a central concern throughout
the entire novel. Genji, at one point, asks Murasaki for just
such an account of herself. They are preparing to distribute
clothing to various persons at the palace in time for the spring
entertainments. Murasaki questions Genji's methods of making his choices:

> ". . . If I may make a suggestion, would it not be better
> to think whether the stuffs will suit the complexions of

---

[8] *Ibid.*, p. 290.   [9] *Ibid.*, p. 412.

their recipient rather than whether they look nice in the box?" "I know just why you said that," Genji laughed. "You want me to launch out into a discussion of each lady's personal charms, in order that you may know in what light she appears to me. I am going to turn the tables. You shall have your own whichever of my stuffs you like, and by your choice I shall know how *you* regard *yourself*." "I have not the least idea of what I look like," she answered, blushing slightly, "after all, I am the last person in the world to consult upon the subject. One never sees oneself except in the mirror. . . ."[10]

Lady Murasaki's powers of observation and her skill in setting them down permit her the widest possible range of subject matter within the purview of the inner world of her characters. Indeed, the reader of *Genji*, surrounded by the rich emotional universe she has provided for him, may have some initial difficulties in persuading himself precisely what the narrowly defined purposes of the novel might be. There seem so many possibilities. The text, which runs over eleven hundred closely packed pages in the one-volume edition of Waley's translation, is obviously planned on an enormous scale, and its structure is organic. Themes and characters appear and disappear, swept along by the movements of time, which moves all before it. *Genji*, unlike some lengthy masterpieces of the twentieth century (one thinks of James Joyce's *Ulysses*, Thomas Mann's *Magic Mountain*, or, for that matter, of Proust), was not planned in such a way that every detail of its structure and design can be referred back to some central, tightly organized conception in the mind of the author. In fact, time in Lady Murasaki's novel flows precisely like a river, occasionally picking up bits of extraneous, even irrelevant, information, which the author was not always at great pains to remove. Judgments on the meaning of particular aspects of the work are more safely made from a close and repeated reading of the entire text, rather than from a careful analysis of any single passage. To give the simplest example: the setting of the story itself undergoes a considerable

[10] *Ibid.*, p. 463.

metamorphosis. The novel begins in the abstract: "At the court of an Emperor (he lived it matters not when), there was. . . ." The name of the country, presumably Japan, is not mentioned at all. By the fourth chapter, however, Lady Murasaki abandons this arrangement and provides more specific information:

> The nun's cell was in a chapel built against the wall of a wooden house. It was a desolate spot, but the chapel itself was very beautiful. The light of the visitor's torches flick-ered through the open door. In the inner room there was no sound but that of a woman weeping by herself; in the outer room were several priests talking together (or was it praying?) in hushed voices. In the neighbouring temples vespers were over and there was absolute stillness; only towards the Kiyomizu were lights visible and many figures seemed to throng the hillside.[11]

Kiyomizu temple, one of the great attractions in Kyoto during the Heian period (and ever since), was constructed in 805. (The temple also plays an important part in Mori Ōgai's "Sanshō the Steward.") Lady Murasaki now places her novel in space and, more roughly, in time. By the time the bulk of the novel is completed, she grows even more specific, iden-tifying both herself and her supposed informants in the text:

> What here follows was told me by some of the still sur-viving gentlewomen of Tamakatsura's household. I myself was inclined to regard much of it as mere gossip, particu-larly where it concerned Genji's descendants, with whom they can have had very little contact. My informants how-ever were indignant at the idea that Genji's or Murasaki's women must necessarily know better than they. "If anyone gets things wrong," they said, "it is far more likely to be Genji's people, who are all so old that their memories are beginning to fail."
> For my part I have made no effort to decide the question, but simply put things down as I was told.[12]

[11] *Ibid.*, p. 73.   [12] *Ibid.*, p. 766.

The Tale of Genji is a unified work (unlike many novels in the Chinese tradition), and it seems to have grown naturally from Lady Murasaki's pen in the fullness of time. An appreciation of that fullness, whatever small inconsistencies may have been permitted, must lie at the beginning of the reader's coming to terms with the larger purposes of the novel.

Before we discuss the possible nature of those purposes, it might be well to sketch the main outlines of the story, which spans three generations. Prince Genji is the son of the Emperor, although not by his principal consort. The major part of the narrative begins when Genji is already a young adult. His best friend is the courtier To no Chujo, and Genji marries his sister, Princess Aoi; ironically this is the only unsatisfactory relationship sustained by Genji, whose grace and wide range of human sympathies help him reach a closeness of spiritual (and often physical) understanding with the many women who inhabit the novel. Genji's adventures encompass the first two thirds of the text. His first love is Fujitsubo, his legal stepmother and consort of the Emperor. Yet her niece Murasaki, the daughter of Fujitsubo's brother, becomes the main object of his affections after the death of his wife, Princess Aoi, who dies after giving birth to Genji's son Yugiri. Genji is intimate with a number of other women, among them the imperious Lady Rokujo, the mysterious Yugao (actually the mistress of his friend To no Chujo), and the Lady of Akashi.

Genji has a child by the Lady of Akashi. When the girl is grown, she marries the young Emperor. Their son, Niou, Genji's grandson, helps carry the story into the third generation. Genji is also, later in life, officially betrothed to Nyosan, an imperial princess. Nyosan, however, deceives him with Kashiwagi, the son of To no Chujo. A child, Kaoru, is born to Nyosan as a result of this illicit affair. Niou and Kaoru both show some resemblance to Genji, but neither shows his extraordinary certainty and wholeness of spirit. After Genji's death, the novel traces the activities of these two young men, concentrating on their affairs with three remarkable sisters who live with their father in seclusion at Uji. The triple portraits of these three women, Agemaki, Kozeri, and above all Ukifune, are at the center of the final sections.

The details of the plot of the novel are endlessly—and fascinatingly—complex. The materials used by Lady Murasaki can be analyzed in any number of ways, but must always be considered in terms of the totality of her conception. Events that occur early in *Genji* do not reveal their full significance until much later in the narrative, when incidents and the emotional states they engender repeat and reinforce each other. Many readers of the novel unfortunately form their impressions of the whole work from reading merely the first book, itself called "The Tale of Genji." Thus they carry away a largely erroneous view of the work as a while. The emotional center of the novel may well lie in Book Four, entitled "Blue Trousers." "Blue Trousers" chronicles the death of Murasaki and gives the reader a last glimpse of Genji before his own death. Time, disappointment, and death hover in the atmosphere in this long section of the novel and prepare the reader for the imperfect and neurotic world that will follow in the last two books. The very first book in the novel, "The Tale of Genji," deals with death as well: the romantic Yugao dies mysteriously, and Lady Aoi's death in childbirth is one of the more harrowing scenes in the entire novel. Nevertheless the optimism and animal vigor of youth sustain Genji, and the reader, through those early trials. By the time of Genji's death, he is sadder and wiser. Book Four shows the mature characters coping with the realities of their lives, admitting frustrations, insecurities, defeats. The glamor of youth has gone, and the honor and compassion developed in middle age are revealed to provide the only satisfactory means to face up to the inevitable compromises that must be made. Genji now merely wants to "finish life without disaster." Lady Murasaki gives his age as forty, just that period chosen by Yoshida Kenkō (on the basis of this novel, perhaps, one might speculate) as the time when "it is seemly for a man to die."

All the fatigues of middle age supply the narrative material for this portion of the novel. The reader sees illness in the declining Murasaki, observes madness in the behavior of Makibashira, the wife of Higekuro. Friends quarrel, and

Genji for a time loses his closeness with To no Chujo. An unhappy marriage is chronicled in the unfortunate experience of
Tamakatsura, the daughter of Yugao and To no Chujo. Both
Murasaki and Genji feel a sense of their own impending
deaths; resignation and melancholy replace energy and laughter. And Genji himself is deceived in love by Nyosan, who
has an affair with Kashiwagi.

Lady Murasaki's views of these unpleasant realities again
surprise us, containing as they do a powerfully evocative
sense of the emotional exhaustion brought on by human
frailty. In particular, Murasaki's fears, the movements of her
mind as she surveys her situation, are portrayed in a fashion
familiar from post-nineteenth-century literary techniques,
where the attempt is made to record the sense of the flow of
impressions and emotions rather than merely to delineate
their logic. On one occasion she muses on the fact that Genji
is required to accept the young Nyosan as his official wife:

> After all, she thought to herself afterwards, the care of this
> girl was a duty that he could not possibly have avoided. It
> had fallen on him as it were from the sky, and to be cross
> with him for accepting it would be ridiculous. If Nyosan
> had been some girl that he had taken a fancy to or gone out
> of his way to befriend, the case would have been different.
> But it was perfectly true that this step had been imposed
> upon him; and Murasaki was determined to show the
> world that she was not going to lose her head. But she
> knew that once people take a dislike to one, it does not
> make much difference how one behaves. . . . For example,
> her stepmother had even held her responsible for
> Makibashira's fall; it was Murasaki's jealousy (so this
> woman asserted) that had forced Genji to plant Tamakat-
> sura in Higekuro's way! No doubt her tortuous imagina-
> tion would not fail to supply equally complicated slanders
> in the present case. For, though generous and long-
> suffering, Murasaki was capable of making judgments that
> were by no means devoid of sharpness. And now, though
> as yet all was well, there came back to her again and again
> the thought that perhaps the dreaded turning-point had

come. His confidence, his devotion, the whole sovereignty in his affections that had been so long her pride, would begin to slip away from her. . . .[13]

The reader now feels in Murasaki a growing sense of apprehension, reinforcing all her moments of incertitude that have come before. Genji's closeness to Murasaki is not in any doubt, yet in her state of fatigue she cannot accept his most genuine protestations. Genji tries to reassure her:

> "It is only with people such as you, whom I have known all their lives, that I am really happy. But you know all this quite well, and there is no use in my repeating it. About Princess Nyosan—of course it was tiresome for you that I was obliged to have her here, but since she came, I have grown even fonder of you than before; a change you would have noticed quickly enough, if it had been my affection towards someone else that was on the increase! However, you are very observant, and I cannot believe you are not perfectly well aware. . . ." "I cannot explain it," she said. "I know that to any outside person I must appear the happiest of women—fortunate indeed far above my deserts. But inwardly I am wretched. . . . Every day."[14]

Genji himself, who eventually loses his contact with Tamakatsura, whose presence always served to remind him of his first great love, her mother Yugao, can blame only himself for his own wretchedness:

> He could not for an instant stop thinking about her, and soon fell into a condition of absent-mindedness and melancholy that was observed by all who met him. It is said that whatever happens to us is ruled by our conduct in previous existences, or, as others would express it, by Fate. But it seemed to Genji that for the miseries into which he constantly found himself plunged, no other person or power could possibly be held responsible. They sprang from his own excessive susceptibility, and from no other cause whatever. He longed to write to her; but it seemed impos-

[13] *Ibid.*, p. 624.   [14] *Ibid.*, p. 651.

sible, now that she was in the hands of the grim, unbend-
ing Higekuro, to address to her the small humours and
absurdities of which their correspondence was usually
composed.[15]

The very sensibility that has earned Genji the sobriquet of
"The Shining One" now brings him only pain and difficulty.
Nevertheless, he and Murasaki manage to cope with their
own destinies; in fact, they approach them with poise, dignity, and a gentle (and greatly attractive) resignation. The
younger generation has no such tact, no such maturity. The
contrast is strongly made in the last two books of the novel,
but the lines are firmly set down even in "Blue Trousers."
Yugiri, Genji's son, is attracted to Princess Ochiba, and he
behaves toward her in a brutal manner that Genji himself
would have found simply inconceivable:

> "It is useless for me to think of returning," Yugiri said to
> Ochiba in an offhand manner, "and I may as well wait here
> as anywhere else. I hope this will not disturb you. When
> the chaplain leaves your mother's room, I shall join him."
> Never before had he behaved in this impertinent manner.
> The only effective answer to his insolence would have been
> to seek shelter in her mother's rooms. But such a course
> seemed under the circumstances too extreme, and she sat
> motionless in her chair, wondering what would come next.
> Nor had she long to wait. For a few minutes afterwards a
> gentlewoman came with a message, and Yugiri, upon
> some excuse or other, accompanied her behind the cur-
> tains. The fog was now so thick, even inside the house, that
> despite the lamp it was almost dark. In sudden terror she
> made for a sliding-door at the back of the room. Dark
> though it was, he darted unerringly upon her tracks, and
> was just in time to seize the train of her dress before she
> closed the door. She shook herself free; but there was no
> bolt or catch on her side, and holding the door to, she stood
> trembling like water.[16]

Book Four seems the central focus for many of the complex

[15] *Ibid.*, p. 586.   [16] *Ibid.*, p. 705.

themes of the novel. There are at least three of them. All are
suggested in the early sections of the novel, find explicit
statement and example in Book Four, and reach final development in Books Five and Six.

The first of Lady Murasaki's grand themes involves an
examination of the real meaning in human life of the passage
of time. The author and her audience shared modes of thinking that found a centrality of human concern in precisely these
questions. The classic definitions of *aware*, that literary virtue
so much bound up with the Heian period, owes much to
Lady Murasaki's treatment and development of that term.
She treats the conception organically, or perhaps one might
say musically. Her readers were quite familiar with the
theme. The concerns of Lady Murasaki are "givens." We
"know" them in the way we quickly come to know the
theme of a movement in a Haydn symphony. The fascination
for the reader comes rather in witnessing how that theme is
treated, "orchestrated," recapitulated, so that the full grandeur, the greater implications, of that theme can be experienced.

Thoughts and actions alike reveal their meaning through
the passage of time. In *Genji*, events presented in one context,
for one set of artistic purposes, are later shown to possess different, larger implications. (This device too is familiar from
Proust.) Genji's early affair with the ill-fated Yugao, for example, takes on a whole new set of overtones when, late in
his own life, he adopts her daughter Tamakatsura. Through
his knowledge of the daughter, Genji comes to a higher consciousness of the nature of the attraction he originally felt for
Yugao, feelings that in turn increase the tenderness he now
feels for the young woman. At first, he keeps his emotions to
himself, but eventually he tells Tamakatsura what he knows
about her mother:

> ". . . how well I remember the conversation in the course
> of which your father first told me how your mother had
> carried you away, and of his long search for you both. It
> does not seem long ago. . . ." And he told her more than he
> had ever done before about the rainy night's conversation
> and his own first meeting with Yugao.

"Gladly would I show the world this Child-flower's beauty, did I not fear that men would ask me where stands the hedge on which it grew." The truth is, he loved your mother so dearly that I cannot bear the thought of telling him the whole miserable story. That is why I have kept you hidden away like a chrysalis in a cocoon. I know I ought not to have delayed. . . . He paused, and she answered with the verse: "Who cares to question whence was first transplanted a Child-flower that from the peasant's tattered hedge was hither brought?" Her eyes filled with tears as in a scarcely audible voice she whispered this reply.[17]

The subsequent entanglements of plot concerning Tamakatsura and her relations with Genji and the others are too complex to explicate in detail here. Yugao has not been mentioned for hundreds of pages,[18] but by means of the new "orchestration" of the theme introduced again halfway through the novel, the full significance of Genji's experience with her becomes apparent. Further, Genji's romantic attachments have an importance for the narrative beyond the protagonist himself, for they serve as paradigms for the final tragic encounters between the three daughters of Prince Hachi with Kaoru and Niou. In these later sections of the novel, however, these variations are often treated ironically.

The passage of time often signals loss. The death of Genji and the dwindling of the spiritual and aesthetic world inhabited by the third generation of characters in the novel represent merely the most explicit example of this theme. The novel begins, like the young Genji, boldly. Relatively little self-reflection concerning time intrudes in the narrative. The first significant hint of such a concern in the consciousness of the major characters comes in Book Three, when Murasaki realizes that time may sweep away Genji's own affection for her:

[17] *Ibid.*, pp. 512-513.

[18] One critical theory concerning the composition of *The Tale of Genji* suggests that the sections of the novel dealing with Tamakatsura were later added to the original text, either by Lady Murasaki herself or by another writer. Such an allegation is difficult to prove and, in any case, does not vitally effect the point I hope to suggest above. The placement of these sections on Tamakatsura are highly effective, whoever may have arranged them.

Murasaki knew that she must be prepared for the worst. It was not easy for her to face what she now believed to threaten her. For years past she had held, beyond challenge or doubt, the first place in Genji's affections—had been the center of all his plans and contrivings. To see herself ousted by a stranger from a place which long use had taught her to regard as her own by inalienable right—such was the ordeal for which she now began silently to prepare herself. He would not, of course, abandon her altogether; of that she was sure. But the very fact that they had for so many years lived together on terms of daily intimacy and shared so many trifling experiences made her, she felt, in a way less interesting to him. So she speculated, sometimes thinking that all was indeed lost, sometimes that the whole thing was her fancy and nothing whatever was amiss.[19]

This consciousness of the passing of time forces Murasaki to take cognizance as well of her own vulnerability. Her feminine reaction is matched not many lines later by Genji's masculine response to his own developing consciousness of a similar vulnerability in himself. He comes to this state of mind during a visit to a sister of the Emperor:

As he had promised to appear at a much earlier hour Princess Nyogo had by now quite given up expecting him, and, much put about by this untimely visit, she bade her people send the porter to the western gate. The man made his appearance a moment later, looking wretchedly pinched and cold as he hastened through the snow with the key in his hand. Unfortunately the lock would not work, and when he went back to look for help no other manservant could anywhere be found. "It's very rusty," said the old porter dolefully, fumbling all the while with the lock that grated with an unpleasant sound but would not turn. "There's nothing else wrong with it, but it's terribly rusty. No one uses this gate now."

The words, ordinary enough in themselves, filled Genji with an unaccountable depression. How swiftly the locks rust, the hinges grow stiff on doors that close behind us! "I

[19] *Ibid.*, pp. 388-389.

am more than thirty," he thought; and it seemed to him impossible to go on doing things just as though they would last . . . as though people would remember. . . . "And yet," he said to himself, "I know that even at this moment the sight of something very beautiful, were it only some common flower or tree, might in an instant make life again seem full of meaning and reality."[20]

The passage of time signals the removal of friends, affections, activities. Genji seeks the possibility of transcending time through beauty, yet, as Lady Murasaki is at pains to show elsewhere in the novel, beauty can serve as a solace, never as a solution. This too is a lesson that Genji will come to learn later. As he grows older, he becomes more and more convinced of the finality of time. Eventually he grows openly nostalgic. A party with the Emperor Suzaku described in Book Three is a particularly telling moment for him. Suzaku reminds Genji of the Feast of Flowers when Genji, as a young man, danced so brilliantly and won the hearts of all:

. . . Suzaku, remembering that famous Feast of Flowers years ago, said to Genji with a sigh: "What wonderful days those were! We shall not see their like again." There were indeed many incidents belonging to that time which even now Genji looked back upon with considerable emotion, and when the dance was over, he handed the wine bowl to Suzaku, reciting as he did so: "Spring comes, and still the sweet birds warble as of old; but altered and bereft are they that sit beneath the blossoming tree."[21]

Genji feels bereft because he has come to understand that, for him, the past will not and cannot be repeated.

These and similar "orchestrations" on the theme of the passage of time first reach the level of explicit statement in "Blue Trousers." By this point in the narrative, the weight of the past is heavy on all the major characters: Genji, Murasaki, and all who surround them. To no Chujo in particular feels a permanent sense of disappointment and loss. Resignation is possible for him, but it is hard to bear. Awareness cannot remove the pain:

[20] *Ibid.*, p. 390.   [21] *Ibid.*, p. 427.

Genji was meanwhile recalling the day when he had been To no Chujo's partner in the Dance of the Blue Waves, and plucking a chrysanthemum he addressed to him the poem: "Though like this flower you have as time goes by put on a deeper hue, do you recall a day when in the autumn wind your sleeve flapped close to mine?" Yes, then indeed (thought To no Chujo) they were partners, and there was little to choose between them in rank and prospects. But now, despite the very important position he held, he knew well enough that, compared with Genji, he was in popular estimation a very insignificant person indeed. "Not to a flower shall I compare thee, who hidest amid the pomp of regal clouds, but to a star that shines out of an air stiller and clearer than our own." Such was To no Chujo's answer. By now the evening wind was stirring among the red leaves that lay heaped upon the courtyard floor, weaving them into patterns of brown and red.[22]

As a means to produce this degree of self-awareness on the part of her major characters, Lady Murasaki sets up patterns of thought, reaction, and behavior in each. They follow their own habits of mind unwittingly at first, then become increasingly conscious of their own attitudes as they grow older. A real cognizance on the part of the major characters of their own nature usually marks the final stage in their maturity. To no Chujo gains this consciousness when he visits his daughter, Lady Kumoi, and her husband Yugiri, Genji's son by Princess Aoi:

At this moment To no Chujo, drawn hither by the beauty of the autumn leaves, came into the garden for a while on his way back from the Palace. The house, full once more of movement and life, looked (thought To no Chujo) just as he had known it on many an autumn day in his parents' lifetime, and as he wandered from one familiar spot to another it affected him strangely to find those whom he had recently thought of as mere children playing the part of dignified masters and possessors amid the scenes where he himself had once submitted to his elders' rule.

[22] *Ibid.*, p. 613.

Yugiri too seemed slightly embarrassed by the situation; he blushed noticeably when giving orders, and his manner was oddly subdued.[23]

To no Chujo's sense of displacement is powerful but small in comparison with that of Genji, who suffers through the affair of Nyosan and To no Chujo's son Kashiwagi. Genji's greatest consciousness of the ravages of time come when, having intercepted a letter, he confronts Nyosan with the evidence of her infidelity:

"It does not in the least surprise me that you should feel as you do. For one thing, novelties are inevitably more interesting, and you have known me since you were a child. But the real trouble is that I am too old for you. It is true. I am hideously old. Indeed, what in the world could be more natural than that an infant like you should desire to escape from me? I only make one condition. So long as your father is alive we must keep up the pretence, tiresome old person though you may find me, that I am still your husband. Afterwards you may do as you like. But I cannot bear that Suzaku should know what has in reality been the end of this wonderful marriage of ours, upon which he built all his hopes. It is not at all likely that he will live much longer. If you do not wish to add to his sufferings, please let us for the present have no more episodes of this kind."[24]

Suddenly, Genji confronts his own past:

But as he said the words he caught in his own voice a familiar intonation. How often, years ago, those responsible for his upbringing had adopted just this tone, and how dreary, how contemptible he had thought their self-righteous homilies. "Boring old man!" That was what she must be thinking, and in sudden shame he relapsed into a complete silence, during which he drew her writing-case towards him, carefully mixed the ink and arranged the paper. Nyosan was by now sobbing bitterly, and her hand shook so much that at first she was unable to write. How very differently must her pen have flowed, Genji mused,

[23] *Ibid.*, p. 611.   [24] *Ibid.*, p. 674.

when she sat down to answer the letter he had found under her cushion. . . .[25]

Genji's remorse makes him melancholy, but he is able to summon sufficient courage to take stock of himself and to grasp the realities of his situation; indeed, Lady Murasaki seems to suggest, his acquiescence to the passage of time permits him the only victories possible. Genji's realization that the familiar patterns of his existence must be altered thus stands in sharp contrast to Kaoru, who, in the last books of the novel, is wedded to his own neurotic pattern of responses to life. Kaoru can escape from nothing. This observation is consciously made, not by Kaoru himself (who would doubtless be incapable of making it) but by Kozeri, one of the three daughters of Prince Hachi with whom he falls in love:

> Kozeri knew well enough that Kaoru had chosen today for his visit because he counted on Niou having to stay late at the Palace. However he seemed to be in a good mood and said nothing that one could possibly object to, though even today there was perceptible in all his conversation a vague background of the usual tragic description. It was difficult to believe that, as he constantly asserted, time had done nothing to reconcile him to his loss. Human beings, Kozeri felt, were not so constituted, and she sometimes felt that his melancholy was becoming a mere matter of habit—was due simply to an inability ever to relinquish, in her presence, the attitude that he had taken up at the start.[26]

Self-knowledge tempers regrets over the passing of time and provides the wise with the only sure means of remaining at peace with themselves and in harmony with others. The theme, expounded subtly by Lady Murasaki in the early portions of the novel, swells in importance until, at the close, the symphony is overwhelming.

A second theme in *The Tale of Genji* that modern readers will identify at once as they read and study the text is the quest for self-identification. The characters devote themselves to that most contemporary of psychological questions, "Who

---

[25] *Ibid*.   [26] *Ibid*., p. 971.

am I?" In Lady Murasaki's view, the question seems best approached (although not fully answered) by examining the role of love as a means to self-definition. Those who have not read the novel carefully may make the mistake of thinking that the burden of her arguments rests in the realm of physical love, in the amours of Genji. The actual text shows something considerably different. Sexual love certainly plays a part, of course, in her concerns, but the span of Lady Murasaki's imagination is enormous. All human relationships—friendly affection, love for children, relations between brother and sister, social friendships, every aspect of possible human connection and affection—make their contribution, forming an organic whole in which the totality often serves to illumine and underscore any one of its particular parts.

The urgent necessity for such a quest leading to self-definition is emphasized early in the novel, when the Emperor secretly sends the boy Genji to have his fortune told by a visiting Korean magician:

> At this time some Koreans came to Court and among them a fortune-teller. Hearing this, the Emperor did not send for them to come to the Palace, because of the law against the admission of foreigners which was made by the Emperor Uda. But in strict secrecy he sent the Prince to the Strangers' quarters. He went under the escort of the Secretary of the Right, who was to introduce him as his own son. The fortune-teller was astonished by the boy's lineaments and expressed his surprise by continually nodding his head: 'He has the marks of one who might become a Father of the State, and if this were his fate, he would not stop short at any lesser degree than that of Mighty King and Emperor of all the land. But when I look again—I see that confusion and sorrow would attend his reign. But should he become a Great Officer of State and Councillor of the Realm I see no happy issue, for he would be defying those kingly signs of which I spoke before.'[27]

Genji's future is immediately shown to be unclear; what-

---

[27] *Ibid.*, pp. 15-16.

ever role he chooses, or has chosen for him, may lead to grief.
His personality is not warped by the ambiguity of his status;
he knows who his parents are (unlike Kaoru) and he finds certainty in his happy relations with his peers. Nevertheless
Genji is always conscious of his unusual status.

Lady Murasaki uses Genji's career to illustrate two aspects
of love that help define her protagonist's own sense of self.
The first is her development of the conception that a human
being always seeks in his amorous life the same configurations by which he defines the sentiment. As those configurations may manifest themselves in a variety of partners, a person may fall in one with one person after another. Yet what
he seeks remains always the same. Kiritsubo, the Emperor's
consort, and Genji's real mother, dies at an early age, grief-
stricken because of her ill-treatment at court. The Emperor
then marries Fujitsubo, who becomes Genji's stepmother. As
a young man, Genji falls in love with her. This ambiguous
relationship is doomed, of course; yet the importance of this
central metaphor on love becomes apparent when Genji
comes to know the young Murasaki, the daughter of Fujitsubo's brother. Genji understands the depth of his love for
Murasaki at precisely the moment he recognizes her resemblance to Fujitsubo:

> How beautiful she was! And, now that it was possible to
> compare them on equal terms, how like in every minutest
> detail of pose and expression to the girl at home! Particu-
> larly in the carriage of her head and the way her hair grew
> there was the same singular charm. For years Murasaki had
> served to keep Lady Fujitsubo, to some extent at any rate,
> out of his thoughts. But now that he saw how astonish-
> ingly the one resembled the other he fancied that all the
> while Murasaki had but served as a substitute or eidolon of
> the lady who had denied him her love. Both had the same
> pride, the same reticence. For a moment he wondered
> whether, if they were side by side, he should be able to tell
> them apart. How absurd! Probably indeed, he said to him-
> self, the whole idea of their resemblance was a mere fancy;
> Fujitsubo had for so many years filled all his thoughts. It

was natural that such an idea should come to him. Unable to contain himself any longer, he slipped out of his hiding-place and gently crept between her curtains-of-state, until he was near enough to touch the train of her cloak.[28]

Variations on this pattern are repeated throughout the novel, and nowhere more telling than in a series of incidents between Yugiri (Genji's son by Princess Aoi) and Murasaki herself. Yugiri bears approximately the same relationship to Murasaki that Genji does to Fujitsubo, and, like his father, he too falls in love with his stepmother. Yugiri himself has some vague unarticulated sense of this attraction, but he shies away from it:

> Yugiri was well-born, handsome, and, in a subdued way, very agreeable in his manners. The gentlewomen of the household took no small interest in him, but he remained somewhat of a mystery to them. With Murasaki he had few dealings and was indeed barely acquainted with her. Why it was that he held aloof from her he would have been at a loss to explain. Was it that some dim instinct warned him against a repetition of his father's disastrous entanglements?[29]

The chord is fully struck, with all its terrible overtones, when Yugiri later catches a glimpse of Murasaki and is overcome with the physical presence of her beauty:

> Morning after morning Murasaki too saw the dew roughly snatched from leaf and flower. She was sitting thus one day on watch at her window while Genji played with the little princess in a neighboring room. It happened that Yugiri had occasion to come across from the eastern wing. When he reached the door at the end of the passage he noticed that the great double-doors leading into Murasaki's room were half-open. Without thinking what he was doing, he paused and looked in. Numerous ladies-in-waiting were passing to and fro just inside, and had he made any

[28] *Ibid.*, p. 205.   [29] *Ibid.*, p. 421.

sound they would have looked up, seen him and necessarily supposed that he had stationed himself there on purpose to spy upon those within. He saw nothing for it but to stand dead still. Even indoors the wind was so violent that the screens would not stand up. Those which usually surrounded the high dais were folded and stacked against the wall. There, in full view of anyone who came along the corridor, reclined a lady whose notable dignity of mien and bearing would alone have sufficed to betray her identity. This could be none other than Murasaki. Her beauty flashed upon him as at dawn the blossom of the red flowering cherry flames out of the mist upon the traveller's still sleepy eye. It was wafted towards him, suddenly imbued him, as though a strong perfume had been dashed against his face. She was more beautiful than any woman he had ever seen.[30]

The pattern is repeated, but not precisely; Genji's actual relations with his stepmother are far more intimate, and far more disastrous, than anything Yugiri might have contemplated. No suggestion of a relationship is ever broached, let alone consummated, and indeed Yugiri never gives way to his feelings until Murasaki's death:

The daylight was still feeble, and he could see very little. But at that moment Genji himself held up the great lamp, bringing it so close to the couch that Yugiri suddenly saw her in all her loveliness. "And why should he not see her?" thought Genji, who knew that Yugiri was peeping. But in a moment he covered his eyes with his sleeve. "It is almost worse to see her now, while she is still unchanged," he said. "One thinks that she will speak, move. . . ." Yugiri brushed away the tears that kept on dimming his eyes. Her hair lay spread across the pillows, loose, but not tangled or disorderly, in a great mass, against which in the strong lamplight her face shone with a dazzling whiteness. Never, thought Genji, had her beauty seemed so flawless as now, when the eye could rest on it undistracted by any ripple of

30 *Ibid.*, p. 528.

sound or motion. Yugiri gazed astounded. His spirit seemed to leave him, to float through space and hover near her, as though it were he that was the ghost, and this the lovely body he had chosen for his habitation.[31]

Father and son are thus drawn together in a moment of unspoken communion.

A second aspect of love connected with the character of Genji involves his predilection for acting the role of a father-figure to various young women. Genji, as Earl Miner has pointed out,[32] has produced enough children to remain credible but not so many as to overcomplicate the plot of the novel; actually, he has fewer children than any other father described in the text. The role of the father bears a certain relationship to that of lover, as Kawabata points out with such tact and skill in *The Sound of the Mountain*, and Lady Murasaki as well plays on this ambiguity with telling effect. Genji's first experience as a surrogate father involves Murasaki, who, when she grows up, actually becomes his consort. Both their roles then change accordingly. Halfway through the novel, Genji befriends Tamakatsura, the daughter of Yugao, his early passion. The danger of the same ambiguity, the same metamorphosis now arises. No one recognizes the pattern more clearly than does Murasaki herself:

> "But you surely cannot mean that I shall *betray* her confidence?" asked Genji indignantly. "You forget," Murasaki replied, "that I was once in very much the same position myself. You had made up your mind to treat me as a daughter; but, unless I am much mistaken, there were times when you did not carry out this resolution very successfully. . . ." "How clever everyone is!" thought Genji, much put out at the facility with which his inmost thoughts were read. But he hastened to rejoin: "If I were in love with Tamakatsura, she would presumably become aware of the fact quite as quickly as you would." He was too much an-

[31] *Ibid.*, p. 732.

[32] See Earl Miner, "Some Thematic and Structural Features of the *Genji' Monogatari*," *Monumenta Nipponica* XXIV, 1-2 (1969), p. 8.

noyed to continue the conversation; however, he admitted
to himself in private that when people come to a conclusion
of this kind, it is hardly ever far from the mark. But surely,
after all, he could judge better than she. And Murasaki, he
reflected, was not judging the case on its merits, but merely
assuming, in the light of past experience, that events were
about to take a certain course. . . .[33]

Later still, Genji is asked by the Emperor Suzaku to play
the role of father and protector to his daughter Nyosan by
officially adopting her as his wife. In this instance, as has been
noted above, things turn out worst of all: Genji carries out his
father's role with greater correctness, and Nyosan betrays
him.

Obviously marriage customs during the Heian period
made ambiguous situations such as these more likely than
they would be in a modern society. Nevertheless Lady
Murasaki pursues such themes with a full knowledge of their
artistic and philosophical possibilities. Genji's kindness and
understanding require appropriate recipients; his beauty of
character, and his own sense of himself, require him to play
the role of Pygmalion from time to time.

In Kaoru, Lady Murasaki recreates certain aspects of Genji's character, and certain patterns in his behavior. For Kaoru,
the ambiguities of his life are harsher and more destructive to
him. Although Genji's social position had been ambiguous,
he at least knew who his parents were. Kaoru does not. He is
"officially" considered to be Genji's son, but the reader
knows he is the illicit offspring of the liaison between Nyosan
and Kashiwagi. Genji attempts to come to know himself.
Kaoru cannot, and his life is marked by the weight of this
ambiguity concerning his origins. And Genji's treatment of
him as a child could not conceal the ambiguous attitude of the
older man towards the boy. Indeed, Genji himself indulges in
fantasy:

> The little boy was asleep in his nurse's quarters; but pres-
> ently he was waked, and crawling into the room made

[33] *Genji*, p. 488.

straight for Genji and grabbed at his sleeve. He was dressed in a little shirt of white floss, over which was a red coat with a Chinese pattern finely worked upon it. The skirts of this garment were remarkably long and trailed behind him in the quaintest way; but it was (as usual with children of that age) quite open at the front, showing his little limbs, white and smooth as a fresh-stripped willow wand. There was certainly something in his smile and the shape of his brow that recalled Kashiwagi. But where had the child got his remarkably good looks? Not from his father, who was passable in appearance, but could not possibly have been called handsome. To Nyosan, curiously enough, he could see no resemblance. Indeed the expression that chiefly gave character to the boy's face (or so Genji contrived to fancy) was not at all unlike his own.[34]

The ambiguity becomes a permanent part of Kaoru's character, and his loneliness and uncertitude, appealing as they are in various ways, give suspicious and egotistical aspects to his personality that, for all the roundness they contribute to Lady Murasaki's portrait, remain, as intended, less than appealing. Kaoru's own consciousness of his troubled state is best revealed in a conversation he has with Ben no Kimi, the wise and kindly servant who looks after Agemaki and her sisters. Kaoru is deeply in love with Agemaki and he attempts to define for Ben no Kimi (and for himself) the precise quality of the affection he feels:

"It is not however love in the ordinary sense of the word for which I ask. What I long so passionately for and have never been able to find is someone to whom I could speak freely and openly about whatever came into my head, however trivial or however secret and intimate the thing might be—it comes perhaps of never having had brothers and sisters or anyone with whom I stood on that sort of footing. I have been terribly lonely—all my sorrows, joys, enthusiasms have been locked up inside me, and if at the present moment my greatest craving is simply for someone

[34] *Ibid.*, p. 694.

to share my life with, to talk to, to be near—is that so very unnatural?"[35]

Sharing, however, comes hardest of all virtues for Kaoru. Even at the end of the novel the reader is by no means certain that he has been able to break out of his self-imposed prison of doubt and suspicion to any degree sufficient to permit him to give himself to anyone. Life seems for Kaoru, as for most of the others in the final books, a "bridge of dreams" that cannot actually be crossed. Like Genji, Kaoru loves several women in the course of searching for the woman who corresponds to his deepest desires. (Again, Lady Murasaki varies the theme: Kaoru loves three sisters, a particular adventure that never befell Genji.) Yet just as Kaoru never really knew his parents, he never really finds his love.

Lady Murasaki provides Niou, his closest companion, with certain attributes missing in Kaoru. Together they share a friendship not unlike that of Genji and To no Chujo. Niou is the other side of Kaoru: he is bold, handsome, and passionate. He shows the faults of impetuosity, jealousy. He is, indeed, the only male character in the novel who exhibits those traits. Niou loves Kozeri. On one occasion, suspicious of her relationship with Kaoru, he determines to find out the truth:

At moments when Niou found himself alone in her rooms he made a hasty search for such documents in likely boxes and drawers; but he found nothing but the briefest and most matter-of-fact communications left lying about or stuck into things in a way that showed them not to have been regarded as of the slightest consequence. But even this was not enough to allay his suspicions. It was obvious, after the perfume incident, that love-letters must exist, even if a superficial search had failed to reveal them. That Kaoru should fall in love with her he had already decided to be inevitable. And why should she resist his advances? They were very well suited to one another. . . .

Niou was working himself up into a frenzy of jealousy. He spent all day at the Nijo-in, but wrote no less than three times to the New Palace. . . .[36]

[35] *Ibid.*, p. 843.   [36] *Ibid.*, p. 931.

At best, Niou and Kaoru represent certain aspects of the splendid wholeness that was Genji. "Genji was dead," writes Lady Murasaki at the beginning of Book Five, "and there was no one to take his place." The one who feels this lack of wholeness the most keenly is Ukifune, who loves both Kaoru and Niou; indeed she unwittingly loves what Genji represents, but that love must remain "a bridge of dreams" as well, since such a man no longer exists. No wonder that, torn between Kaoru's sensitiveness and the terrible power of Niou's passion, she, like the Maiden Unai in the *Manyōshū* poem, tries to drown herself. (And again, Lady Murasaki does a variation on that paradigm by having her remain alive.)

The third theme of importance in the novel manifests Lady Murasaki's convictions concerning the central importance of a developed sensibility. Sensibility, that exceptional openness to emotional impressions possessed by Genji, Murasaki, and certain other important characters in the novel, makes possible a comprehension of the conflicting evidence that life presents. For Lady Murasaki, only the possession of a cultivated sensibility permits the grasp of the often hidden consonance between emotion and idea, between what one feels and one grasps intellectually. Thus, for the author, the cultivation and the discipline of such a sensibility remain the highest goal of all. All the major characters in the novel undergo such a process of refinement. In a larger sense, too, the novel is meant to serve as a means to help bring about the development of such a sensibility in its readers. Such an emphasis on sensibility brings the world of the novel closer to our contemporary conceptions of the self. Yet, although the mechanisms of introspection Lady Murasaki delineates are familiar, the mental world inhabited by her characters remains considerably different from our own. We rapidly sense the appositeness of the reactions of her characters; their thoughts often need explication.

In this regard, it may be useful to mention several conceptions common to Buddhist belief in the Heian period that Lady Murasaki shared with her contemporaries.[37] One con-

---

[37] For a more detailed consideration of these questions, see Chapter IV of Ivan Morris, *The World of the Shining Prince* (New York, 1964).

cerns the concept of *mappō*, "the latter days of the law." The
general sense of decline, and the elements of decadence that
were thought to attend the coming of the period (calculated to
be roughly during Lady Murasaki's lifetime and afterwards),
were familiar to her contemporaries through numerous references in the Lotus Sutra and other Buddhist religious documents studied in Heian times. The future seemed to offer only
gloom and decay. Some scholars have seen the dark and broken atmosphere that pervades the final third of *The Tale of
Genji* as evidence of Lady Murasaki's conviction that the high
point of her civilization had passed.

A second belief common to the period centered on *karma* or
reincarnation. In its crudest, folklike form, such a concept
suggested a belief in a rebirth in a next life, higher or lower on
the scale of creation depending on the merits one has acquired
during one's present lifetime. Such a view seems simplistic at
best to a modern reader; Lady Murasaki, too, was at pains to
take a much more sophisticated view of the doctrine.
Nevertheless the conception provides her with numerous opportunities for scenes of self-scrutiny for many important
characters in the novel. Most often, a conviction in the efficacy of *karma* creates sentiments of remorse. In one particularly telling scene, for example, Genji's stepmother feels herself prey to a terrible guilt over her illicit relationship with
Genji, a union that resulted in the birth of a child (later to
reign as the Emperor Ryozen):

> The Lady Abbess too was at this time in great distress.
> The sin of the Heir Apparent's birth was a constant weight
> upon her heart. She felt that she had up to the present es-
> caped more lightly than her *karma* in any degree warranted
> and that a day of disastrous reckoning might still be at
> hand. For years she had been so terrified lest her secret
> should become known that she had treated Genji with ex-
> aggerated indifference, convinced that if by any sign or
> look she betrayed her partiality for him their attachment
> would at once become common knowledge at Court. She
> called to mind countless occasions when, longing for his
> sympathy and love, she had turned coldly away. The result
> of all her precautions did indeed seem to be that, in a world

where everything that anyone knows sooner or later gets repeated, this particular secret had, so far as she could judge by the demeanour of those with whom she came in contact, remained absolutely undivulged. But the effort had cost her very dear, and she now remembered with pity and remorse the harshness which this successful policy had involved.[38]

Even Genji, late in his life, feels the weight of his *karma* when Nyosan gives birth to Kaoru, his "official" son, but, of course, fathered by Kashiwagi:

> At the first ray of morning sunlight a child was born. It was hard indeed for Genji to receive this news, and to be told too that the child was a boy, with all the paternal pride and thankfulness that the occasion (if he were not to betray his secret) so urgently demanded. As things were, he was certainly glad that it was a boy; for with a girl's upbringing he would have been expected to take much more trouble, whereas a boy can be left to his own devices. But should the child, when it grew up, show a striking resemblance to Kashiwagi, this would be far more likely to attract notice in a boy than in a girl. With how strange an appropriateness had he been punished for the crime that never ceased to haunt his conscience![39]

As Ivan Morris has pointed out, many Japanese commentators have found in this atmosphere of retribution the major theme of the novel, and, by the same token, he is surely correct when he comments further that "it is surely an over-simplification of The Tale of Genji to imagine that its purpose is to expound any particular theory or moral."[40]

Certainly Lady Murasaki finds an importance in the religious sensibility. For her, the cultivation of that sensibility, rather than the intellectual apprehension of sophisticated Buddhist doctrine, represents, in human and literary terms at least, the higher level of accomplishment. A desire for introspection, and the emotional state engendered by such a desire, most often evoke religious sentiments in the novel. And, always, the nature of the attitude with which one approaches

[38] *Genji*, p. 243.   [39] *Ibid.*, p. 682.   [40] Morris, *Shining Prince*, p. 41.

the religious experience is crucial. Early in the narrative, Lady Murasaki provides a passage that serves to illustrate the range of Genji's sympathies with the religious ideal. At this juncture, he is recovering from the shock of the death of his young wife, Princess Aoi:

> Genji gathered about him a number of doctors famous for their understanding of the Holy Law and made them dispute in his presence. Yet even in the midst of scenes such as these, calculated to impress him in the highest degree with the futility of all earthly desires, one figure from the fleeting world of men still rose up importunately before him and haunted every prayer. One day at dawn by the light of a sinking moon the priests of the temple were making the morning offering of fresh leaves and flowers before an image that stood near by. He could hear the clink of the silver flower-trays as they scattered chrysanthemum and maple leaves of many hues around the Buddha's feet. It seemed to him then that the life these people led was worth while, not merely as a means to salvation but for its own pleasantness and beauty.[41]

Art and beauty play a central role in religion and justify its practices to those with sufficient sensibility to be attracted to its larger purposes. Art can inform the instinct for religion just as it can inform the instinct for life itself.

And art serves other purposes as well: it disciplines the sensibility and reinforces it in the search for self-definition. Art, especially the art of literature, is chosen by Lady Murasaki as a means to permit a number of characters in the novel to grasp the significance of their own lives, and the meaning of their own relationships with others. Tamakatsura, for example, uncertain about her own future, examines the complex etiquette of her situation by reading novels:

> However kind her father might be, it was impossible that he should take more trouble about her than Prince Genji was doing; indeed, To no Chujo, not having once set eyes on her since she was a mere infant, might well have ceased

[41] *Genji*, p. 208.

to take any interest in her whatever. She had lately been reading a number of old romances and had come across many accounts of cases very similar to her own. She began to see that it was a delicate matter for a child to force itself upon the attention of a parent who had done his best to forget that it existed, and she abandoned all idea of taking the business into her own hands.[42]

Murasaki too attempts to find solace and meaning in her reading of fiction:

> On the nights when Genji was away, Murasaki used to make her women read to her. She thus became acquainted with many of the old-fashioned romances, and she noticed that the heroes of these stories, however light-minded, faithless, or even vicious as they might be, were invariably represented as in the end settling down to one steady and undivided attachment. If this were true to life, then Genji was, as he himself so often said, very differently constituted indeed from the generality of mankind. Never, she was convinced, never as long as he lived would his affections cease to wander in whatever direction his insatiable curiosity dictated. Say what he might, wish what he might, the future would be just what the past had been.[43]

A genuine sensibility intuits the real nature of things and has the capacity to perceive, if only fleetingly, the grandeur and the sadness of life itself. Such a sensibility comes from a participation in, and an observation of, the movements of everyday life as manifested in time, as well as from the study of art and the contemplation of the religious ideal. All such activities of the spirit represent elements in a necessary training. Self-awareness on the part of an individual that he possesses such a sensibility, rather than any particular set of convictions he may hold, represents Lady Murasaki's highest ideal. This sensibility concerning sensibility, to put it another way, represents in psychological terms the quality of *mono no aware*, that highest literary virtue in the traditional canon of taste.

The ultimate grandeur of Genji's personality can be expli-

[42] *Ibid.*, p. 487.   [43] *Ibid.*, p. 653.

cated in terms of *mono no aware*. His grasp of the beauty, and
of the sadness, of life in all its refulgence, makes him the pinnacle of Lady Murasaki's, and the reader's, admiration. From
this perspective, all of his adventures and amours can be seen
for what they are: devices on the part of the author to permit
differing aspects of Genji's understanding and compassion to
show themselves. In every truly important way, Genji is a
deeply good man. He is loyal to everyone he knows, kind
even to those who spite him, and anxious to help all those
with whom he comes in contact. He too, like Koremori in
The Tale of the Heike, feels the pull of retirement from the
world, but, unlike Koremori, he remains in the world for the
sake of others. (In this regard, Kaoru's views on the subject
serve almost as a parody of Genji's.) Genji, in fact, acts out in
a secular fashion the role of a *Boddhisatva*, one who, in
Mahāyāna Buddhism, turns away from his own salvation in
order to help all others to attain the same goal.

To suggest that the character of Genji may be intended to
serve in some fashion as a religious symbol may seem startling to a modern reader, and that reaction in itself testifies to
the psychological skill with which Lady Murasaki has constructed her narrative. The text of the novel, in any case, certainly suggests that Genji's significance to those around him
was enormous:

> In the country at large Genji's loss was felt and lamented
> at every turn. The spectacle of life lost all its glamour; it
> seemed as though a sudden darkness had spread over the
> whole world. Of the depression which reigned at his two
> palaces it is needless to speak; and here another loss—that of
> Murasaki—weighed constantly on the minds of those who
> were left behind, and of the two bereavements was indeed
> perhaps felt the more keenly. For she had died very young,
> and her memory, like the flowers whose blossoming is
> shortest, was the more highly prized.[44]

The significance of Genji's death, lightly touched on here,
is explained in a more explicit fashion by Kaoru, who is, of

---

[44] *Ibid.*, p. 751.

course, also more personal in his statements concerning the meaning of Genji's death:

> "Genji's death," he said to Ben no Kimi presently, "happening when I was a mere child made—now that I think in looking back on it—a disastrous impression on me. I grew up feeling that nothing was stable, nothing worthwhile, and though in course of time I have risen to a fairly high position in the state and have even managed to win for myself a certain degree of celebrity, these things mean nothing to me. I would much rather have spent my time in some such quiet place as this. And now Prince Hachi's death has made it less possible for me than ever to seek satisfaction in the ordinary pleasures of the world."[45]

Genji's compassion, stability, and energy disappear now from the world of the novel, and, with that disappearance, the horizon darkens forever. At one point in the latter sections of the novel, the death of Genji is directly compared to the death of Buddha, and his loss is seen to be, in its way, almost as great. Kobai, Kashiwagi's brother, makes the comparison to the Daughter of Prince Sochi:

> "Not that I ever knew Genji very well; enough however to realize what must be the feelings of those to whom his death was a real and intimate loss." Kobai stood silent for a while, and then, as though glad to busy himself with something that would help him to shake off a train of melancholy reflections, he helped the boy to pluck a spray of blossom and get ready to go off to Court.
> "Perhaps after all," Kobai added, "Niou will one day surprise us as Ananda surprised the Assembly. I do not want to bore him, but for the sake of old remembrances I will write a word or two for you to take with the flowers. . . ."[46]

Ananda, a disciple of Buddha, was an imposing figure at the First Assembly held after Buddha's death. Niou, Kobai suggests in the comparison, may rise to the occasion in a similar fashion, but so far he has not done so.

[45] *Ibid.*, p. 829.   [46] *Ibid.*, p. 762.

Despite hints of Lady Murasaki's *boddhisatva* concept, the novel is a masterpiece of narrative fiction, not remotely a religious tract. Still, the author's concern for the truths of religious insight and the meaning of that insight on the developing personalities of her characters give *The Tale of Genji* a profundity denied any wholly secular work.

Such are some of the themes with which Lady Murasaki invests her vast and evocative novel. A full analysis of the complex literary means she has used in its construction would require explications beyond the scope of this essay. Nevertheless, a few general principles can be set down as an aid in approaching such a lengthy and demanding text.

First, taking *The Tale of Genji* as a whole, the reader cannot fail to be struck by the skill with which the author has imposed a carefully wrought symmetry on the novel's pattern of shifting densities. The novel begins with only a few characters. Gradually, more and more are added, so that the middle books are thick with the doings of a dozen or more major characters, and countless minor ones. At the death of Genji, the world begins to shrink again. In the last books, as in the first, only a few personages are presented, who manage to live on with difficulty, in the shadows cast by all the activity that has come before. Such an overall design resembles that employed in the early Japanese narrative scroll paintings, involving the same principles of motion, harmony, and time. A narrative scroll, as it is unrolled, slowly fills and quickens with life, then tapers off at the end. As with these scroll paintings, increased movement in time permits Lady Murasaki to introduce a wider and still wider variety of personalities. The center portions of *The Tale of Genji* find room to include a number of charming vignettes, many of the same sort that make the scroll paintings themselves so vivid. Some of these characters are comic: the crusty old governor of Akashi, the governor of Hitachi, Ukifune's boorish stepfather, or the outrageous Lady of Omi, an illegitimate child of To no Chujo. The humorous characters, in particular, are often included at the expense of the provincials and the lower classes, yet even the broadest sketches are carried out within the bounds of decorum and good taste. Lady Murasaki's world seems replete.

Yet not complete in itself. The scroll painters often suggested the presence of vague and evocative scenes (a glimpse of mountains through an open doorway, figures in a distant forest) beyond the area circumscribed by their central conception. A similar sensation of opening out exists in *The Tale of Genji*, in narrative terms. The author includes a certain number of additional characters who inhabit still different worlds from the one she presents in her novel. Often the attitudes of these characters are crucial in motivating the central personages of *Genji*; yet the reader is given only the briefest glimpse of them. Their very remoteness serves as a useful technique to create a sense of a still larger universe, in which the world inhabited by the major characters plays only a part. Genji's deep attachments to Asagao and to Lady Rokujo, for example, are dwelt upon throughout the novel, yet the reader sees little of them. Like Genji, the reader is kept in a state of restless suspense concerning these unrealized relationships. Lady Rokujo's hauteur, so important in establishing the tone of certain early sequences in the novel, is mirrored later by the attitudes of the icy First Princess, of whom the reader is given only the briefest glimpse. Through such devices, the psychological world inhabited by the characters in the novel takes on a movement, a shifting perspective, consonant with that found in the great works of narrative visual art created during the same period.

Other general principles of structure—Lady Murasaki's organic, symphonic technique, and her systems of parallels in the emotional responses of the various generations of her characters—have been discussed above in other contexts. Such a pattern of repetition and variation is not merely visible in the configurations of the characters she has created. Incidents too are repeated. Two different characters find themselves in the same circumstances. Each reacts differently. One encounter helps define the nature of the other. The effect is not unlike the reciprocity between the two juxtaposed images that make up a well-wrought *haiku*. One small example may suffice to suggest the technique. Early in the novel Genji, passionately in love with the mysterious Yugao, remains with her throughout the night. She lives in a rather ordinary quarter of the capital and his pride of possession is matched by his

sense of wonder and surprise at the new and plebian world he
discovers outside the confines of his decorous and ceremoni-
ous life at the palace. For Genji, all of life, even this experience, is an adventure:

> What a queer place to be lying in! thought Genji, as he
> gazed round the garret, so different from any room he had
> ever known before. It must be almost day. In the neighbor-
> ing houses people were beginning to stir, and there was an
> uncouth sound of peasant voices: "Eh! How cold it is! I
> can't believe we shall do much with the crops this year." "I
> don't know what's going to happen about my carrying-
> trade," said another; "things look very bad." Then (bang-
> ing on the wall of another house), "Wake up neighbour.
> Time to start. Did he hear, d'you think?" and they rose and
> went off each to the wretched task by which he earned his
> bread.
>
> All this clatter and bustle going on so near her made the
> lady very uncomfortable, and indeed so dainty and fastidi-
> ous a person must often in this miserable lodging have suf-
> fered things which would make her long to sink through
> the floor. But however painful, disagreeable, or provoking
> were the things that happened, she gave no sign of noticing
> them. That, being herself so shrinking and delicate in her
> ways, she could yet endure without a murmur the exas-
> perating banging and bumping that was going on in every
> direction, aroused his admiration, and he felt that this was
> much nicer of her than if she had shuddered with horror at
> each sound. But now, louder than thunder, came the noise
> of the threshing-mills, seeming to near that they could
> hardly believe it did not come from out of the pillow itself.
> Genji thought his ears would burst.[47]

Toward the end of the novel, the introspective Kaoru also
finds himself spending the night in a dilapidated house in the
capital, talking with Ukifune. He too awakes to the sounds
of early morning:

> It was beginning to grow light, but it seemed that in this
> part of the town the dawn was heralded, not by the crow-

[47] Ibid., p. 63.

ing of cocks, but by the raucous voices of pedlars crying their wares—if indeed that was what they were doing, for the noises they made were entirely unintelligible. There seemed to be whole tribes of them. He looked out. There was something ghostly about them as, seen against the grey morning sky, they struggled along with strange packages piled high on their heads. Apart from everything else the unfamiliarity of the whole experience fascinated him. Presently he heard the watchman unlock the gates and go off.[48]

Kaoru and Genji undergo the same experience, yet Kaoru's gentler response is quite in consonance with his own reflective nature. Genji is distracted by the energy of the moment; Kaoru, distant, uses that moment for reflection on what he sees. The pattern is repeated, the mood changed. Each incident is made appropriate for the character involved; each scene in turn helps build up the reader's impressions of the nature of the character experiencing it. Such natural reciprocity of character and incident (to repeat Henry James's phrase) remains a fundamental technique employed in the novel.

Such a reciprocity is also echoed in the exquisite care with which Lady Murasaki has matched the emotional responses of her characters with the settings in which those characters find themselves. The curious and modest dwelling of Yugao, the mysterious house amidst the thickets, the palace at Uji, the country dwellings at Akashi, are rendered with a palpable atmosphere that reinforces the moods and characters of their inhabitants. Some of Lady Murasaki's reinforcements naturally involve cultural overtones that are bound to escape Western readers. An elaborate analysis might be made, for example, of the consonance between the hours of the day, or of the changing seasons, and of the emotional colorations traditionally assigned them, as revealed in the shifting emotional states of her characters. Nagai Kafū's highly developed sense of the literary possibilities of the intimate bond between mood and setting may well find its *locus classicus* in *The Tale of Genji*. Similar examples are numerous, and any careful reader of the text will begin to pick them up almost immediately.

Symbols, often symbolic objects, also play an important

[48] *Ibid.*, p. 990.

role in unifying the text. The repeated appearance of such objects in *Genji*, like the snakes in *The Setting Sun* or the caged birds in *A Portrait of Shunkin*, creates a powerful cumulative effect. One telling example concerns the *nademono* (literally, "rubbing objects"), sacred images that, after use in purification rites, are thrown into a stream. The first mention of *nademono* in the text occurs in a playful way. Later, mention of these objects takes on an increasingly ominous significance. Kaoru is the first to mention the term. In the last book of the novel, "The Bridge of Dreams," he goes in search of Ukifune. He suspects that her sister Kozeri knows her whereabouts:

> . . . with tears in his eyes, yet half in jest, Kaoru recited a poem in which he wondered whether, just as the touch of the *nademono* cleanses the worshipper of his sin, so the mere presence of Ukifune at his side might not relieve him of his pain. But in her answer Kozeri reminded him that, after its use, the *nademono* is thrown into the stream—"when hands enough have soiled it." "You will I am sure forgive my pointing out that the allusion was not very happily chosen."[49]

The exchange seems to have little significance at that moment, other than perhaps to show Kozeri's coolness of temperament and Kaoru's slightly overwrought condition. Later, however, this brief conversation comes to take on powerful implications. Ukifune, hearing of the swiftness of the river flowing by her home, decides to drown herself. She has grown close to Kaoru; she feels herself soiled from her contact with Niou. Unwittingly she acts out the poetic exchange between Kaoru and her sister Kozeri. For his part, Kaoru comes to take cognizance of the power of the same image. After her disappearance, Kaoru thinks Ukifune to be dead. He reflects bitterly on the ultimate significance of his attachment to her. "Yes, it was by his doing that she had died, as surely as though he had cast her with his own hands into that hated stream."[50] Such variations on a motif, spaced through-

---

[49] *Ibid.*, p. 972.   [50] *Ibid.*, p. 1060.

out relevant sequences of the narrative, constitute a rhythm of great power.

Whatever the techniques employed by Lady Murasaki in constructing her novel, she invariably applies them with a graceful deftness. The reader seldom feels himself manipulated; rather, he finds himself exploring with ever greater wonder a world the author has prepared for him to enter. Arthur Waley, in his Introduction to Book II of his translation of *Genji*, characterizes the virtues of Lady Murasaki's style as "elegance, symmetry, and restraint," an apt description that helps suggest in turn the discretion with which she has assembled her literary materials. Ragged ends, the structures underneath, are almost never visible, certainly not in Waley's recreation, in any case.

A close analysis of *The Tale of Genji* will yield many details of structure that will give ever greater pleasure to a careful reader. In the end, however, the chief profit to be gained from the novel doubtless lies in the experience of reading, rereading, and contemplating the psychological portraits Lady Murasaki has created. Her evocative sense of the mysteries of time and of its relationship to a growth toward self-identity are firmly and happily rooted in her depiction of dozens of personages, delineated with a simply extraordinary finesse, each with the profundity of a unique psychological world made comprehensible to the reader. The portraits are rendered so credible that the vast differences between the characters' social and even philosophical outlook and our own quickly recede. We are left with a powerful underlying image of the realities of life, in all its possibilities, disappointments, and, certainly, its tragedies. One might speculate at length on the fact that no major character in the novel obtains what he or she desires. Genji achieves no high position, nor fathers any children whom he can fully admire. Murasaki, worse still, can give birth to no children at all, thus failing in her most important function to him. The failures of Kaoru and Niou have been remarked on above. Yugao dies as a young woman. Tamakatsura falls victim to an unhappy marriage, Kashiwagi dies after the illicit relationship that destroys him and Princess Nyosan. Agemaki, Kozeri, and Ukifune all suffer terribly as their own temperaments, personalities, and in-adequacies are placed at the mercy of Karou and Niou. The list is endless.

Lady Murasaki goes on to suggest, however, levels of un-derstanding beyond these individual tragedies. She dwells rather on the possibility of freeing the personality, through the cultivation of a sensibility able to accept and transcend in-dividual pain. In this respect, *The Tale of Genji* is both the oldest Japanese novel and the newest. Most of the themes, techniques, and insights found in the novels and stories dis-cussed elsewhere in this study can be found somewhere in this vast novel. And, however much we understand and enjoy those other works, we are always surprised and delighted to return to *The Tale of Genji* again and to find it, the more we come to know of the Japanese literary heritage, all the more evocative, all the more profound. Nothing prepares us for a masterpiece.

XII

Tradition and Contemporary Consciousness:
Ibuse, Endō, Kaiko, Abe

KAWABATA YASUNARI, in a lecture given in 1969, shortly after he was awarded the Nobel Prize for Literature, gave voice to his concerns over the future development of Japanese literature:

> I write primarily novels, but I wonder whether the novel is still the most suitable art form or literary form for the present age, and I also wonder whether the age of the novel might not be coming to an end, or even the age of literature itself might not be vanishing. . . . In Japan, almost a century after the importation of Western literature, nothing has reached the heights of the Japanese type of literary achievement represented by Murasaki Shikibu of the Heian period, or of Bashō of the Tokugawa period; literature is probably declining and weakening.[1]

Kawabata seemed particularly fearful concerning the effect of imported literary ideals and techniques on the native tradition; for him such writers as Sōseki and Ōgai (who seem the most obvious candidates for the category of writers he mentions below) were forced to abandon too much:

> Even after the beginning of the Meiji period in 1868, great men of letters appeared together with the rise of the modern Japanese nation, but they had to spend their youthful time and energy in the study and introduction of Western literature. Many of them had to engage in the task of enlightening their countrymen during most of their lives and were unable to reach maturity in their own creation grounded in the Japanese and Oriental traditions. Thus I tend to think they were victims of their age.[2]

[1] Kawabata Yasunari, *The Existence and Discovery of Beauty*, tr. by V. H. Viglielmo, bilingual edition (Tokyo, 1969), p. 42.
[2] *Ibid.*, pp. 43-44.

Kawabata goes to considerable lengths to define what for him constitutes that native sensibility and the beauty that it can produce. Such beauty, for Kawabata, springs from the particular yet suggests the infinite. In such a tradition, the jux-taposition of specific images grounded in a close observation of nature serves to suggest a larger, transcendental concern. Kawabata himself used that technique in his own work, as any reader of *Snow Country* or *The Sound of the Mountain* will be aware. In such novels, these traditional poetic techniques serve as central a purpose in the narrative construction as in the poetry of Issa or Bashō.

Shortly after delivering his warning, Kawabata died, and indeed the two other major contemporary writers of interna-tional recognition whose work paid greatest heed to the Japanese past—Tanizaki Junichirō and Mishima Yukio—vanished from the scene as well. Some critics, both in Japan and in the West, have gone so far as to suggest that, in terms of narrative fiction at least, the Japanese literary past may be dead.

Certainly, new developments in postwar Japanese literature are easy enough to find. The thematic focus has changed. The contemporary world of Japan is far more cosmopolitan, and far more intellectually troubled, than at any time previously. Dazai Osamu, the first important novelist to chronicle that change, takes up the same concept of "victims" chosen by Kawabata. Dazai manifests all the malaise felt by postwar Japanese intellectuals in that telling passage from *The Setting Sun*: "Victims. Victims of a transitional period of morality. That is what we . . . certainly are."

Kawabata and Dazai share the use of the term, yet Dazai does more than catch the atmosphere and define his position. He posits hope as well. Self-awareness of the status of a vic-tim can bring with it a desire to escape that status and begin a search for values. Such a search did, in fact, begin early in the postwar period and still continues today. Kawabata and Dazai have passed on their burden to other writers who have since continued to face up to their own pain of awareness and to find their own methods to escape from the philosophical pov-erty and political hypocrisy they have seen all around them.

In this sense, at least, much of the more ambitious postwar fiction written in Japan is thoroughly contemporary in spirit.

Of the writers available in English translations to those Western readers who wish to examine the range of such literary accomplishment, I have chosen four works by four men who speak most directly to these concerns.[3] All sense the status of the victim; all search for a means of escape. These four novels have all been written within the past ten years. The shifts in thematic concerns and the changes in methods of narrative technique developed to deal with this contemporary world will be immediately obvious. Yet some persistent similarities with older traditions will emerge as well.

IBUSE MASUJI

The novel *Kuroi Ame* (Black Rain) was written in 1966 by the highly respected author Ibuse Masuji (born 1898). Ibuse is roughly the contemporary of Kawabata. It might be expected that, for a man whose tastes and attitudes were formed in the earlier part of this century, his literary style and philosophical outlook would remain somewhat more traditional than those of younger authors. Such, in certain ways at least, is the case; yet Ibuse was among the first major writers to face up to the meaning of the word "victim," in the largest sense, for in *Black Rain*, he was able to treat the horrors of atomic war— the bombing of Hiroshima—in an artistic way.[4] For such

---

[3] There are other writers who might be considered, in particular Ōe Kenzaburō (born 1935) and Takeda Taijun (born 1912). Translations of their most representative works are not, as of this writing readily available, however.

[4] Ibuse was born in Hiroshima, and one might speculate on the relationship of this fact to his ability to examine the question of the bombing of that city in human rather than in purely political terms. Works written from the latter point of view, and with a predictably anti-American bias, of course abound. Tanaka Chikao (born 1905), the distinguished modern playwright, was born in Nagasaki, and his 1959 play *Maria no kubi* (The Head of the Madonna) is similarly a compassionate and humane account of the holocaust there. (For details of the play see my article on Tanaka in the summer 1976 issue of *Monumenta Nipponica*.) In both cases, evidently, the childhood experiences of these writers in their respective cities allowed them to compose their works from a personal, and indeed a poetic, point of view.

purposes, he required a certain objectivity toward his theme. This he provided by giving himself a period of twenty years before composing the novel. That perspective permitted Ibuse to write what seems incontestably his masterpiece.

The story of the novel concerns a white-collar worker named Shizuma Shigematsu and his niece Yasuko. The narrative is constructed from several elements. The basic layer consists of a straightforward third-person account portraying certain events that take place some time after the war. Interspersed with this text are extracts from diaries kept by both Shigematsu and Yasuko at the time of the bombing in August 1945. The title of the novel is explained by the following reference in Yasuko's war diary:

> I wasn't aware until Uncle Shigematsu told me that my skin looked as though it had been splashed with mud. My white short-sleeved blouse was soiled in the same way, and the fabric was damaged at the soiled spots. When I looked in the mirror, I found that I was spotted all over with the same color except where I have been covered by my air-raid hood. I was looking at my face in the mirror, when I suddenly remembered a shower of black rain that must have fallen about 10 a.m. Thundery black clouds had borne down on us from the direction of the city, and the rain from them had fallen in streaks the thickness of a fountain pen. It had stopped almost immediately. It was cold, cold enough to make one shiver, even in midsummer. . . . I washed my hands at the ornamental spring, but even rubbing the marks with soap wouldn't get them off. They were stuck fast on the skin. It was most odd. . . .[5]

Yasuko has been marked, literally as well as psychologically, by the holocaust. When a prospective husband is found for her, the young man's family requests assurances that she has no defects in health because of the bombing. Father and niece alike realize that such assurances cannot truthfully be given.

Yasuko's experience of the black rain is juxtaposed against

[5] Ibuse Masuji, *Black Rain*, tr. by John Bester (Tokyo and Palo Alto, 1969), pp. 34-35.

many greater horrors suffered in the city. In particular, Shigematsu's diary presents the reader with overwhelming scenes of destruction, often based on the author's interviews with survivors. Ibuse balances these accounts to show the dignity, good humor, and resilience in the behavior of those ordinary citizens who remain, for him, the ultimate victims. Nothing in their culture can withstand this final frightening onslaught of the West, here shown in its most powerful symbolic presence, the atomic bomb. Ibuse uses indirect means to chronicle the effect of this force. One particularly telling scene shows Shigematsu and his family, on their way out of the burning city, as they stop at the gate of a friend's home. The explosion has destroyed it:

> It had been an imposing mansion, with a splendid old-style garden. Now, however, it was completely razed to the ground. Where the main building and clay-walled storehouse had once stood was an arid waste scattered with broken tiles. The stone on which Yasuko was sitting was almost certainly a rock from the garden inside the grounds. Rock though it was, a thin layer had been burned away all over it.
>
> "That rock's granite, you know," I said. "I expect it was covered with moss only this morning." It was a scene of cruel desolation. Where the ornamental pond had been was an uneven stretch of blackish mud, and at the foot of a rounded hillock of earth lay the blackened skeletons of three large pine trees. Beside the trunk of the thickest of the three stood a narrow, square pillar of stone. Why it alone should have remained standing was a mystery. The owner had once told me that an ancestor of his, several generations back, had had it erected there. It was somewhat over ten feet tall, and instead of the usual long description it had the single character "Dream" carved on it, about two and a half feet from the top. Some high-ranking priest was said to have written the original, and the effect was doubtless considered stylish and rather sophisticated in its day, but at present, style and sophistication alike failed utterly.[6]

[6] *Ibid.*, p. 103.

Here, the past is the victim. For Shigematsu, alive at this moment of horror, the present seems incapable of holding any meaning. He wanders aimlessly around, helping to search for missing persons. He reads the Buddhist memorial services for the dead. In the midst of these random experiences, he gradually comes to realize that the ordinary citizens of Hiroshima have the ability to live on. In the simplicity of their modest concerns, he finds not only comfort but hope:

> The balustrade of every bridge I crossed bore messages written on pieces of paper stuck on the stone, or scrawled on the bridge with charcoal. The number was astonishing. Some of the pieces of paper were fluttering in the breeze. Large numbers of people were scanning them, like the crowd that gathers before the bulletin board outside a newspaper office. Very occasionally, someone would stop, write something, and go off again in a great hurry. The messages were all simple in the extreme, yet they seemed to convey something of the circumstances of the people who had written them. I jotted down a few of the sentences from pieces of paper on the balustrade of the Motokawa Bridge:

> To Kōnosuke: Come to your Aunt's home at Gion—Father.
> Father and Mother: Let me know where you are now—Mayumi, c/o Mr. Abe, Sakurao, Hatsukaichi.
> Papa: The boy is worrying where you are—Hasue, c/o Yaichi Sehara, Midorii.
> Worried about members of the class. Will come here every day at ten—Taizō Ogawa, Class IIA, Industrial High School.
> Grandfather, Grandmother, and Emiko missing. To Shōji and Natsuyo: Come to Mr. Tokurō Ida's in Ōkawa-chō—Yasuoka.
> To Mr. Ikuo Nishiguchi of Kamiya-chō: Please leave your present address and I will return the debt. Thank you. From your acquaintance in Nakahiro-chō.
> To Yaeko: Stop in at Mihara on your way back to Fuchū—from your Father.[7]

---

[7] *Ibid.*, pp. 189-190.

The existence of such unaffected human sympathy gives Shigematsu the courage to continue himself. He does all he can to develop the same sense of courage in his niece. The climax of the central narrative comes when Yasuko falls ill from radiation sickness. Shigematsu and his family can no longer escape the status of victims. He now must find a new kind of courage, another hope. He receives an essential clue when reading the diary of one who actually survived such a sickness. According to that testimony, only the will-power to go on living can effect a cure. Reading the document, Shigematsu is forced to realize that his niece will doubtless be incapable of summoning such will power. Yet he becomes convinced that his culture can survive. A memory reminds him of the possibilities of renewal. He recalls the moment when he listened to the broadcast of the Emperor's message of surrender:

The broadcast had begun, but all I could hear from the courtyard was fragments of speech in a low voice. I made no effort to follow the sense, but walked up and down by the canal, occasionally stopping and standing still for a moment. The canal had solid stone banks about six feet deep, and the bed was flat and paved all over with stones. The water was shallow, but absolutely clear, and the effect was immensely refreshing.

How had I never realized that there was such an attractive stream so near at hand? In the water, I could see a procession of baby eels swimming blithely upstream against the current. It was remarkable to watch them: a myriad of tiny eels, still at the larval stage, none of them more than three or four inches in length.

"On you go, on up the stream!" I said to them encouragingly. "You can smell fresh water, I'll be bound!" Still they came on unendingly, battling their way upstream in countless numbers. They must have swum all the way up from the lower reaches of the river at Hiroshima. Newborn eels usually swim into the rivers from the sea in mid-May. Within the first mile from the estuary they are still flat and transparent, like willow leaves, and the fishermen of the bays around Hiroshima call them "sardine eels," because of their likeness to sardine fry. By the time they reached here, though, they looked like real eels, about as big as a large loach but far slenderer and more graceful in their movements. I wondered where they had been swimming on August 6, when Hiroshima had been bombed. I squatted down by the edge of the canal and compared their backs, but all I saw was different shades of gray. None of them showed any signs of harm.[8]

The tiny eels, like the simple citizens of Hiroshima, move in consonance with the processes of nature. Both are free, saved by their unassuming and unspoken dignity. They have the will to survive. Shigematsu's sudden flash of insight makes him aware in turn that he too still possesses his Japanese sensibility. For Ibuse (and for Kawabata like him), such a sensibility posits an intimate relationship to nature and to her movements. Closeness to the natural flow of life will heal, restore. For Ibuse, to escape the status of a victim requires the cultivation of that sensibility, as a means to recover human dignity.

ENDŌ SHŪSAKU

The remaining three writers discussed below are equally concerned with this Japanese sensibility and of the shocks it has received. Endō Shūsaku (born 1923) has painstakingly examined the tradtitional Japanese sensibility and its limitations. The perhaps too-often discussed "conflict of East and West" that began in Japan in the nineteenth century, and to which the atomic bomb made the most horrendous of contributions, finds a strong reflection in Endō's personal life. He was brought up a Catholic, an Easterner with a Western faith. Such a dual heritage troubles him:

> I received baptism when I was a child . . . in other words, my Catholicism was a kind of ready-made suit . . . I had to decide either to make this ready-made suit fit my body or get rid of it and find another suit that fitted. . . . There were

[8] *Ibid.*, pp. 296-297.

many times when I felt I wanted to get rid of my Catholi-
cism, but I was finally unable to do so. It is not just that I
did not throw it off, but that I was unable to throw it off.
The reason for this must be that it had become a part of me
after all. The fact that it had penetrated me so deeply in my
youth was a sign, I thought, that it had, in part at least, become coextensive with me. Still, there was always that feeling in my heart that it was something borrowed, and I
began to wonder what my real self was like. This I think is
the "mud swamp" Japanese in me. From the time I first
began to write novels even to the present day, this confrontation of my Catholic self with the self that lies underneath
has, like an idiot's constant refrain, echoed and reechoed in
my work. I felt that I had to find some way to reconcile the
two.[9]

Endō's personal world is a complex one in every way. He
has travelled widely, including a period of study in France,
about which he has written with eloquence and a certain acer-
bity. The confrontation he feels between these two ways of
life and thought have naturally found their way into his fiction, notably in *Chinmoku* (Silence), written, like Ibuse's *Black
Rain*, in 1966.[10] In *Silence*, Endō sets up an aesthetic distance
from his material not of twenty but of over three hundred
years, in order to observe the first clashes of sensibility between East and West. The sources for his novel, like Ibuse's,
are largely factual: he examines the lives of several Portuguese
Catholic priests who continued to serve as missionaries to
Japan after the promulgation of the edicts banning the Christian faith early in the seventeenth century. The protagonist of
the novel is an amalgam of several of these men, to whom
Endō gives the name Sebastian Rodrigues; he comes to Japan
to work with the secret Christians, mostly poor farmers and
fishermen. In the course of his adventures, Rodrigues meets

[9] See Endō Shūsaku, *Silence*, tr. by William Johnson (Rutland and Tokyo,
1969), pp. 12-13.
[10] In the same year, Endō wrote a play entitled *Ogon no kuni* (The Golden
Country), a variation on the story told in *Silence*. The play was a considerable
success in its Tokyo production and was subsequently translated into English
by Francis Mathy.

others who assume a powerful role in guiding his own unhappy pilgrimage toward self understanding: Inouye, a kind
of Grand Inquisitor appointed by the government to ferret
out and punish the secret Christians; Ferreira, an apostatized
priest who now works for the Japanese anti-Christian authorities; and Kichijirō, a Japanese Christian who, weak and
frightened, apostatizes, takes up his faith again, then gives it
up a second time in a perpetual circle of hesitation and doubt.

Rodrigues, the protagonist, is portrayed in considerable
roundness and depth. In this instance Endō shows a most unusual ability in creating a non-Japanese character who is both
credible in psychology and understandable in motivation.
The novel is at least partially intended as an examination of
the spiritual changes that come over the Western sensibility of
Rodrigues in the "mudswamp of Japan." Early in his stay, he
is hidden in a hut in a remote and mountainous area in order
to avoid capture by the government authorities. This en-
forced leisure gives him time to write back to his colleagues in
Europe, and in one of those letters he first poses the problem
of the "silence of God" to which the title of the novel refers:

> . . . even as I write these words I feel the oppressive
> weight in my heart of those last stammering words of
> Kichijiro on the morning of his departure: "Why has Deus
> Sama imposed this suffering on us?" And then the resent-
> ment in those eyes that he turned upon me. "Father," he
> had said, "what evil have we done?"
>
> I suppose I should simply cast from my mind these
> meaningless words of the coward; yet why does his plain-
> tive voice pierce my breast with all the pain of a sharp nee-
> dle? Why has Our Lord imposed this torture and this perse-
> cution on poor Japanese peasants? No, Kichijiro was trying
> to express something different, something even more
> sickening. The silence of God. Already twenty years have
> passed since the persecution broke out; the black soil of
> Japan has been filled with the lament of so many Christians;
> the red blood of priests has flowed profusely; the walls of
> the churches have fallen down; and in the face of this terri-

ble and merciless sacrifice offered up to Him, God has remained silent. This was the problem that lay behind the
plaintive question of Kichijiro.[11]

Rodrigues has begun dimly to perceive the implications of
the fact that his religion and his culture are bound up together
and that, further, his own religious sensibilities can bring only
destruction to those whom he is bound in good conscience to
love. Later, after he leaves his place of hiding, Rodrigues
undergoes his own "Temptation in the Wilderness." In this
most poetic section of the novel, he travels to a remote and
beautiful mountain area. There he suddenly encounters his
own personal Satan in the person of Kichijiro, who, after asking his help, betrays him to the authorities.

Arrested by the police, Rodrigues is finally forced to understand the harm he and his faith have brought to Japan. Inouye, the government official, tells him in an interview that
"Christianity is of no use for Japan." Soon after, Rodrigues
receives another harrowing testimony to the fact. He is led to
watch a group of priests and peasants who are to be put to
death by drowning. Rodrigues has been assigned an interpreter, who is to explain to him the significance of the scene
he is forced to watch. The interpreter, frightened and en-
raged, finally bursts out as follows:

> "This is a horrible business. No matter how many times
> one sees it, it's horrible," said the interpreter getting up
> from his stool. Then suddenly reeling on the priest with
> hatred in his eyes he said: "Father, have you thought of the
> suffering you have inflicted on so many peasants just be-
> cause of your dream, just because you want to impose your
> selfish dream upon Japan. Look! Blood is flowing again.
> The blood of those ignorant people is flowing again."[12]

Rodrigues finally learns that he will be expected to re-
nounce his faith. He must apostatize by putting his foot on a
painted picture of Christ as a final proof that he has abandoned his religion. Ferreira, the former priest, provides him
with the logic to succumb to this final temptation:

[11] *Silence*, p. 97.   [12] *Ibid.*, pp. 217-218.

"My weakness?" Rodrigues shook his head; yet he had no self-confidence. "What do you mean? It's because I believe in the salvation of these people. . . ."

"You make yourself more important than them. You are preoccupied with your own salvation. If you say that you will apostatize, these people will be taken out of the pit. They will be saved from suffering. And you refuse to do so. It's because you dread to betray the Church. You dread to be the dregs of the Church, like me." Until now Ferreira's words had burst out as a single breath of anger, but now his voice gradually weakened as he said: "Yet I was the same as you. On that cold, black night I, too, was as you are now. And yet is your way of acting love? A priest ought to live in imitation of Christ. If Christ were here.
. . ."

For a moment Ferreira remained silent; then he suddenly broke out in a strong voice: "Certainly Christ would have apostatized for them."[13]

Rodrigues is being asked to give up his Western sensibilities, his own sense of identity, as much as he is his Christian faith. Stress on the importance of the self, on abstract concepts, on personal salvation, places the Western mentality at considerable odds with the Japanese sensibility, which emphasizes intuitive understanding and the processes of nature. Like Ibuse, Endō finds a flexibility in his own tradition that serves to protect and permit survival; and in this particular novel, at least, he poses his concerns over the possible meeting of the two traditions in a negative configuration. The message is the same: those who abandon their Japanese sensibility (in this case, for Christianity) will become the victims. Endō, like his character the interpreter, finds the imposition of the Western ego on the Japanese the most dangerous gift of all.

KAIKO TAKESHI

The remaining two novels deal with the world of contemporary Japan directly, sketching the atmosphere of what has

[13] *Ibid.*, p. 268.

been termed "Japan, Inc.," a society in which the values of the marketplace have come to reign supreme. The creation of a greatly increased material prosperity has led, in the eyes of many Japanese intellectuals, to a vacuum in which no moral or spiritual fulfillment seems possible. A similar problem has been diagnosed in virtually every advanced country in the world, but many Japanese insist the hedonism resulting from this prosperity has been particularly destructive to traditional values of financial and indeed emotional frugality and restraint. All larger purposes, personal or national, seem to disappear. Mishima Yukio called the postwar period an "age of languid peace," and he found in its atmosphere the ultimate corruption of Japanese civilization:

> Although it is true that we are living in a period of languid peace, we do not have an appropriate ideology or philosophy of life that enables us to live with a sense of spiritual satisfaction. People in this country do not know how to live in an age of peace: their lives seem to be floating along without direction.
>
> A hint at the reason for this can be gleaned from Arnold Toynbee's book *Hellenism* in which the author points out that the Hellenistic Greeks lived in an age of languid peace and eventually succumbed to ennui. He cites the early Christians who were, by contrast, constantly oppressed and exposed to danger of life and limb. He concludes that because they lived under such perilous conditions they gained a treasure which many never come to possess: the vitality one gains from living in danger.[14]

Mishima turned for his answer to the politics of the right, a move found distasteful to a majority of his contemporaries, but, however unsatisfactory his answer may have seemed to them, his grasp of the problem seems evident. And the problem he poses is the same that troubles Dazai, Ibuse, and Endō: how can one avoid living as a victim of these circumstances?

One examination of the nature of these circumstances that includes as well the hint of a possible answer lies in the 1972

[14] See Mishima Yukio, "An Ideology for an Age of Languid Peace," in *The Japan Interpreter*, Vol. 7, #1, Winter 1971, p. 79.

novel *Natsu no yami* (Darkness in Summer) written by the highly acclaimed young novelist Kaiko Takeshi (born 1930). *Darkness in Summer* is a thoroughly contemporary book. Kaiko's narrative focuses on two characters, the progatonist and his mistress, and he follows their Genet-like search for salvation through sin. Kaiko's methods, however, are his own and the novel is both original and quite powerful.

Kaiko's objective distance from the contemporary scene is established not in terms of time, as in the case of Endō and Ibuse, but in terms of distance, psychological and actual. The author has created the two highly alienated characters and placed them in Europe. They wish literally to get as far away as they can from their heritage. In fact, the protagonist, as he comes to know the girl better, is astounded to discover that she is even more alienated than he:

> . . . she ranted at Japan and the Japanese in relation to everything she could think of.
>
> Behind the venemous, cutting edge of these imprecations, there was an unmistakable air of loneliness. As I listened, I could finally guess, though vaguely, what had sustained her through these past ten years, about which I knew nothing. The girl who could not live in Japan . . . and yet who was too proud to surrender and had therefore established herself as an exile, probably had no other choice but to live as an orphan here too. She must have lived on the strength she drew from her hatred of Japan and the Japanese. She must have survived the annihilating early mornings and the frightful but intimate evenings, exuding hatred, the way a shell exudes slime. Working as an interpreter for a touring group, or a dishwasher at a restaurant, or a cigarette girl in a cabaret, or a typist at a Japanese commercial firm, she had eked out a living. The hatred that burst open and poured out so breathlessly was a result of the hands that had almost dissolved in detergent, the stereotyped routine comments that had almost frozen her lips, the thick fog of smoke that had nearly constricted her throat, and the rough walls of the desolate toilet. It must also have risen from the leftover meals consisting of fat

meat covered with crushed cigarette stubs or fish that had become completely cold. The slimy simpering wet eyes in the darkness, the gigantic worm-like white fingers taking out a wallet, the thick lips glistening with saliva, and the roar of cymbals filled with hollow passion—while all these things beat against her and almost broke her, she somehow tenaciously withstood them all and lived on in the garret, cultivating her hate.[15]

These are people trying to escape their natural sensibilities. At the beginning of the novel, the strongest emotion expressed by both is one of self-disgust. The protagonist, who had been a newspaper reporter in Vietnam, prior to the beginning of the narrative, learned there that he was unable to face reality altogether. Thereafter he preferred to lose himself in a personal oblivion, so as to try to conceal his own bad faith from himself. He had come to an awareness of this weakness in himself during a visit to an Indochinese opium den:

> . . . in the beginning I hesitated, ashamed of my fat body, but as I watched the boy in the dim lamplight preparing the pipe with a thoroughly professional yet somehow sweet gesture, I ceased to worry. The texture of the long bamboo pipes from Laos, on which bits of ivory were inlaid, the boy's flat nose floating in the scanty light, his lively, mischievous eyes, and his placid, expert sluggishness seduced me into a warm reassurance, and the useless soul-searching, which until then had been such a burden, mattered no longer. Gradually, languidly, I merged into the darkness, into the gurgling sounds that were both active and unobtrusive, the darkness filled with snoring and sighs, hesitant yet uncontrollable deep exhalations, the sound of grinding teeth, the salty smell of perspiration, the sour-sweet smell of infected feet, and the peculiar scent of opium. I lost my hands, my abdomen, my shape.[16]

He becomes a victim to his own weakness as well as to the

[15] Kaiko Takeshi, *Darkness in Summer*, tr. by Cecilia Segawa Seigle (New York, 1973), pp. 118-119.
[16] *Ibid.*, p. 100.

weakness of his times; nothing around him seems to contain sufficient meaning. He can only scoff. At one point, the girl asks the protagonist about his contemporaries, home in Japan. To him, they seem no better off:

> "Well . . . the ones who stayed at university are assistant professors by now, and those who succeeded to their fathers' businesses are presidents. At the news service, they are desk head or deputy department chief. They have all grown fat or bald, and their faces are so completely changed that I can't tell them apart. If they get together, they talk about sickness or golf. Diabetes and blood pressure are popular topics. If you start to talk about illness, they come alive. Another subject to talk about is During the War, when they were children and ate horse fodder like pressed beans and weeds—that's another good conversational gambit. You can talk about it for hours on end. If they are forbidden to talk about sickness and pressed beans, it's as good as tying their hands behind their backs and throwing them into a river. Pressed beans are a particularly good subject. You can really be carried away by it.[17]

There seems no way out of the swamp.

Kaiko now introduces some movement in this moral stagnation. The pair go off on a fishing trip to the mountains, presumably in Austria. During the trip, the protagonist for the first time loses his agonizing sense of self and his distrust with that self:

> After I wound the reel three or four times and bent the pole in a curve, the line tensed momentarily. An electric shock ran through the pole to my hand, from my hand to my entire body. I jerked suddenly, and the hook probably pierced the fish's lip and bit into the bone. The line began to cut the water and skimmed to the left and right.
> "It's hooked, hooked, hooked!" I shouted.
> "Really!" she cried, half incredulous, and stood up, letting go of the oars. The boat swayed sluggishly. We came

---

[17] *Ibid.*, pp. 196–197.

back to life. I was revitalized in a second. Instantly my body ceased to dissolve and once again became a tangible entity. All my flesh became firm, I resumed my outward shape, and was dazzled. Sensations pulsed through me, and my body responded with joy. Ruthlessness, irritation, and malice disappeared. I could look at her, not out of the corner of my eyes, but face to face.[18]

Like Ibuse, Kaiko finds in a renewed contact with nature the means by which a genuine sensibility can be regained. Later, after making love, the protagonist finds a moment of perfect peace and tranquillity, the one instant of transcendental repose in the novel:

I was replete, free of all complexity and self-disgust. Thoughts could not possibly take shape unless my consciousness was in ferment. No thought, no writing, no words could sprout. My tongue and my fingers did not indulge in their usual tricks. I was as pure and modest as an animal. Cattle were roaming in the meadow and a bell was ringing. I am the cattle, the bell, and the sky.[19]

This sense of repose gained, even if only momentarily, sets him to choosing a new course of action. The protagonist leaves the girl to return to Vietnam to search out the meaning of reality there, even though, as he confesses, "it is not his war." Still, he insists, second-hand reality is better than none. The novel ends with the sound of trains, empty of passengers, running back and forth between East and West Berlin. Whether the ultimate meaning of the protagonist's quest is similarly empty remains a possibility concerning which the author makes no direct comment; but Kaiko does make clear that, having glimpsed even for an instant the real nature of his own sensibility, the protagonist has escaped his status as victim.

ABE KŌBŌ

The newest of the novels that speaks to the theme of victim is *Hako otoko* (The Box Man) written in 1973 by Abe Kōbō

[18] *Ibid.*, pp. 139-140.   [19] *Ibid.*, p. 146.

(born in 1924). Abe has always been a fashionable writer. His early work, especially in the theater, shows the powerful influence of Marxism, so important in the Japanese intellectual scene during the early postwar years. With the composition of his novel *Suna no onna* (Woman in the Dunes) in 1962, Abe confirmed his interest in portraying a Kafkaesque world that stresses the qualities of irrationality, surrealism, and the unknowing in contemporary life. His writing is the most conspicuously "avant-garde," at least in the popular sense of that term, in Japan today.

Abe Kōbō's victims resemble Kaiko's in their complete alienation and despair. Like Kaiko's victims too, they retreat, but in a different direction. Rather than disappearing from Japan, they disappear into themselves. They literally abandon society and live in boxes. This retreat provides Abe his own necessary aesthetic distance from his subject matter. The opening paragraph of the book quickly suggests the paradoxes that will follow:

MY CASE

This is the record of a box man.

I am beginning this account in a box. A cardboard box that reaches just to my hips when I put it over my head. That is to say, at this juncture the box man is me. A box man, in his box, is recording the chronicle of a box man.[20]

Abe follows this with a set of instructions.

INSTRUCTIONS FOR MAKING A BOX

Materials:

1 empty box of corrugated cardboard
vinyl sheet (semitransparent)—20 inches square
rubber tape (water resistant)—about 8 yards
wire—about two yards
small pointed knife (a tool)
(to have on hand, if necessary: 3 pieces of worn canvas and one pair of work boots in addition to regular work clothes for streetwear.)
Any empty box a yard long by a yard wide and about four feet deep will do . . .[21]

---

[20] Abe Kōbō, *The Box Man*, tr. by Dale Saunders (New York, 1975), p. 3.
[21] *Ibid*.

The narrative then chronicles the withdrawals from society of Boxmen A, B, C, and D, often in an atmosphere of purposeful confusion. The idea of withdrawal from society, despite its current fashionableness as a subject, is actually a familiar theme in Japanese culture and literature, as earlier discussions of *The Tale of Genji* and *The Tale of the Heike* make clear. Indeed, even the concept of a portable house has a distinguished pedigree, as the following paragraph from the medieval diary "An Account of My Hut," written about 1212 by Kamo no Chōmei, will indicate:

> Before I was aware, I had become heavy with years, and with each remove my dwelling became smaller. The present hut is of no ordinary appearance. It is a bare ten feet square and less than seven feet high. I did not choose this particular spot rather than another, and I built my house without consulting any diviners. I laid a foundation and roughly thatched a roof. I fastened hinges to the joints of the beams, the easier to move elsewhere should anything displease me. What difficulty would there be in changing my dwelling? A bare two carts would suffice to carry off the whole house, and except for the carter's fee there would be no expenses at all.[22]

Even the little poem written by the Box Man:

> From the human chrysalis that is the box man,
>   Even I know not
>   What kind of living being will issue forth.[23]

resembles many a medieval poem on rebirth and transcendence.

Abe, like Kaiko, shows his victim to have an extremely negative image of himself; aware of his status as a victim, he is ashamed as well of his desire to escape that fate. The box man has one vivid childhood memory of an attempt to escape:

> An unpleasant recollection suddenly occurs to me. It concerns the student entertainment program in primary

[22] Kamo no Chōmei, "An Account of My Hut," in Donald Keene, ed., *Anthology of Japanese Literature* (New York, 1955), p. 206.
[23] *The Box Man*, p. 41.

school. I was generally not popular and was thus assigned a
trifling role, perhaps because no one else wanted it. It was
the part of a horse by the name of Dunce, but for all of that
I remember romping around in the greatest of high spirits.
However, when it came time for me to go on stage, the
short lines I was to deliver at only one point during the play
would not come no matter how hard I tried to get them
out. When I gave up and started to leave the stage, my
classmate who played the role of the horse's owner, in an
excess of anger, gave me a boot in the pants. That made me
no less angry, and I kicked him back, whereupon he fell,
struck his head on the floor, and lost consciousness. I have
no recollection at all of how the play was subsequently dis-
continued. But it was soon after that that I became terribly
nearsighted and squeezed some glasses out of my miserly
parents. Myopia developed because I deliberately used to
read books and magazines with fine print in dark places. *I
just wanted to run away from seeing and being seen.*[24]

The victim realizes quite consciously the degradation of his
position:

The truth was more fragmented, like a picture puzzle
with many pieces missing and filled with flights of imagination. Although I am perhaps not I, was it necessary for me
to go on living and going to the trouble of writing these
notes? I may seem to be repeating, but a box man is an ideal
victim. If I had been the doctor, I should have at once offered a cup of tea. Being a doctor, it would be easy for him
to slip in a drop of poison. Or . . . perhaps . . . had I already
been made to drink the cup of tea? I wondered. Perhaps I
had. It was possible. Certainly there was no proof that I
was still alive.[25]

Abe's literary strategies emphasize wit and satire. He pro-
pounds a situation but offers no solution. In his central
paradox, both those in society and out of it seemed doomed
to remain victims, although for different reasons. *The Box
Man* represents more of an intellectual game than a serious,

---

[24] *Ibid.*, p. 85.   [25] *Ibid.*, p. 111.

speculative work, yet its very facile brilliance suggests the nervous sense of despair felt by the author over the state of the world as he finds it.

The literary styles of these four novels vary widely. Ibuse, with his mixture of diary and narrative, seems closest to the traditional Japanese literary techniques. Endō and Kaiko write in a lucid and objective style effective for their purposes but without any particular linguistic or stylistic innovations. Abe's style is closer to that of Kafka, or Beckett, than to any Japanese model. The Western reader of these works, how-ever, cannot fail to be struck by a certain consonance among them, not only in the shared concern they reveal over the sig-nificance of contemporary life (as was indicated in the previ-ous section) but in the sensibilities of the men who wrote them. Insofar as all four authors partake of an inherited Japanese sensibility, one might further speculate as to whether the long literary tradition created by that sensibility has left any traces in their own work, even though the novels are gen-erally written in an avowedly international style.

By way of example, one might begin the quest for the man-ifestation of such a heritage by citing again Kawabata's re-marks concerning the importance of discovering beauty in the commonplace things of life, that beauty which exists "in the particular circumstances of that which exists naturally in those circumstances." The ability to posit the transcendental beauty that conceals itself in the reality of specific objects has remained a fundamental principle in Japanese aesthetics. Like Bashō, Kawabata found a mystic dignity in the smallest things in creation. So, in their own ways, do the four authors discussed in this chapter. A few citations will serve to indicate the workings of this particular sensibility.

In *Black Rain*, Ibuse's skill in piling up specific observations to suggest a larger emotional state is never better displayed than in the sections of Shigematsu's diary as he tries to escape the city. The following passage is particularly vivid:

> When I got to the near side of the Yokogawa railway bridge, I found over two thousand refugees squatting on the grass embankment below. Almost no one except the

young made any move to cross. The bridge must have been more than a hundred feet up, and a glimpse of the river below was enough to make one's limbs go weak. Even so, it was the only way to get to the other side. The people squatting there, almost all of whom were injured, seemed to be in a state of apathy, without even the will to get across. Some of them simply sat in silence, gazing at one fixed spot in the sky.

Most of them, however, kept their eyes averted from the mushroom cloud. Quite a few of the injured lay sprawled on their backs on the bank. The one exception was a woman who had her arms stretched out toward the cloud and kept screaming in a shrill voice: "Hey, you monster of a cloud! Go away! We're nonbelligerents! D'you hear—go away!" Oddly for one who seemed so lively she made no attempt to cross the bridge.

Suddenly, I could no longer bear waiting about indecisively. I made up my mind: I would cross the bridge. I set off in the wake of a young man who was bleeding from the shoulder, avoiding as far as possible looking at the waters below. About nine-tenths of the way across, passage was blocked by the freight train lying on its side, but after much difficulty I succeeded in getting past by crawling flat on my face. About halfway along the train, where the river below was shallow, I spied a mass of onions that had tipped out and lay in heaps below.[26]

Just at the emotional climax engendered by the addition of these powerful images, Ibuse suddenly creates a *haiku*-like juxtaposition: comparing the humanity spilling over the bridge to a heap of onions. But more than a metaphor is involved. As in a good *haiku*, one image defines the other; one is as significant as the other. Here, both images bespeak disorder, waste. Through such a technique, even the humblest object can, at least reciprocally, take on the greatest significance.

Endō too finds occasion to express his intuitions over the connotative power of objects, even in a narrative committed

---

[26] Ibuse, *Black Rain*, p. 56.

by the nature of his subject matter to a considerable emphasis
on action and psychological development. Here is a paragraph describing the movements of Rodrigues just after his
capture by the Japanese authorities:

> Through the village they went, and then out again into
> the paddy fields. The road went downhill until at last a dry
> breath of salty wind blew into the sunken flesh of the
> priest's cheeks. Below was a harbor—if, indeed, it could be
> called a harbor, for it was no more than a landing-place of
> black pebbles heaped together with two forlorn little boats
> pulled up on the beach. While the guards were pushing
> poles under the boats, the priest picked up the peach-
> colored shells that were lying in the sand and played with
> them in his hands. They were the only beautiful things he
> had seen in this long, long day. Putting one to his ear he
> listened to the faint, muffled roar that issued forth from its
> deepest center. Then quite suddenly a dark shudder shook
> his whole being and in his hand he crushed that shell with
> its muffled roar.
> "Get on board!" came the order.[27]

In the midst of great danger, the priest is suddenly moved
to witness, through a humble object, the enormity of nature.
Such a moment marks a step in his own unwitting *rapproche-
ment* with a culture that will soon bring him to his downfall.
Throughout the novel Rodrigues suffers from the tensions between two ways of being. The psychological pull of
"mudswamp Japan" on him is expressed with great delicacy
through his confrontation with the small and simple shells he
touches here.

Kaiko's tone is ironic, his style nervous. His use of specific
objects in the following passage is planned to produce a
humorous effect. Such principles of juxtaposition, however,
bear a close resemblance to those employed by Ibuse in the
passage cited above. At this particular moment, the protagonist is attempting to go to sleep:

> Drifting on dim, vague, and hazy waves, I try to think

[27] Endō, *Silence*, pp. 155-156.

about the objects on which I have slept for the past forty years: quilts, beds, foam rubber, down, straw, hammocks, chairs, benches at railroad stations, train coaches, meadows, floors of freight cars, baled cargoes, pavements, ridges between rice fields, village roads, behind garbage dumps, on dead leaves in a jungle, on the bellies of women—it has been almost enough to make me dizzy. In spite of the fact I came into intimate contact with almost too many places and too great a variety of objects, I have forgotten most of these things, and those I can remember are pitifully few. Should this not be called ingratitude? How is it that my obliviousness runs so deep?[28]

The reader is plunged from one texture, one shape, one surface, to another. In the case of Ibuse, the ultimate juxtaposition involved the image of the wounded with the image of the onions. In Kaiko's text, the juxtaposition is with the "I" of the narrator. The passage thus becomes a peculiar but telling bit of autobiography. Finally, here is Abe's Box Man, examining the contexts of his own box:

When I first started living in a box, there was a time when I was quite unable to abandon the common idea of convenience and stored away willy-nilly things I didn't even know how to use, not to mention those articles that seemed as if they might come in handy. My baggage was endlessly increased with various items: a tin can on which were embossed three Technicolor nudes holding a golden apple (surely they would serve some purpose), a precious stone (perhaps an ancient implement), a slot-machine ball (it would come in handy for moving heavy things), a Concise English-Japanese dictionary (indispensable sometime, one never knew), a high heel, painted gold (the shape was interesting, and it might be used in place of a hammer), a 125 watt, 6 amp. house socket (it would be a problem if it wasn't around when I needed it), a brass doorknob (attached to a string, that could be a dangerous weapon), a soldering iron (surely useful for something), a key ring

---

[28] Kaiko, *Darkness*, p. 93.

with 5 keys (it was not impossible that sometime in the future I would come on a lock one of them would fit), a cast-iron nut one and five eighths inches in diameter (suspended from a string, it could be a seismograph and would also be handy as a weight when I dried film.) When it got so that I couldn't move for the cramped quarters, I was at last vividly aware of the necessity for throwing them all out.[29]

Like Kaiko, Abe juxtaposes against his list of objects the personality of the man who collected them. The confused and miscellaneous contents of the box serve to define the cluttered mentality of the Box Man. Each object represents nothing noteworthy in itself, yet taken as a whole the list symbolizes all the eclectic waste of contemporary civilization. A few objects suggest a whole world.

Such lists, such juxtapositions, find precedents in the traditions of Japanese literature, from those in *The Pillow Book* of Sei Shōnagon to passages in the comic novels of Ihara Saikaku. Here, from a work by the latter, is a paragraph assembled to produce the same kind of comic effect later sought by Kaiko and Abe:

> This particular day was a special occasion for the people of the neighborhood because the common well was being cleaned. The people living in rented houses on the side lanes participated in this cleaning and kept water on the boil for tea to be served to the workmen. After most of the dirty water had been scooped out, the bottom of the well was scraped and up came a variety of things mixed in with pebbles. A kitchen knife, the disappearance of which had puzzled people, came to light, and so did a bunch of seaweed into which a needle had been thrust. I wonder why that was done. Then, on further search, more things came up including some old pony-design coppers, a naked doll without a face, a one-sided sword-handle peg of crude workmanship, and a patched-over baby's bib. You can never tell just what you will find at the bottom of an uncovered, outside well.[30]

[29] Abe, *The Box Man*, p. 71.
[30] Ihara Saikaku, *Five Women Who Loved Love*, tr. by Wm. Theodore de Bary (Rutland and Tokyo, 1956), pp. 76-77.

Abe and Kaiko both reveal, perhaps unconsciously, their debt to a literary legacy. The debt, it might be further argued, can be defined in terms of an inherited sensibility that naturally manifests itself in similar verbal constructions. All four writers share an innate conviction that reality, in some degree, can be grasped through intuitive awareness of the invisible connection between the specific (no matter how insignificant) and a larger metaphysical truth beyond. Bashō stated the importance of such a dialectical relationship clearly:

> What is important is to keep our mind high in the world of true understanding, and returning to the world of our daily experience to seek therein the truth of beauty. No matter what we may be doing at a given moment, we must not forget that it has a bearing upon our everlasting self which is poetry.[31]

Certain qualities in the writing of Ibuse, Endō, Kaiko, and Abe suggest that the long traditions of Japanese narrative have not been altered altogether. True, most of the classical references, the literary homages to earlier works, have disappeared. But the long history of this created sensibility—aesthetic, aristocratic, mystic—still remains. Even in its newest guise that sensibility continues to exercise a considerable force, and a powerful appeal.

[31] See Matsuo Bashō, *The Narrow Road to the Deep North and Other Travel Sketches*, tr. by Nobuyuki Yuasa (Baltimore, 1966), Introduction, p. 28.

XIII

A Few Final Remarks

WESTERN views of Japanese literature have been greatly
altered since the latter decades of the nineteenth century,
when sudden and intensive contact between the West and
Japan brought about the first examinations of the native muse
by outside observers. At first, many were disappointed by
what they found. Nothing seemed to answer to their rightful
expectations. W. G. Aston, in his 1899 *A History of Japanese
Literature*, the first book in English on the subject, made a
number of judgments on Japanese literature and the Japanese
literary tradition that reflect more about his own sensibilities
and those of his epoch than about the authors and works he
spent so much time and effort in studying. Concerning *The
Tale of Genji*, for example, he wrote as follows:

> Japanese critics claim for the *Genji* that it surpasses any-
> thing of the kind in Chinese literature, and even deserves to
> be ranked with the masterpieces of European fiction.
> None, however, but an extreme Japonophile (the species is
> not altogether unknown) will go so far as to place Murasaki
> no Shikibu on a level with Fielding, Thackeray, Victor
> Hugo, Dumas, and Cervantes. On the other hand, it is un-
> just to dismiss her summarily with the late M. George
> Bousquet as "cette ennuyeuse Scudéry japonaise," a verdict
> endorsed by Mr. Chamberlain.[1]

Many modern readers may be tempted to agree with the
first part of the statement and to reject the second. Aston was,
of course, merely attempting to be honest in representing his
own perceptions. It must be said as well that he continues, de-
fending Lady Murasaki as follows:

> There are in *Genji* pathos, humour, an abundant flow of
> pleasing sentiment, keen observation of men and manners,

[1] W. G. Aston, *A History of Japanese Literature* (reprint edition, Rutland,
Vermont and Tokyo, 1972), pp. 96-97.

an appreciation of the charms of nature, and a supreme
command of the resources of the Japanese language, which
in her hands reached its highest point of excellence.
Though never melodramatic, she gives us plenty of incident, and is seldom dull. A scholar, she abhorred pedantry
and fine writing, the bane of so many of the modern
novelists of Japan.[2]

From a Victorian point of view, the assessment is just; indeed, Lady Murasaki's literary techniques and narrative structures do not resemble at all those of Thackeray, Hugo, and
the others for which Mr. Aston found high esteem. These
principles of narrative structure, and the philosophical differences they suggest, seem to have been the major source of
confusion in his evaluation of the entire Japanese literary tradition.

Our contemporary view of that tradition and its accomplishments certainly finds Japanese fiction far more appealing.
In the first place, more of it is available in English, thanks to
the continuing efforts of so many gifted translators. Secondly,
many Americans, particularly in the postwar years, have visited Japan, and, finding themselves caught up in the energy of
a sophisticated people so different and yet so appealing, have
enjoyed an attempt to grasp the nature of that remarkable culture by means of literary documents. In addition, there is an
ever greater number of general readers who, even without
any direct contact of any kind with Japanese culture, find in
this literature much that is personally compelling. Such an attitude might be expected toward more or less contemporary
Japanese works, created by means of a literary expression
fairly close to that currently employed in the West. Yet contemporary readers find works throughout the history of the
whole tradition (and especially *The Tale of Genji*) to hold
great appeal. Some qualities that pervade the whole history of
that literature are coming to find a response in our vastly different culture.

What is the nature of this appeal? Particular reasons will
remain as various as the tastes of individual readers. One gen-

[2] *Ibid.*, p. 97.

eralization however might be advanced as a tentative hypothesis: our modern perception of the centrality of the unconscious in human emotion, response, and action has given us a new view of man, a view very different from that held by those of Aston's generation. This perception, in turn, permits us to appreciate a literature where such concerns have always played an important role.

Erich Kahler, in describing the development of the modern consciousness in the literature and the art of twentieth-century Europe and America, has insisted upon an important distinction. "The unconscious no longer remained a mere *object* of conscious acts of exploration; it seized upon the artistic *act itself* and emerged as the very *enactor* of artistic creation."[3] Kahler is prepared to admit the importance of the unconscious in modern art but feels impelled to insist that artistic discipline remains vital, even when the unconscious holds the central place in the act of creation. The modern artists he most admires (he specifically mentions Kafka and Picasso in this connection), Kahler concludes, "have given the greatest conscious care to the form of conveying their experiences. Such scrupulous control, the effect of a long-trained meditative sensibility, is apparent in their creations."[4]

Kahler's conception has a certain utility as a means of evaluating the traditions of Japanese literature, for that tradition always recognized the central importance of a "long-trained meditative sensibility." In the Japanese tradition, the unconscious, guided and stimulated by long discipline, comes to apprehend profound realities intuitively and to convey those apprehensions in highly controlled literary forms. Such is the *mono no aware* sought in the *haiku* and *waka* poetry, where complex rules of composition shelter and direct, but do not command, the sensibility of the poet. Similar terms of reference apply to narrative works as well, as this book has hopefully made clear. Bashō's diaries, as was pointed out above on several occasions, provide a prose section that frames each poetic situation, thus preparing the reader for the

[3] Erich Kahler, *The Disintegration of Form in the Arts* (New York, 1968), p. 37.
[4] *Ibid.*, p. 38.

leap into lyrical response. Bashō's techniques can be traced back in some fashion at least as far as *Tales of Ise*, and these strategies of combining lyric and narrative impulses are as important to Sōseki in *Kusamakura* or Kawabata in *Snow Country* as they were to Lady Murasaki. Such a poetically structured narrative that can successfully propel a story like "The River Sumida" shows no affinity with the structures of Dickens or Thackeray. Such a structure does, however, seem closer to certain trends in narrative composition. Consider the statement by Alain Robbe-Grillet that "lifelike, spontaneous, limitless, a story must, in a word, be natural."[5] The evocative quality of the reality conveyed by many Japanese works, traditional and contemporary, shows more sympathy with our contemporary psychology than with the mental worlds inhabited by a Becky Sharp or a Joseph Andrews, however much we admire the work of a Thackeray or a Fielding for other, equally valuable qualities. The intuitive forms of Japanese fiction, always fluid, approximate a world consonant with our own.

[5] Alain Robbe-Grillet, *For a New Novel*, tr. by Richard Howard (New York, 1965), p. 31.

APPENDIX I

As an aid to the reader who may wish to sample one of the earliest examples of the Japanese art of fiction, I include here, with the kind permission of Donald Keene, his new translation of the Taketori monogatari *(The Tale of the Bamboo Cutter), a tale discussed in Chapter IV of the present study.*

Taketori monogatari
(The Tale of the Bamboo Cutter)

Translated by Donald Keene*

Many years ago there lived a man they called the Old Bamboo Cutter. Every day he would make his way into the fields and mountains to gather bamboo, which he fashioned into all manner of wares. His name was Sanuki no Miyakko. One day he noticed among the bamboos a stalk that glowed at the base. He thought this was very strange, and going over to have a look, saw that a light was shining inside the hollow stem. He examined it, and there he found a most lovely little girl about three inches tall. The old man said, "I have discovered you because you were here, among these bamboos I watch over every morning and evening. It must be you are meant to be my child."

He took the little girl in his hands and brought her back home. There he gave the child into the keeping of his old wife, for her to rear. The girl was incomparably beautiful, but still so small they put her in a little basket, the better to care for her.

It often happened afterwards that when the Old Bamboo Cutter gathered bamboo he would find a stalk crammed with gold from joint to joint, and in this way he gradually became very rich.

The child shot up under their loving care. Before three months had passed she stood tall as a grown woman, and her

* Copyright © by Donald Keene

parents decided to celebrate her coming of age. Her hair was combed up and they dressed her in trailing skirts. The greatest pains were lavished on her upbringing—they never even allowed her to leave her curtained chamber. This child had a purity of features quite without equal anywhere in the world, and the house was filled with a light that left no corner dark. If ever the old man felt in poor spirits or was in pain, just to look at the child would make the pain stop. All anger too would melt away.

For a long time afterwards the old man went on gathering bamboo, and he became a person of great importance. Now that the girl had attained her full height, a diviner from Mimuroto, Imbe no Akita by name, was summoned to bestow a woman's name on her. Akita called her Nayotake no Kaguya-hime, the Shining Princess of the Supple Bamboo. The feast given on the occasion of her name-giving was graced by diversions of every kind and lasted three days. Men and women alike were invited and grandly entertained.

The Suitors

Every man in the realm, whether high or low of rank, could think of nothing but of how much he wanted to win Kaguya-hime, or at least to see her. Just to hear the rumors about her made men wild with love. But it was not easy for those who perched on the fence nearby or lurked around her house, or even for those inside, to catch a glimpse of the girl. Unable to sleep peacefully at night, they would go out into the darkness and poke holes in the fence, attempting in this foolish way to get a peep at her. It was from this time that courting a woman came to be known as "nightcrawling."

But all their prowling around the place, where no one showed the least interest in them, was in vain. Even when they made so bold as to address the members of the household, no answer was forthcoming. Many a young noble, refusing to leave the vicinity, spent his nights and days without budging from his post. Suitors of shallower affections decided eventually that this fruitless courtship was a waste of time and ceased their visits.

Five among them, men renowned as connoisseurs of beauty, persisted in their suit. Their attentions never flagged, and they came courting night and day. These were Prince Ishizukuri, Prince Kuramochi, the Minister of the Right Abe no Mimuraji, the Grand Counsellor Ōtomo no Miyuki, and the Middle Counsellor Isonokami no Marotari. Whenever these men heard of any woman who was even moderately good-looking, and the country certainly had many such, they burned to see her; and when they heard about Kaguya-hime they wanted so badly to meet her that they gave up all nourishment and spent their time in brooding. They would go to her house and wander aimlessly about, even though nothing was likely to come of it. They wrote her letters that she did not even deign to answer; they penned odes bewailing their plight. Though they knew it was in vain, they pursued their courtship, undaunted by hindrances, whether the falling snows and the ice of mid-winter or the blazing sun and the thunderbolts of the summer.

One day they called the Bamboo Cutter to them, and each in turn got down on his knees and rubbed his hands, imploring the old man, "Please give me your daughter!"

But the old man replied, "The child was not of my begetting, and she is not obliged to obey my wishes." And so the months and the days went by.

Confronted by this situation, the gentlemen returned to their houses, where, lost in despondent thoughts, they prayed and offered petitions to the gods, either to fulfill their love or else to let them forget Kaguya-hime. But, however they tried, they could not put her from their minds. Despite what the old man had said, they could not believe that he would allow the girl to remain unwedded, and this thought gave them hope.

The old man, observing their ardor, said to Kaguya-hime, "My precious child, I realize you are a divinity in human form, but I have spared no efforts to raise you into such a great, fine lady. Will you not listen to what an old man has to say?"

Kaguya-hime replied, "What request could you make of me to which I would not consent? You say I am a divinity in human form, but I know nothing of that. I think of you and you alone as my father."

"Oh, how happy you make me!" exclaimed the old man. "I am now over seventy, and I do not know if my end may not come today or tomorrow. In this world it is customary for men and women to marry and for their families then to flourish. Why do you refuse to be wedded?"

Kaguya-hime said, "How could I possibly do such a thing?"

The old man replied, "You are a transformed being, it is true, but you have a woman's body. As long as I am alive, you may, if you choose, remain unmarried, but one day you will be left alone. These gentlemen have been coming here faithfully for months and even years. Listen carefully to what they have to say, and choose one of them as your husband."

"All I can think is that I should certainly regret it if, in spite of my unattractive looks, I married a man without being sure of the depth of his feelings, and he later proved fickle. No matter how distinguished a man he may be, I wouldn't be willing to marry him unless I were sure he was sincere," said Kaguya-hime.

"That's exactly what I myself think," answered the old man. "Now, what must a man's feelings be before you are willing to marry him? All these gentlemen have certainly shown unusual devotion."

Kaguya-hime said, "Shall I tell you the depth of sentiments I require? I am not asking for anything extraordinary. All five men seem to be equally affectionate. How can I tell which of them is the most deserving? If one of the five will show me some special thing I wish to see, I will know his affections are the noblest, and I shall become his wife. Please tell this to the gentlemen if they come again."

"An excellent solution," the old man said approvingly.

Towards sunset the suitors gathered as usual. One played a flute, another sang a song, the third sang from score, and the others whistled and beat time with their fans. The old man appeared while this concert was still in progress. He said, "Your visits during all these months and years have done my humble house too great an honor. I am quite overwhelmed. I have told Kaguya-hime that my life is now so uncertain I do not know whether today or tomorrow may not be my last day, and I have suggested to her that she consider carefully and choose one of you gentlemen as her husband. She insists, however, on being sure of the depth of your feelings, and that is only proper. She says she will marry whichever of you proves his superiority by showing her some special thing she wishes to see. This is a fine plan, for none of you will then resent her choice." The five men all agreed that it was indeed an excellent suggestion, and the old man went back into the house to report what had happened.

Kaguya-hime declared, "I should like Prince Ishizukuri to obtain for me from India the stone begging-bowl of the Buddha. Prince Kuramochi is to go to the mountain in the Eastern Sea called Hōrai and fetch me a branch of the tree that grows there, with roots of silver and trunk of gold, whose fruits are pearls. The next gentleman is to bring me a robe made of the fur of Chinese fire-rats. I ask Ōtomo, the Grand Counsellor, please to fetch me the jewel that shines five colors, found in a dragon's neck. And Isokami, the Middle Counsellor, should present me with a swallow's easy-delivery charm."

The old man said, "These are indeed difficult tasks. The gifts you ask for are not to be found anywhere in Japan. How shall I break the news of such difficult assignments?"

"What is so difficult about them?" asked Kaguya-hime.

"I'll tell them, at any rate," said the old man and went outside. When he had related what was expected of them, the princes and nobles exclaimed, "Why doesn't she simply say, 'Stay away from my house!'?" They all left in disgust.

The Stone Begging-Bowl of the Buddha

Nevertheless, Prince Ishizukuri felt as though his life would not be worth living unless he married the girl, and he reflected, "Is there anything I would not do for her, even if it meant traveling to India to find what she wants?" He realized, however, being a prudent man, how unlikely he was to find the one and only begging-bowl, even if he journeyed all eight thousand leagues to India. He left word with Kaguya-hime that he was departing that day for India in search of the begging-bowl and remained away for three years. At a mountain temple in Tochi district of the province of Yamato he obtained a bowl that had stood before the image of Binzuru and was pitch-black with soot. He put the bowl in a brocade bag, fastened it to a spray of artificial flowers, and carried it to Kaguya-hime's house. When he presented the bowl, she looked it over suspiciously. Inside she found a note and opened it: "I have worn out my spirits on the roads over sea and mountains; in quest of the stone bowl my tears of blood have flowed."

Kaguya-hime examined the bowl to see if it gave off a light, but there was not so much as a firefly's glimmer. She returned the bowl with the verse, "I hoped that at least the sparkle of the fallen dew would linger within—why did you fetch this bowl from the Mountain of Darkness?"

The Prince threw away the bowl at the gate and replied with this verse, "When it encountered the Mountain of Brightness it lost its light perhaps; I discard the bowl, but shamelessly cling to my hopes." He sent this into the house, but Kaguya-hime no longer deigned to answer. When he discovered she would not even listen to his pleas, he departed, at a loss for words. Because he persisted in his suit even after throwing away the bowl, people have ever since spoken of surprise at a shameless action as being bowled over.

The Jewelled Branch from Paradise

Prince Kuramochi, a man of many devices, requested leave of the court, saying he intended to depart for Tsukushi to take a cure at the hot springs. He sent word at the same time to Kaguya-hime that he was off in search of the jewelled branch. When he left the capital he was accompanied as far as Naniwa by his full staff of retainers, but when he was about to sail from Naniwa he announced he would henceforth travel incognito, taking with him only personal servants instead of his customary large retinue. The others returned to the capital once they had seen him off. The Prince, having convinced everyone that he had indeed departed, ordered his ship to be rowed back to port three days later.

Prior to his departure the Prince had made detailed arrangements: six metalsmiths, acclaimed as the treasures of the age, were hired; a house that outsiders would have difficulty approaching was built for them; and a furnace enclosed by triple walls was erected. The craftsmen were installed in the house, where they were joined by the Prince himself, who devoted the revenues of all his sixteen domains to the expenses of fashioning the jewelled branch. When completed, it differed in no particle from Kaguya-hime's description. Having carried through his plan so brilliantly, the Prince secretly left for Naniwa with the branch.

He sent word ahead to his household, informing them of his return by ship, and acted as if his journey had been a terrible ordeal. Many people went to Naniwa to welcome him. The jewelled branch was placed in a long wooden chest, covered suitably, and carried ashore. Word soon got around, and rumor had it Prince Kuramochi was bringing back an *udonge* blossom to the capital. When Kaguya-hime heard this, she thought, her heart sinking, "I have been outwitted by this prince."

Just then there was a knocking at the gate, and an attendant proclaimed Prince Kuramochi's arrival. "The Prince has come here without even changing his travelling clothes," he said. The old man, impressed, went out to greet the Prince.

"I have brought back, at the risk of my life, the jewelled branch I was sent for," the Prince announced. "Please show it to Kaguya-hime."

The old man took it inside. The Prince had attached a note to the branch: "Even had it cost me my life, I should not have returned empty-handed, without breaking off the jewelled branch."

While the lady was scanning this verse in dismay, the Old Bamboo Cutter rushed in and declared, "The Prince has brought back from Paradise a jewelled branch that answers exactly the description of the one you requested. What more can you ask of him? He has come directly here in his travelling clothes, not even stopping at his own house. Please accept the Prince as your husband without further ado." The lady, not saying a word, brooded disconsolately, her head resting on her arm.

"I'm sure there is nothing further to be said at this point," said the Prince, confidently stepping up on the verandah as he spoke. The old man, considering that this was indeed the case, said to Kaguya-hime, "In all Japan there is not another such jewelled branch. How could you refuse him now? Besides, he's a man of splendid character."

She answered, "It was my reluctance to refuse outright what you asked of me, Father, that made me request such impossible things." She found it most exasperating that the Prince should have surprised her in this way by bringing back the branch. The old man busied himself with preparing the nuptial chamber.

The old man asked the Prince, "What was the place like where you found the branch? What a marvellously beautiful and impressive thing it is!"

The Prince replied, "Three years ago, along about the tenth day of the second moon, I boarded ship at Naniwa and put out to sea. I realized that I had no guidance as to the direction I should head, but I told myself that unless I succeeded in my mission, life would not be worth living, and I decided to let the ship be carried ahead at the mercy of the uncertain winds. I reflected that if I died, my struggles would be over; but I was determined that as long as life was left me, I would keep sailing on, in the hope that eventually I might reach the mountain called Hōrai. The ship, drifting on the waves, was rowed farther and farther from Japan. As we moved along, we sometimes encountered waves so rough I thought we would surely sink to the bottom of the sea. Sometimes too we were blown by the winds to strange lands where the people, who looked like demons, attacked and tried to kill us. Sometimes, losing all track of our bearings, we drifted blindly on the sea. Sometimes too our food ran out, and we barely subsisted on roots or shells we took from the sea. And sometimes unspeakably horrible monsters rose in our path, intending to devour us.

"It happened too on our journey, at places where there was

no one to help us, that we were afflicted by sicknesses of every kind, and had nowhere to turn for comfort. We drifted on the sea, letting the ship wander as it pleased. Then, at about eight o'clock in the morning on the five-hundredth day of our journey we faintly perceived in the distance a mountain rising from the sea. All of us aboard the ship strained our eyes for a better look. The mountain soared imposingly over the waves, tall and gracefully shaped. This, I thought, was undoubtedly the place I was looking for; but somehow I felt afraid, and for two or three days I sailed around the mountain, surveying it. One day we noticed a woman dressed like some celestial being emerge from the mountain and walk here and there, dipping water with a silver bowl. I went ashore and asked her the name of the mountain. She answered, 'This is the mountain of Hōrai.' Words cannot describe my delight at hearing these words. I asked her then, 'With whom have I the pleasure of speaking?' 'My name is Ukanruri,' she replied, and so saying went back into the mountain.

"I examined the mountain, but could discover no way to climb it. As I walked around its slopes I saw flowering trees of a kind unknown in this world. Streams of gold, silver and emerald color gushed from the mountain, and spanning them were bridges of many different precious stones. Nearby stood some brilliantly glittering trees. The one whose branch I took was the least impressive, but since it fitted exactly the lady's description, I broke off this spray of blossoms.

"The mountain was incomparably lovely. Nothing in this world even faintly suggests its delights. But now that I had obtained the branch, I was in no mood to dawdle. I boarded ship and, being favored by the wind, returned in a little over four hundred days. Perhaps I owe it to the Buddha's vow to save all mankind that the wind blew me safely to Naniwa. Yesterday I left Naniwa for the capital, and I have come directly here, without so much as changing my brine-soaked clothes."

The old man, having heard the Prince through, sighed and recited the verse: "Through all the generations men have gathered bamboo in mountains and fields, have they ever experienced such unbroken hardships?"

The Prince responded, "My heart which for so long has been prey to anxiety today is at peace." He composed this reply to the old man's verse: "Now that my sleeve has tried today, I am sure I can forget the many pains I have suffered."

Just then a band of six men burst into the garden. One of them held forth a letter inserted in a presentation stick. He said, "I am Ayabe no Uchimaro, an artisan of the Office of Handicrafts. I beg to report that I served this gentleman by making a jewelled branch for him, working for over a thousand days, so devotedly I gave up all normal nourishment. This was no small sacrifice, but he has yet to give me any reward. Please, sir, pay me now so I can take care of my assistants." He proffered the note. The Old Bamboo Cutter shook his head in perplexity, wondering what the workman was talking about. The Prince stood there dumbfounded, looking utterly disconcerted.

Kaguya-hime, hearing what had happened, exclaimed, "Bring me that letter!" She examined it, and this is what it said: "For a thousand days the Prince remained in hiding together with us lowly workmen, and he ordered us to make him a magnificent jewelled branch. He promised he would even give us official posts as our reward. Recently we thought the matter over carefully, and it occurred to us that the branch was surely the one demanded by Kaguya-hime, the Prince's future lady. That is why we have come to this household, to receive our just reward."

"Yes," the men insisted, "We must be paid!" At their cry Kaguya-hime, whose spirits had been steadily darkening as the day drew to a close, suddenly burst into merry laughter. She called the old man to her, and said, "I thought the branch really came from a tree in Paradise, but obviously it is a disgraceful counterfeit. Please send it back at once."

The old man nodded and said, "Now that we know the branch is definitely not genuine, it is a simple matter to return it."

Kaguya-hime's spirits had been completely restored. To the Prince's poem she now sent the reply: "Wondering if your story might be true, I examined the jewelled branch, but it was a sham, like your words." She sent back the branch. The

Old Bamboo Cutter, embarrassed that he had tried so hard to persuade the girl to marry the Prince, shut his eyes, pretending to sleep. The Prince, uncomfortable whether he stood or sat, waited outside uneasily until it grew dark, when he slunk off.

Kaguya-hime summoned the workmen who had presented their grievances. "Happy men!" she cried, and bestowed generous rewards on them. The men were delighted, and left saying, "We got exactly what we wanted." On the way home, however, they were intercepted by Prince Kuramochi, who had them thrashed so severely the blood flowed. Their rewards did them little good, for every last gift was snatched away, and they had to run off for dear life.

The Prince said, "No greater disgrace could befall me in this existence. I have failed to win the girl, and I am mortified to think how the world must despise me." He went off all by himself deep into the mountains. His palace functionaries and personal attendants set off in parties in search of him, but, being unsuccessful, they could only conclude that he probably was dead.

The Prince disappeared for several years, wishing to avoid being seen by his people. It was from this time that people began to speak of someone as being stony-hearted if he astonishes others by trying to pass off as genuine a false stone.

The Robe Made of Fire-Rat Fur

The Minister of the Right Abe no Mimuraji was a man of wealth and the master of a flourishing household. That year a gentleman named Wang Ching arrived aboard a Chinese merchant ship, and Abe no Mimuraji wrote him a letter asking him to buy and send what had been described as a robe of fire-rat fur. He entrusted this letter to Ono no Fusamori, an especially reliable retainer. The man took the letter to Wang Ching and presented it, together with a sum in gold. Wang opened and read the letter, then wrote the reply: "Robes made from the fur of fire-rats are not obtainable in my country. I have indeed heard of such things, but have yet to see one. If any really existed, surely someone would have brought one to China. This will entail some very difficult negotiations. However, on the chance that one may have been imported into India, I shall make enquiries at the houses of the rich men there. If my search proves unsuccessful, I shall return the money with your servant."

The Chinese ship left for China, only presently to return to Japan. The Minister, learning that Fusamori was in Japan and on his way to the capital, sent a swift-footed horse to meet him. Fusamori mounted the horse and rode from Tsukushi to the capital in a bare seven days. He brought a letter from Wang Ching: "I have managed with great difficulty, by sending my men everywhere, to acquire the robe of fire-rat fur I am now forwarding. A robe of this fur has never been easy to obtain, whether now or in the past. I was informed that long ago a great Indian priest had brought one to China, and that it was now preserved in a mountain temple to the west. Eventually, with the assistance of the authorities, I was able to purchase it. The officials told my man that the money you sent was insufficient, and I was therefore obliged to add some of my own. I should appreciate it if you would kindly remit fifty ounces of gold by the return voyage of the ship. Please return the robe if you are unwilling to send the money."

When the Minister read these words he exclaimed, "How can he suggest such a thing? He's only asking for a trifle more money, after all. Of course I'll give it to him. How wonderful that he found the robe and sent it to me!" He made a deep bow in the direction of China.

The box containing the robe was inlaid with precious stones and glittered resplendently. The fur itself was a bluish-black, and the hair-tips shone with a golden light. This obviously was a treasure of incomparable beauty. Its beauty indeed was even more remarkable than its vaunted imperviousness to flame. "I can see why Kaguya-hime should have wanted it so," said the Minister. "What a magnificent robe it is!" He placed the robe in a box, attached the box to a branch, and beautified himself with great care, imagining he would spend that very night at her house. He composed a poem to take along: "I have burnt with the flames of boundless love, but today I wear with dry sleeves the fur robe that does not burn in fire."

The Minister took the box to Kaguya-hime's gate and waited there. The Bamboo Cutter came out, accepted the gift, and showed it to Kaguya-hime. "What a lovely robe it is!" she said as she examined it, "But I still cannot be sure it is the genuine fur."

The Bamboo Cutter answered, "That may be so, but I'll invite him in anyway. In all the world there is not another such fur robe. You'd best accept it as genuine. Don't make people suffer so!" He invited the Minister inside and seated him.

The old woman, seeing the Minister ushered to the place of honor, was also convinced in her heart that this time the girl would be wed. The old man had grieved that Kaguya-hime was still single and worried himself over finding a suitable husband for her, but she was so resolutely opposed that he naturally had never tried to force her.

Kaguya-hime said to the old man, "If this fur robe does not burn when it is put in fire, I shall admit that it is genuine and do what is required of me. You say you have never seen its like and that you have no doubt but that it is genuine, but I should like to test it in fire."

"That is quite reasonable," said the old man, and so informed the Minister.

The latter replied, "I secured this fur robe, which was not even to be had in China, with the greatest difficulty. What doubt could there be? All the same, please do test it in the flames at once."

Kaguya-hime asked someone to place it in the fire, where it burned brightly. "Just as I thought," said Kaguya-hime, "The robe was an imitation." The Minister, seeing this, turned the color of leaves of grass. Kaguya-hime was enchanted. She wrote a poem in response to the Minister's, and put it in the box: "Had I known it would burn, leaving not a trace, I should not have worried so, but kept the fur robe away from the flames." The Minister departed.

People crowded around the old man's house and asked, "We hear that Minister Abe has brought a robe of fire-rat fur and is living with the lady. Is he here now?" Someone answered, "When they put the fur into the fire it burst into flames, so Kaguya-hime won't marry him." Those who heard the story transmitted it, and ever since people have said that when a plan is not carried out it falls into Abe-yance.

The Jewel in the Dragon's Neck

Ōtomo no Miyuki, the Grand Counsellor, called together all the members of his household and announced, "A dragon carries a shining five-colored jewel in his neck. Anyone who can get one for me will have whatever he desires."

His men, hearing these words, said, "Your lordship's commands are exceedingly gracious. But such jewels are not easy to come by, and how could we possibly get one from a dragon's neck?"

The Grand Counsellor retorted, "Servants should try to fulfill their master's orders, even if at the risk of their lives. I am not asking for something from India or China that cannot be found in Japan. Dragons are constantly rising from the sea and descending from the mountains in this country. What makes you think it is so difficult?"

"In that case," said the men, "We shall say no more. However difficult it may be, we will go and search for the jewel as you command."

The Grand Counsellor smiled. "You have acquired quite a reputation for being faithful servants of your master. How could you disobey my orders?" He sent them off in search of the jewel in the dragon's neck, stripping his palace of all its silk, cotton, and copper coins to provide them with the means of paying for their food along the way.

"Until you return we shall refrain from eating animal food," he promised, "But don't come back without the jewel!"

The servants departed, each with his instructions. "He told us not to return without the jewel from the dragon's neck— let's just hie ourselves off in whatever direction our feet happen to take us. What a crazy thing to ask of us!" grumbled the servants. They divided up the valuables they had been given; then some returned to their own homes while others set off for places they had long wished to visit. All abused the Grand Counsellor for having issued such unreasonable orders, impossible to execute even if they came from a father or master.

The Grand Counsellor next announced: "I should be exposing myself to ridicule if I asked Kaguya-hime to live here without even altering the place." He proceeded to build a magnificent house for her, its walls lacquered and sprinkled with gold, and its roof thatched with silken threads of many colors. The rooms were furnished with indescribable splendor, and paintings on figured damask hung in each alcove. The Grand Counsellor, certain that Kaguya-hime would become his bride, set his concubines to work making preparations for the wedding and, neglecting his first wife completely, spent his days and nights alone.

The Counsellor waited every day for the men he had despatched, but no news had come by the New Year. In his impatience, he disguised himself and went in great secret to the region of Naniwa, accompanied by only two retainers. There he made enquiries: "Have you heard anything about the men of the Grand Counsellor Ōtomo, who sailed off to slay a dragon and take the jewel in its neck?"

"What a strange story!" replied a boatman with a laugh "We have no boats here that do that kind of work."

The Grand Counsellor thought, "What an irresponsible answer for a boatman to give! He doesn't know who I am. That's why he talks that way." He reflected a while, then said to himself, "I am strong enough with my bow to shoot dead any dragon that shows itself. I'll get the jewel for myself. I won't wait for these rascals to come straggling home." He boarded a ship and sailed round from one arm of the sea to the next, until he reached the distant ocean off Tsukushi.

What happened then? A terrible gale began to blow, everything went dark around them, and a storm tossed the ship helplessly hither and thither, until they lost all track of direction, and it seemed that the wind would surely blow the ship out into the middle of the ocean. The waves lashed again and again at the ship, sucking it down, and lightning flashed almost on top of the vessel. The Grand Counsellor cried out in utter bewilderment, "I've never been in such a horrible predicament before. What will become of me?"

The steersman replied, "In all the years I have been sailing the seas, I've never seen such a terrible storm. If the ship doesn't go down, it's sure to be struck by lightning. And even if by some good fortune the gods spare our lives, we'll probably be blown all the way to the South Seas. It's all because I serve such a crazy master that I must die like a fool!" He wept.

The Grand Counsellor, hearing these words, cried, in between violent bouts of vomiting, "When aboard ship I trust in what the steersman says as in a great mountain. Why do you say such disheartening things?"

The steersman answered, "How should I know how to help you? I'm not a god. It's all because you were looking for a dragon to kill that the wind has been blowing and the waves raging. On top of everything else, we're even getting thunderbolts rained down on our heads. This storm has been blown up by a dragon's breath. Make your prayers to the gods, and don't delay!"

"A good suggestion," said the Grand Counsellor. "God of steersmen, hear my words! I intended in my foolishness to kill a dragon. But from now on I'll never disturb so much as the tip of a dragon's hair." He bellowed this assurance in a loud voice, now standing, now sitting, shouting and weeping all the while. Gradually the thunder abated, perhaps because he had repeated these words at least a thousand times. Lightning still flashed a little, and the wind blew hard as ever, but the steersman commented, "You see—the storm was a dragon's doing. The wind now is favoring us. It's blowing us in the right direction." The Grand Counsellor paid no attention to these words.

The wind blew for three or four days and brought them back to land. The sailors recognized the coast as Akashi in Harima. The Grand Counsellor, however, imagining that they must have been driven ashore somewhere in the South Seas, heaved a great sigh and lay flat on his face. The men aboard the ship reported to the government office on shore, and the local officials went to call on the Grand Counsellor. Even then he was unable to rise, but continued to lie on his face at the bottom of the ship. They spread a mat for him in a pine field, and unloaded him from the ship. Then, for the first time, he realized that he was not in the South Seas, and with great difficulty managed to stand. He looked like a man with some horrible sickness—his belly bulged out grotesquely and he seemed to have plums for eyes. The officials could not hold back their smiles when they looked at him.

The Grand Counsellor gave orders to the officials to have a sedan chair prepared for him, and he was borne home, groaning all the way. When he arrived, the men he had sent out, who had somehow got word of his return, appeared and informed him, "We couldn't get the jewel in the dragon's neck, and that's why we didn't come back to serve you. We've returned now that you've found out how difficult it is to get the jewel. We're sure you won't punish us too severely."

The Grand Counsellor sat up. "You did well not to bring one back. Dragons belong to the same species as the thunder, and if you had tried to capture the jewel, many of you would have been killed. And if you had actually caught a dragon, it certainly would have meant the death of me. I'm glad you didn't catch one! That cursed thief of a Kaguya-hime was trying to kill us! I'll never go near her house again. And don't you go wandering around there either!" He bestowed on the men who had failed to bring back the jewel what little remained of his fortune. When his first wife, from whom he had separated, heard about this, she laughed until her sides ached. The roof that had been thatched with silken threads was pillaged completely by kites and rooks, to line their nests.

People asked, "Has the Grand Counsellor Ōtomo gone off to find the jewel in a dragon's neck?" "No," said others, "Where his eyes should be he has stuck stones that look like plums." "Oh," they answered, "that's plumb foolish." And from that time on people spoke of any ill-starred venture as being plumb foolish.

The Easy-Delivery Charm of the Swallows

The Middle Counsellor Isonokami no Marotari gave orders to the men in his employ to report if any swallows were building nests. "Yes, sir," they said, "But why do you need this information?" He answered, "I intend to get the easy-delivery charm that a swallow carries."

The men said variously, "I've killed many swallows in my

time, but I've never seen anything of that description in a swallow's belly." "How do you suppose a swallow manages to pull out the charm just when it's about to give birth?" "It keeps the charm hidden, and if any man gets a glimpse of it, it disappears."

Still another man said, "Swallows are building nests in all the holes along the eaves of the Palace Kitchen. If you send some dependable men there and set up perches from which they can observe the swallows, there are so many swallows that one of them is sure to be giving birth. That will give your men the chance to grab the charm."

The Middle Counsellor was delighted. "How perfectly extraordinary!" he said, "I had never noticed! Thank you for a most promising suggestion." He ordered twenty dependable men to the spot, and stationed them on lookout perches built for their task. From his mansion he sent a steady stream of messengers asking if the men had successfully obtained the easy-delivery charm.

The swallows, terrified by all the people climbing up to the roof, did not return to their nests. When the Middle Counsellor learned of this, he was at a loss what to do now. Just at this point an old man named Kuratsumaro who worked in the Palace Kitchen was heard to remark, "I have a plan for his Excellency if he wishes to get a swallow's easy-delivery charm." He was at once ushered into the presence of the Middle Counsellor and seated directly before him.

Kuratsumaro said, "You are using clumsy methods to get the charm, and you'll never succeed in that way. The twenty men on their lookout perches are making such a racket that the swallows are much too frightened to come close. You should tear down the perches and dismiss all the men. One man only, a dependable man, should be kept in readiness inside an open-work basket that has a rope attached to it. As soon as a swallow starts to lay an egg, the man in the basket should be hoisted up with the rope. Then he can quickly grab the charm. That is your best plan."

"An excellent plan indeed," said the Middle Counsellor. The perches were dismantled and the men all returned to the palace. The Counsellor asked Kuratsumaro, "How will we know when the swallow is about to give birth, so the man can be hoisted up in time?"

Kuratsumaro answered, "When a swallow is about to give birth it raises its tail and circles around seven times. As it is completing its seventh turn you should hoist the basket immediately and the man can snatch the charm."

The Counsellor was overjoyed to hear Kuratsumaro's words. "How wonderful to have my prayers granted!" he exclaimed, "And to think you're not even in my service!" He removed his cloak and offered it to the old man. "Come tonight to the Palace Kitchen," he said, dismissing him.

When it grew dark the Middle Counsellor went to the Kitchen. He observed that swallows were indeed building nests and circling the place with lifted tails, exactly as Kuratsumaro had described. A man was put in a basket and hoisted up, but when he put his hand into the swallow's nest he called down, "There's nothing here!"

"That's because you aren't searching in the proper way!" the Counsellor angrily retorted. "Is there nobody competent here? I'll have to go up there myself." He climbed into the basket and was hoisted up. He peered into a nest and saw a swallow with its tail lifted circling about furiously. He at once stretched out his arm and felt in the nest. His fingers touched something flat. "I've got it! Lower me now; I've done it myself!" he cried. His men gathered round, but in their eagerness to lower him quickly they pulled too hard, and the rope snapped. The Middle Counsellor plunged down, landing on his back atop a kitchen cauldron.

His men rushed to him in consternation and lifted him in their arms. He lay motionless, showing the whites of his eyes. The men drew some water and got him to swallow a little. At length he regained consciousness, and they lowered him by the hands and feet from the top of the cauldron. When they at last felt they could ask him how he was, he answered in a faint voice, "My head seems a little clearer, but I can't move my legs. But I am happy anyway that I managed to get the easy-delivery charm. Light a torch and bring it here. I want to see what the charm looks like." He raised his head and opened his hand only to discover he was clenching some old droppings the swallows had left. "Alas," he cried, "It was all to no avail!" Ever since that time people have said a project that goes contrary to expectations "lacks charm."

When the Middle Counsellor realized he had failed to obtain the charm, his spirits took a decided turn for the worse. His men laid him inside the lid of a Chinese chest and carried him home. He could not be placed inside his carriage because his back had been broken.

The Middle Counsellor attempted to keep people from learning he had been injured because of a childish escapade. Under the strain of this worry he became all the weaker. It bothered him more that people might hear of his fiasco and mock him, than that he had failed to secure the charm. His anxiety grew worse each day, until he felt in the end it would be preferable to die of illness in a normal manner than lose his reputation.

Kaguya-hime, hearing of his unfortunate condition, sent a poem of enquiry: "The years pass, but the waves do not return to the pines of Suminoe, where I wait in vain; you have failed to find the charm, I am told, is it true?"

He asked that her poem be read to him. Then he lifted his head very feebly, barely able to write in great pain while someone else held the paper: "My efforts were in vain, and now I am about to die in despair; but will you not save my life?" With these words he expired. Kaguya-hime was rather touched.

From this time something slightly pleasurable has been said to have a modicum of charm.

The Imperial Hunt

The Emperor, learning of Kaguya-hime's unrivaled beauty, said to a maid of honor, Nakatomi no Fusako by name, "Please go and discover for me what kind of woman Kaguya-hime is, this beauty who has brought so many men to ruin and refuses to marry."

Fusako, obedient to his command, departed. When she arrived at the Bamboo Cutter's house the old woman deferentially showed her in. The maid of honor said, "I have been ordered by His Majesty to ascertain whether Kaguya-hime is as beautiful as people say. That is why I am here now."

"I shall tell her," said the old woman and went inside. "Please," she urged Kaguya-hime, "Hurry out and meet the Emperor's messenger."

Kaguya-hime replied, "How can I appear before her when I am not in the least attractive?"

"Don't talk nonsense! Do you dare to show such disrespect to someone sent here by the Emperor?"

"It doesn't make me feel especially grateful to think the Emperor might wish to summon me," answered Kaguya-hime. She showed no sign of relenting and meeting the lady. The old woman had always considered Kaguya-hime as being no different from a child she had borne herself, but when the girl spoke so coldly, it much embarrassed her, and she could not reprimand Kaguya-hime as she would have liked.

The old woman returned to the maid of honor and said, "I must apologize, but the girl is terribly obstinate and refuses to see you."

The maid of honor said, "I was ordered by His Majesty to verify her appearance without fail. How can I return to the Palace without seeing her? Do you think it proper for anyone living in this country to be allowed to disobey a royal command? Please do not let her act so unreasonably!" She intended these words to shame Kaguya-hime, but when the latter was informed, she refused all the more vehemently to comply. "If I am disobeying a royal command, let them execute me without delay," she declared.

The maid of honor returned to the Palace and reported what had happened. The Emperor listened and said merely, "You can see she's quite capable of causing the deaths of a great many men." He seemed to have given up all thought of summoning Kaguya-hime into his service, but he still had his heart set on her, and refused to accept defeat at her hands. He sent for the old man and stated, "I want this Kaguya-hime you have at your place. Word has reached me of the beauty of her face and figure, and I sent my messenger to look her over, but she returned unsuccessful, unable to obtain so much as a glimpse of the girl. Did you bring her up to be so disrespect-ful?"

The old man humbly replied, "The girl absolutely refuses to serve at Court. I am quite at a loss what to do about her. But I'll go back home and report your Majesty's command."

The Emperor asked, "Why should a child you have raised with your own hands refuse to do what you wish? If you present the girl for service here, you can be quite sure I will reward you with court rank."

The old man returned home, overjoyed. He related this conversation to Kaguya-hime, concluding, "That was what the Emperor told me. Are you still unwilling to serve him?"

Kaguya-hime answered, "I absolutely refuse to serve at the Court. If you force me, I'll simply disappear. It may win you a court rank, but it will mean my death."

"Never do such a dreadful thing!" cried the old man. "What use would position or rank be to me if I couldn't be-hold my child? But why are you so reluctant to serve at the Court? Would it really kill you?"

"If you still think I am lying, send me into service at the Court and see if I don't die. Many men have showed me most unusual affection, but all of them in vain. If I obey the Em-peror's wishes, no sooner than he expresses them, I shall feel ashamed how people will consider my coldness to those other men."

The old man replied, "I don't care about anyone else. The only thing that disturbs me is the danger to your life. I'll re-port that you are still unwilling to serve." He went to the Palace and informed the Emperor, "In humble obedience to Your Majesty's command, I attempted to persuade the child to enter your service, but she told me that if I forced her to serve in the Palace, it would surely cause her death. This child was not born of my body. I found her long ago in the moun-tains. That is why her ways are not like those of ordinary people."

The Emperor commented, "She must be a transformed be-ing. There's no hope, then, of having her serve me, but at least I should like somehow to get a glimpse of her."

"I wonder how this could be arranged," said the old man.

The Emperor said, "I understand, Miyakkomaro, your house is near the mountains. How would it be if, under pretext of staging an imperial hunt, I stopped by for a look at her?"

"That is an excellent plan," said the old man. "If Your Majesty should happen to call at a time when she does not expect a visitor, you can probably see her." The Emperor at once set a date for the hunt.

During the course of the hunt the Emperor entered Kaguya-hime's house and saw there a woman so lovely she shed a radiance around her. He thought, this must be Kaguya-hime, and approached. She fled into the adjoining room, but the Emperor caught her by the sleeve. She covered her face, but his first glimpse was enough to convince him that she was a peerless beauty. "I won't let you go!" he cried. But when he attempted to take her away with him, Kaguya-hime declared, "If I had been born on earth I would have served you. But if you try to force me to go with you, you will find you cannot."

The Emperor said, "Why can't I? I'll take you with me!" He summoned his palanquin, but at that instant Kaguya-hime suddenly dissolved into a shadow. The Emperor realized to his dismay and disappointment that she was indeed no ordinary mortal. He said, "I shall not insist any longer that you come with me. But please return to your former shape. Just one look at you and I shall go." Kaguya-hime resumed her original appearance.

The Emperor was still too entranced with Kaguya-hime's beauty to stifle his feelings, and he displayed his pleasure with the old man for having brought about the meeting. Miyakkomaro, for his part, tendered a splendid banquet for the Emperor's officers. The Emperor was bitterly disappointed to return to the Palace without Kaguya-hime, and as he left the Bamboo Cutter's house he felt as though his soul remained behind. After he had entered his palanquin he sent this verse to Kaguya-hime: "As I go back to the Palace my spirits lag; I turn back, I hesitate, because of Kaguya-hime, who defies me and remains behind."

To this she wrote in reply, "How could one who has lived

her life in a house overgrown with weeds dare to look upon a jewelled Palace?"

The Emperor felt there was less reason than ever to leave when he saw this poem, but since he could not spend the night with Kaguya-hime, he had no choice but to return. When he saw again the Palace ladies who usually waited on him they seemed unworthy even to appear in Kaguya-hime's presence. Indeed, the very ladies he had always considered more beautiful than other women, when compared to Kaguya-hime seemed scarcely worthy of the name of human beings. He ceased visiting his consorts, finding no pleasure in their company. He wrote letters only to Kaguya-hime, and her answers were by no means unkind. He used also to send her poems attached to flowers or branches that struck him as especially attractive.

The Celestial Robe of Feathers

They passed some three years in this way, each consoling the other. At the beginning of the next spring Kaguya-hime seemed more pensive than usual as she watched the Moon rise in all its splendor. Some one nearby admonished her, "People should avoid staring the Moon in the face." But when no one was around, Kaguya-hime would often gaze at the Moon and weep bitterly. At the time of the full moon of the seventh month she sat outside, seemingly lost in thought.

Her maidservants informed the Bamboo Cutter: "Kaguya-hime has always looked with deep emotion at the Moon, but she has seemed rather strange of late. She must be terribly upset over something. Please keep an eye on her."

The old man asked Kaguya-hime, "What makes you look so pensively at the Moon?"

She answered, "When I look at the Moon the world seems lonely and sad. What else would there be to worry me?"

He went over to Kaguya-hime and looked at her face. She definitely appeared melancholy. He asked, "My dear one, what are you thinking of? What worries you?"

"I am not worried about anything. But everything seems so depressing."

"You shouldn't look at the Moon," the old man said. "Whenever you do, you always seem so upset."

"How could I go on living if I didn't look at the Moon?" Each night, as the Moon rose, she would sit outside, immersed in thought. On dark moonless nights she seemed to emerge from her reverie, but with the reappearance of the Moon she would sometimes sigh and weep. Her maids whispered to one another, "There really does seem to be something disturbing her," but no one, not even her parents, knew what it was.

One moonlight night towards the middle of the eighth month Kaguya-hime, sitting outside, suddenly burst into a flood of tears. She now wept without caring whether or not people saw. Her parents, noticing this, asked in alarm what was troubling her. Kaguya-hime answered, still weeping, "I have intended to tell you for a long time, but I was so sure I would make you unhappy that I have kept silent all this while. But I can be silent no more. I will tell you everything. I am not a creature of this world. I came from the Palace of the Moon to this world because of an obligation incurred in a former life. Now the time has come when I must return. On the night of the full moon people from my old country will come for me, and I will have no choice but to go. I was heartbroken to think how unhappy this news would make you, and that is why I have been grieving ever since this spring." She wept copiously.

The old man cried, "What's that you say? I found you in a stick of bamboo when you were no bigger than a poppy seed, and I have brought you up until now you stand as tall as I. Who is going to take my child away? Do you think I'll let them?" He added, "If they do, it will kill me." His distraught weeping was really unbearable to behold.

Kaguya-hime said, "I have a father and mother who live in the City of the Moon. When I came here from my country I said it would be just for a short while, but already I have spent many years in this land. I have tarried among you, without thinking of my parents on the Moon, and I have become accustomed to your ways. Now that I am about to return I feel no great joy, but only a terrible sadness. And yet though it is

not by my choice, I must go." They both wept uncontrolla-
bly. Her maids, who had been in her service for years,
thought how unspeakable parting would be, and how much
they would miss her noble and lively disposition, to which
they had grown so familiar. They refused all nourishment and
grieved no less than the others.

When the Emperor learned what had occurred, he sent a
messenger to the Bamboo Cutter's house. The old man went
out to receive him, weeping profusely. His beard had turned
white from sorrow, his back was bent, and his eyes were
swollen. He was just fifty this year, but his troubles seemed to
have aged him suddenly. The imperial messenger transmitted
the Emperor's words: "I am informed that you have been afflicted by a grave misfortune—is it true?"

The Bamboo Cutter, weeping, answered the message,
"On the night of the full moon men are coming from the City
of the Moon to fetch Kaguya-hime. I am deeply honored by
His Majesty's kind enquiry, and beg him to send soldiers here
on that night, to catch anyone who may arrive from the
Moon."

The messenger departed and, after reporting to the Emperor on the old man's condition, repeated his request. The
Emperor said, "If I, who had but a single glimpse of
Kaguya-hime, cannot put her from my thoughts, what must
it be like for her parents, who are used to seeing her day and
night, to lose her?"

On the fifteenth, the day of the full moon, the Emperor issued orders to the different guards headquarters, and, desig-
nating as his official envoy the Junior Commandant of the
Palace Guards, Takano no Okuni, sent a force of some two
thousand men from the Six Headquarters to the Bamboo
Cutter's house. No sooner did they arrive than a thousand
men posted themselves on the wall and a thousand on the
roof. Together with the numerous members of the household
they formed a defense that left no openings. The defenders
were equipped with bows and arrows, and inside the main
house the womenfolk were stationed, guarding it.

The old woman sat in the strong-room of the house, holding Kaguya-hime in her arms. The old man, having tightly

barred the door, stood on guard at the entrance. He declared, "Do you think anybody, even if he comes from the Moon, is going to break through our defences?" He called to the roof, "Shoot to kill if you see anything flying in the sky, no matter how small!"

The guards answered, "With defenses as strong as ours we're sure we can shoot down even a mosquito. We'll expose its body as a warning to the others." Their words greatly reassured the old man.

Kaguya-hime said, "No matter how you lock me up and try to guard me, you won't be able to resist the men from the Moon. You won't be able to use your weapons on them. Even if you shut me up in this room, when they come everything will open before them. Resist them though you may, when they come even the bravest man will lose heart."

"If anyone comes after you, I'll tear out his eyes with my long nails," cried old man. "I'll grab him by the hair and throw him to ground. I'll put him to shame by exposing his behind for all the officers to see!" He shouted with anger.

"Don't talk in such a loud voice," cautioned Kaguya-hime. "It would be shocking if the men on the roof heard you. I am very sorry to leave you without ever having expressed my gratitude for all your kindnesses. It makes me sad to think that fate did not permit us to remain together for long, and I must soon depart. Surely you know it will not be easy for me to leave without ever having shown in the least my devotion to you, my parents. When I have gone outside and have sat looking at the Moon I have always begged for just one more year with you, but my wish was refused. That was what made me so unhappy. It breaks my heart to leave you after bringing you such grief. The people of the Moon are extremely beautiful, and they never grow old. Nor have they any worries. Yet, I am not all happy to be returning. I know I shall miss you and keep wishing I could be looking after you when you are old and helpless." She spoke in tears.

"Don't talk of such heartrending things!" the old man exclaimed. "No matter how beautiful those people may be, I won't let them stand in my way." His tone was bitter.

By now the evening had passed. About midnight the area

of the house was suddenly illuminated by a light more dazzling than that of high noon, a light as brilliant as ten full
moons put together, so bright one could see the pores of a
man's skin. Then down from the heavens men came riding on
clouds, and arrayed themselves at a height some five feet
above the ground. The guards inside and outside the house,
seemingly victims of some supernatural spell, quite lost their
will to resist. At length they plucked up their courage and
tried to ready their bows and arrows, but the strength had
gone from their hands, and their bodies were limp. Some val-
iant men among them, with a great effort, tried to shoot their
bows, but the arrows glanced off harmlessly in all directions.
Unable to fight boldly, like soldiers, they could only watch
on stupified.

Words cannot describe the beauty of the raiment worn by
the men who hovered in the air. With them they had brought
a flying chariot covered by a parasol of gauzy silk. One
among them, apparently their king, called out, "Miyakkomaro, come here!" The old man, who had assumed such an air
of defiance, prostrated himself before the stranger, feeling as
if he were in a drunken stupor. The king said, "You childish
old man! We sent the young lady down into the world for a
short while, in return for some trifling good deeds you had
performed, and for many years we have bestowed riches on
you, until you are now like a different man. Kaguya-hime
was obliged to live for a time in such humble surroundings
because of a sin she had committed in the past. The term of
her punishment is over, and we have come, as you can see, to
escort her home. No matter how you weep and wail, old
man, you cannot detain her. Send her forth at once!"

"I have been watching over Kaguya-hime for more than
twenty years," the old man answered. "You speak of her having come down into this world for 'a short while.' It makes
me wonder if you are not talking about some other Kaguya-
hime living in a different place." He added, "Besides, the
Kaguya-hime I have here is suffering from a serious illness
and cannot leave her room."

No answer met his words. Instead, the king guided the
flying chariot to the roof, where he called out, "Kaguya-hime!

Why have you lingered such a long time in this filthy place?"
The door of the strong room flew open, and the lattice-work
shutters opened of their own accord. The old woman had
been clutching Kaguya-hime in her arms, but now the girl
freed herself and stepped outside. The old woman, unable to
restrain her, could only look up to heaven and weep.

Kaguya-hime approached the Bamboo Cutter, who lay
prostrate, weeping in his bewilderment. "It is not by my own
inclination that I leave you now," she said. "Please at least
watch as I ascend into the sky."

"How can I watch you go when it makes me so sad? You
are abandoning me to go up to Heaven, not caring what may
happen to me. Take me with you!" He threw himself down,
weeping.

Kaguya-hime was at a loss what to do. She said, "Before I
go I shall write a letter for you. If ever you long for me, take
out the letter and read it." In tears she wrote these words:
"Had I but been born in this world I should have stayed with
you and never caused you any grief. To leave this world and
part from you is quite contrary to my wishes. Please think of
this cloak, that I leave with you, as a memento of me. On
nights when the Moon shines in the sky, gaze at it well. Now
that I am about to forsake you, I feel as though I must fall
from the sky, pulled back to this world by my longing for
you."

Some of the celestial beings had brought boxes with them.
One contained a robe of feathers, another the elixir of immortality. "Please take some of the elixir in this jar," said a celestial being to Kaguya-hime. "You must be feeling unwell after
the things you have had to eat in this dirty place." He offered
her the elixir and Kaguya-hime tasted a little. Then, thinking
she might leave a little as a remembrance of herself, she
started to wrap some of the elixir in the cloak she had dis-
carded, when a celestial being prevented her. He took the
robe of feathers from its box and attempted to throw it over
her shoulders, but Kaguya-hime cried out. "Wait just a moment! They say that once you put on this robe your heart
changes, and there are still a few words I must say." She
wrote another letter.

The celestial beings called impatiently, "It's late!"

"Don't talk so unreasonably!" exclaimed Kaguya-hime. With perfect serenity she gave the letter to someone for delivery to the Emperor. She showed no signs of agitation. The letter said: "Although you graciously deigned to send many people to detain me here, my escorts have come and will not be denied. Now they will take me with them, to my bitter regret and sorrow. I am sure you must find it quite incomprehensible, but it weighs heaviest on my heart that you may consider my stubborn refusal to obey your commands an act of disrespect." To the above she added the verse: "Now that the moment has come to put on the robe of feathers, how longingly I recall my lord!" Kaguya-hime attached to the letter some elixir of immortality from the jar and, summoning the commander of the guards, directed him to offer it to the Emperor. A celestial being took the gift from her hands and passed it to the commander. No sooner had the commander accepted the elixir than the celestial being put the robe of feathers on Kaguya-hime. At once she lost all recollection of the pity and grief she had felt for the old man. No cares afflict anyone who once puts on this robe, and Kaguya-hime, in all tranquillity, climbed into her chariot and ascended into the sky, accompanied by a retinue of a hundred celestial beings.

The old man and woman shed bitter tears, but to no avail. When her letter was read to them, they cried, "Why should we cling to our lives? For whose sake? All is useless now." They refused to take medicine, and never left their sick-beds again.

The commander returned to the Palace with his men. He reported in detail the reasons why he and his men had failed with their weapons to prevent Kaguya-hime from departing. He also presented the jar of elixir with the letter attached. The Emperor felt much distressed when he opened the letter and read Kaguya-hime's words. He refused all nourishment, and permitted no entertainments in his presence.

Later, the Emperor summoned his ministers and great nobles and asked them which mountain was closest to Heaven. One man replied, "The mountain in the province of Suruga. It is near both to the capital and to Heaven." The Emperor

thereupon wrote the poem: "What use is it, this elixir of immortality, to one who floats in tears because he cannot meet
her again?"

He gave the poem and the jar containing the elixir to a messenger with the command that he take them to the summit of
the mountain in Suruga. He directed that the letter and the jar
be placed side by side, set on fire, and allowed to be con-
sumed in the flames. The men, obeying this command,
climbed the mountain, taking with them a great many soldiers. Ever since they burnt the elixir of immortality on the
summit, people have called the mountain by the name Fuji,
meaning immortal. Even now the smoke is still said to rise
into the clouds.

APPENDIX II

A Brief Bibliography for Further Reading

For those readers who may wish to read works by the major authors discussed in this study, the following list may serve as a simple guide to works in translation currently available. It is by no means exhaustive. English titles are given, followed by the Japanese original titles in roman letters. In cases where the title has not been translated, a tentative translation is provided in parentheses.

Chapter II. Tanizaki Junichirō
Diary of a Mad Old Man (Futen rōjin nikki), translated by Howard Hibbett, New York: Knopf, 1965.
The Key (Kagi), translated by Howard Hibbett, New York: Knopf, 1961.
The Makioka Sisters (Sasame yuki, "Thin Snow"), translated by Edward G. Seidensticker, New York: Knopf, 1958.
Seven Japanese Tales, translated by Howard Hibbett, New York: Knopf, 1963.
Some Prefer Nettles (Tade kuu mushi), translated by Edward G. Seidensticker, New York: Knopf, 1955.

Chapter III. Natsume Sōseki
And Then (Sore Kara), translated by Norma Moorefield, Baton Rouge, Louisiana State University Press, 1978.
Botchan ("Master Darling"), translated by Alan Turney, Tokyo and Palo Alto: Kodansha, 1972.
Grass on the Wayside (Michikusa), translated by Edwin McClellan, Chicago: University of Chicago Press, 1970.
I Am a Cat (Wagahai neko de aru), translated by Shibata Katsue and Kai Motonari, Tokyo: Kenkyusha, 1961.
Kokoro ("The Heart"), translated by Edwin McClellan, Chicago: Henry Regnery, 1957.
Light and Darkness (Meian), translated by V. H. Vigleilmo, Honolulu: The University Press of Hawaii, 1971.
Mon ("The Gate"), translated by Francis Mathy, London: Peter Owen, 1972.

Sanshirō (the title of this novel is a proper name), translated by Jay Rubin, Seattle: University of Washington Press, 1977.

The Three Cornered World (Kusamakura), translated by Alan Turney, London: Peter Owen, 1965.

The Wayfarer (Kōjin), translated by Beongcheon Yu, Detroit: Wayne State University Press, 1967.

Chapter VII. Ueda Akinari

Tales of Moonlight and Rain (Ugetsu monogatari), translated by Leon M. Zolbrod, London: George Allen & Unwin, 1974.

Tales of the Spring Rain (Harusame monogatari), translated by Barry Jackman, Tokyo: The Japan Foundation, 1975.

Chapter VIII

Nagai Kafū

Edward Seidensticker, *Kafū the Scribbler*, Stanford: Stanford University Press, 1965. This volume contains biographical information on the author as well as translations of extended exerpts from a number of his works.

Geisha in Rivalry (Ude kurabe), translated by Kurt Meissner and Ralph Friedrich, Tokyo and Rutland, Vermont: Charles E. Tuttle, 1963.

Mori Ōgai

The Incident at Sakai and Other Stories, edited by David Dilworth and J. Thomas Rimer, Honolulu: The University Press of Hawaii, 1977. This volume contains ten of Ōgai's best known historical stories. An additional selection of his late historical writings can be found in the companion volume, *Saiki Kōi and Other Stories*, Honolulu: The University Press of Hawaii, 1977.

Vita Sexualis, translated by Ninomiya Kazuji and Sanford Goldstein, Tokyo and Rutland, Vermont: Charles E. Tuttle, 1972.

The Wild Geese (Gan), translated by Ochiai Kingo and Sanford Goldstein, Tokyo and Rutland, Vermont: Charles E. Tuttle, 1959.

Chapter IX. Kawabata Yasunari

Beauty and Sadness (Utsukushisa to kanashimi to), translated by Howard Hibbett, New York: Knopf, 1975.

House of the Sleeping Beauties and Other Stories (Nemureru bijo), translated by Edward G. Seidensticker, Tokyo and Palo Alto: Kodansha, 1969.
The Lake (Mizuumi), translated by Reiko Tsukimura, Tokyo and Palo Alto: Kodansha, 1974.
The Master of Go (Meijin), translated by Edward G. Seidensticker, New York: Knopf, 1972.
Snow Country (Yukiguni), translated by Edward G. Seidensticker, New York: Knopf, 1955.
The Sound of the Mountain (Yama no oto), translated by Edward G. Seidensticker, New York: Knopf, 1970.
Thousand Cranes (Senbazuru), translated by Edward G. Seidensticker, New York: Knopf, 1959.

Chapter X. Dazai Osamu
No Longer Human (Ningen shikkaku), translated by Donald Keene, New York: New Directions, 1955.
The Setting Sun (Shayō), translated by Donald Keene, New York: New Directions, 1956.

Chapter XI. Murasaki Shikibu
The Tale of Genji (Genji monogatari), translated by Arthur Waley, London: George Allen & Unwin, 1935, 1952. This edition is also available at this writing in a Random House Modern Library edition.
The Tale of Genji, translated by Edward G. Seidensticker, New York: Knopf, 1976.
The Diary of Murasaki Shikibu (Murasaki Shikibu nikki) in *Diaries of Court Ladies of Old Japan*, translated by Ann Shepley Omori and Kochi Doi, Tokyo: Kenkyusha, 1935, reprinted 1961.

Chapter XII
Ibuse Masuji
Black Rain (Kuroi ame), translated by John Bester, Tokyo and Palo Alto: Kodansha, 1969.
Lieutenant Lookeast and Other Stories (Yōhai taichō), translated by John Bester, Tokyo and Palo Alto: Kodansha, 1971.

Endō Shūsaku

The Sea and Poison (Umi to dokuyaku), translated by Michael Gallagher, London: Peter Owen, 1972.

Silence (Chinmoku), translated by William Johnston, Tokyo and Rutland, Vermont: Charles E. Tuttle, 1969.

Wonderful Fool (Obaka San), translated by Francis Mathy, London: Peter Owen, 1974.

Kaiko Takeshi

Darkness in Summer (Natsu no yami), translated by Cecilia Segawa Seigle, New York: Knopf, 1973.

Abe Kōbō

The Box Man (Hako otoko), translated by Dale Saunders, New York: Knopf, 1974.

The Face of Another (Tanin no kao), translated by Dale Saunders, New York: Knopf, 1966.

Inter Ice Age 4 (Daishi kampyōki), translated by Dale Saunders, New York: Knopf, 1970.

The Ruined Map (Moetsukita chizu), translated by Dale Saunders, New York: Knopf, 1969.

The Woman in the Dunes (Suna no onna), translated by Dale Saunders, New York: Knopf, 1964.

Index